Conservation and Agriculture

WITHDRAWN

Conservation and Agriculture

edited by
J.G. HAWKES
Professor of Botany
in the University of Birmingham

Duckworth

First published in 1978 by
Gerald Duckworth & Co. Ltd
The Old Piano Factory
43 Gloucester Crescent, London NW1

© by Gerald Duckworth & Co. Ltd 1978

ISBN 0 7156 1032 5

Photoset in Great Britain by
Specialised Offset Services Limited, Liverpool
and printed by
Page Bros (Norwich) Ltd, Norwich

CONTENTS

PART III: GENE POOL CONSERVATION
IN AGRICULTURE

PART IV: FORESTRY CONSERVATION
AND DEVELOPMENT

PART V: AN ASSESSMENT OF THE GREEN
REVOLUTION IN INDIA

PART VI: ECODEVELOPMENT: THE WAY AHEAD

PART VII: CONCLUSIONS

Preface

Man's power over his environment, whether to destroy, conserve or develop, has become frighteningly immense. The world is coming to realise that decisions of a political nature, both nationally and through international agreement, are needed to regulate and control man's actions. But what kinds of decisions are needed?

This book attempts to set out some of the ways in which man's effect on the natural environment might be regulated and developed. Only by rational discussions on scientific, sociological and political levels can we hope to make the right decisions for the future.

The chapters and discussions which follow are based on part of a symposium entitled 'Man and His Environment'. The symposium was the main academic event in celebrating the centenary of the founding of Birmingham University's parent institution, Sir Josiah Mason's Science College.

At the end of the symposium it was felt that a considerable degree of progress and understanding had been achieved by the bringing together of scientists from many disciplines. The parts of the conference reported here have attempted to present the thoughts, arguments and conclusions relating to the balance between the apparently opposing trends of conservation and development of the natural environment.

As editor of this book and one of the symposium organisers I should like to thank those who kindly provided chapters and took part in the discussions. My thanks are due also to the chairmen of sessions and the many other conference members who spoke in the discussions; my apologies for referring to them by surname only, in the interest of brevity. A list of their full names appears on page xi.

Finally, I should like to record my thanks to my assistant, David Langley, for help in preparing the manuscript, checking the proofs and assembling the index.

1 May 1976   J.G.H.

Contributors†

Dr. E. Bennett, FAO, Via delle Terme di Caracalla, 00100-Rome, Italy

Don Brothwell, Institute of Archaeology, 31-34, Gordon Square, London WC1H 0PY

Dr. J. Burley, University of Oxford, Department of Forestry, Commonwealth Forestry Institute, South Parks Road, Oxford OX1 3RB

J.M. Davidson, Countryside Commission, John Dower House, Crescent Place, Cheltenham, Gloucestershire GL5 3RA

Professor G.W. Dimbleby, Institute of Archaeology, 31-34, Gordon Square, London WC1H 0PÝ

Sir Otto Frankel, CSIRO, Division of Plant Industry, P.O. Box 1600, Canberra City, ACT 2601, Australia

Dr. M. Gane, Nature Conservancy Council, Calthorpe House, Calthorpe Street, Banbury, Oxfordshire OX16 8EX

M.S. Gill, Centre of South Asian Studies, University of Cambridge, Laundress Lane, Cambridge CB2 1SD

Dr. D.R. Harris, Department of Geography, University College London, Gower Street, London WC1E 6BT

J.C. Harriss, Centre of South Asian Studies, University of Cambridge, Laundress Lane, Cambridge CB2 1SD

J.L. Henson, Rare Breeds Survival Trust, Cotswold Farm Park, Bemborough, Guiting Power, Cheltenham, Gloucestershire

Dr. M.W. Holdgate, The Institute of Terrestrial Ecology, 68, Hills Road, Cambridge CB2 1LA

Dr. M.D. Hooper, The Institute of Terrestrial Ecology, Monks Wood Experimental Station, Abbots Ripton, Huntingdon PE17 2LS

Professor Sir Joseph Hutchinson, St. John's College, Cambridge CB2 1TP

† The meeting was held in the University of Birmingham during September 1975.

Dr. R.W.J. Keay, Executive Secretary, The Royal Society, 6, Carlton House Terrace, London SW1Y 5AG

Dr. R. Kemp, University of Oxford, Department of Forestry, Commonwealth Forestry Institute, South Parks Road, Oxford OX1 3RB

Dr. K.F.S. King, Assistant Director General, Forestry Department, FAO, Via delle Terme di Caracalla, 00100-Rome, Italy

Professor H. Thorpe, Department of Geography, University of Birmingham, P.O. Box 363, Edgbaston, Birmingham B15 2TT

Participants in discussion

Dr. E. Bennett
D. Brothwell
Dr. J. Burley
J.M. Davidson
Professor G.W. Dimbleby
Professor L.H. Finlayson
Sir Otto Frankel
Dr. M. Gane
Dr. K.R. Gray
Dr. D.R. Harris
Professor J.G. Hawkes
J.L. Henson
Dr. M.W. Holdgate
Dr. M.D. Hooper
Sir Joseph Hutchinson

Dr. R.W.J. Keay
R.H. Kemp
Dr. K.F.S. King
Dr. R.N. Lester
Dr. S. Limbrey
Dr. M.K. McPhane
L.D.C. Owen
Professor E.W. Russell
Sir Leslie Scarman
Dr. H.A. Sencer
Professor H. Thorpe
Dr. T.L.V. Ulbricht
Professor C.H. Waddington
Dr. J.T. Williams

Introduction

J.G. Hawkes

In any discussion of man's relation to his environment, that of the natural or biotic environment must assume a special importance, since it is on this which he must rely for his food.

Not so long ago, probably nine or ten thousand years back, man changed from a species of relatively few numbers to one which is now threatening to engulf the earth. This change came by his invention of agriculture. The knowledge that he could cultivate plants and domesticate animals to provide a more certain and abundant source of food was not gained suddenly. It may have taken thousands of years but, once gained, the material benefits were immense, and they enabled him to increase his numbers and to change the original natural ecosystems to an unprecedented extent.

In the twentieth century the effect of man on his environment has been even more marked, so much so that there is grave danger of environmental degradation and a collapse of many of the self-regulating support systems on which the biotic environment normally relies. It is thus a matter of urgent concern that, through discussion and debate, through experiment and calculation, we should try to formulate plans and blue-prints for our survival.

Of course, the biotic environment is only one aspect of the whole syndrome of change and balance, which includes other matters such as energy, non-renewable resources, health, urbanism and pollution. All these things interact and should be related closely in our decision-making. Yet, the complexity of the total situation necessitates a first examination of its individual parts and it is the natural or biological part of our environment which is treated in this book.

The theme of the book is the attempt to find a balance between environmental conservation and the various processes of development in agriculture, forestry and other activities which man imposes on the land. Is a single balance possible and, if so, where does it lie? If not, what are the data which must be used to arrive at the various balances for various regions and conditions? What are the differences which must be taken into account when comparing the tropical and the temperate regions of the earth or the developing and developed countries? How do soil and rainfall influence the balance and how do politics and economics?

In this book some writers have taken Britain as an example; others have taken an overview of the world as a whole, while others have concerned themselves with the tropics and the problems of development and conservation in developing countries. Obviously, much is left out, for it would take more than a handful of people to discuss all the world problems relating to conservation and development in the natural environment. Yet something is perhaps better than nothing, and this is what we have attempted to set out.

Since the chapters which follow cover a number of themes, they have been grouped together into parts or sections.

Part One examines the effect of agriculture on the natural environment, in which the historical changes brought about by man are related to the evidence of forest clearance and destruction, the evidence for ancient field patterns and the changing pattern of human settlement. The changes in animals brought about by man during the pre-agricultural and agricultural period are also examined. Of considerable importance to us at present is a study of the environmental impacts of traditional and modern agricultural systems, since we are coming to realise that much of relevance can be learned from traditional systems. Thus, this first section sets the stage, as it were, by examining the early impact of man on his environment – a process which is of course still continuing.

In Part Two we look at the recent changes in land use in Britain and the studies being made to effect a balance of use in relation to needs. In fact, one should speak of balances rather than a single balance, since the level or type of use must vary according to a complex interplay of many factors. An attempt here is made to examine positive conservation policies in highly developed landscapes. The final chapter in this section deals with nature reserves, or biosphere reserves as they are called, in a world context with an attempt to outline a philosophy of conservation. Here we are considering not the 'reserves' of developed countries, which are in most instances highly influenced by man, but those of areas with low populations, generally in developing countries, where there is considerable hope of conserving intact parts of the natural ecosystems and the threatened species which many of them contain. So the contrast in this section is between a positive land management policy in a highly populated industrialised country on the one hand with many conflicting pressures and uses, and the true biosphere reserves on the other in regions of low population density and almost completely natural ecosystems.

Part Three switches to a very different theme, that of the conservation of gene pools of crop plants and their wild relatives as well as the genetic diversity of domestic cattle. A wide genetic base in our domesticated plants and animals is now seen to be essential for the present and future needs of plant and animal breeders. Yet the genetic diversity which has developed in the ancient centres of origin and variation where domestication first began is under grave threat. Hence, the process of conservation of rare breeds and ancient variability in reserves, farm parks, seed banks and the like is essential if man as a species is going to survive and solve the problem of hunger, which is still so widespread. It is pointed out, however, that social and political action is needed as well as scientific research to help solve such problems.

Part Four turns now to forestry and forest resources. These are dwindling more and more rapidly in this latter half of the twentieth century, where the tropical rain forests and all the non-tree species associated with them are in grave danger of extinction. As with crop plants and farm animals, so with forest trees – an erosion or diminution of genetic variability is clearly seen. Even many species themselves and whole ecosystems are disappearing rapidly. Such a process of change and destruction can be slowed down and, in many instances, halted altogether. The biosphere reserves described in a previous section are of obvious importance in this connection. Where biosphere reserves are not appropriate much of the world's forests still need to be preserved, with systems of management and utilisation appropriate to soil and climate and to the social and political background of the countries concerned. Here again, as was discussed in part two, active management and the striking of a balance between conservation and development is all-important.

The green revolution in India is the subject dealt with in Part Five. This is of the greatest importance, since much has been claimed in over-glowing terms of the green revolution – the introduction of high-yielding 'miracle strains' of wheat, rice and maize that was to have solved all the food problems of the developing world. The reaction which set in subsequently claimed the reverse, that the green revolution was no less than an ecological and social disaster. The truth lies between these two extremes and we see in a country like India that good economic and social organisation, together with the use of good local and introduced varieties, can provide tremendous increases of yield, bringing well-being and prosperity. Where the social and economic organisation is lacking, mere plant breeding or the introduction of highly bred varieties from outside can do very little good.

In Part Six the first steps are taken towards an evaluation and a summing up of evidence presented in the previous chapters. Here, the 'balancing act', as it was frequently referred to in the discussion, is set out. This balance between food production and environmental conservation must be developed as a means of assessing options for the present and the future. The process of planned 'ecodevelopment' leads us to see that there is no single balance, but a series of them, which depend on the pressures and circumstances acting on a country or region at any particular point in time. A complete discussion period followed, introduced by a paper emphasising the dangers inherent in applying solutions based on temperate climate conditions to the tropics and vice versa.

The final chapter sums up the conclusions reached on the basis of the previous chapters and the discussions which followed them. Far from being 'doomsters', the participants of the symposium which this book is reporting ended on a note of cautious optimism. They concluded that development and constructive conservation must be linked together into a synthetic whole and should not be regarded as conflicting opposites which can never be reconciled.

PART I
AGRICULTURE AND THE NATURAL ENVIRONMENT

1. Changes in ecosystems through forest clearance

G.W. Dimbleby

So that we are not thinking in too much of a vacuum this chapter will be based largely on conditions in western Europe, but the principles discussed are, of course, of much wider relevance. In this setting we cannot discuss man and his environment without recognising that the presence of man inevitably implies some degree of disruption of the ecological *status quo*. He had at his disposal – long before the advent of agriculture – the powerful ecological tool of fire (Oakley, 1956), and there is evidence that he may even have practised some form of animal husbandry (Simmons & Dimbleby, 1974), though we cannot say whether this would have modified the environment perceptibly. The tools of Palaeolithic and more especially Mesolithic man were also capable of removing woody vegetation, albeit on a limited scale. We shall see later that even these simple practices could have a detectable impact on the environment. Once agriculture came in, of course, these factors were intensified; only in low latitudes can crops be grown under any degree of tree cover, and if pastoralism is practised the light-demanding herbage equally requires the removal of the ecological dominants, the trees.

Primary forest

To some degree man has been operative in our landscapes throughout the postglacial period. In the first few thousand years his numbers were small and the forest cover was still adjusting to the ameliorating climate. We can see some level of stability in the Atlantic period (Zone VIIa), when the mixed deciduous forest had become generally established below a certain altitude (the actual height is still a matter of conjecture: Simmons, 1975), soils had been developing long enough to have reached maturity and man was still in the Mesolithic stage with a low population.

Throughout Britain south of the Scottish Highlands the forest cover

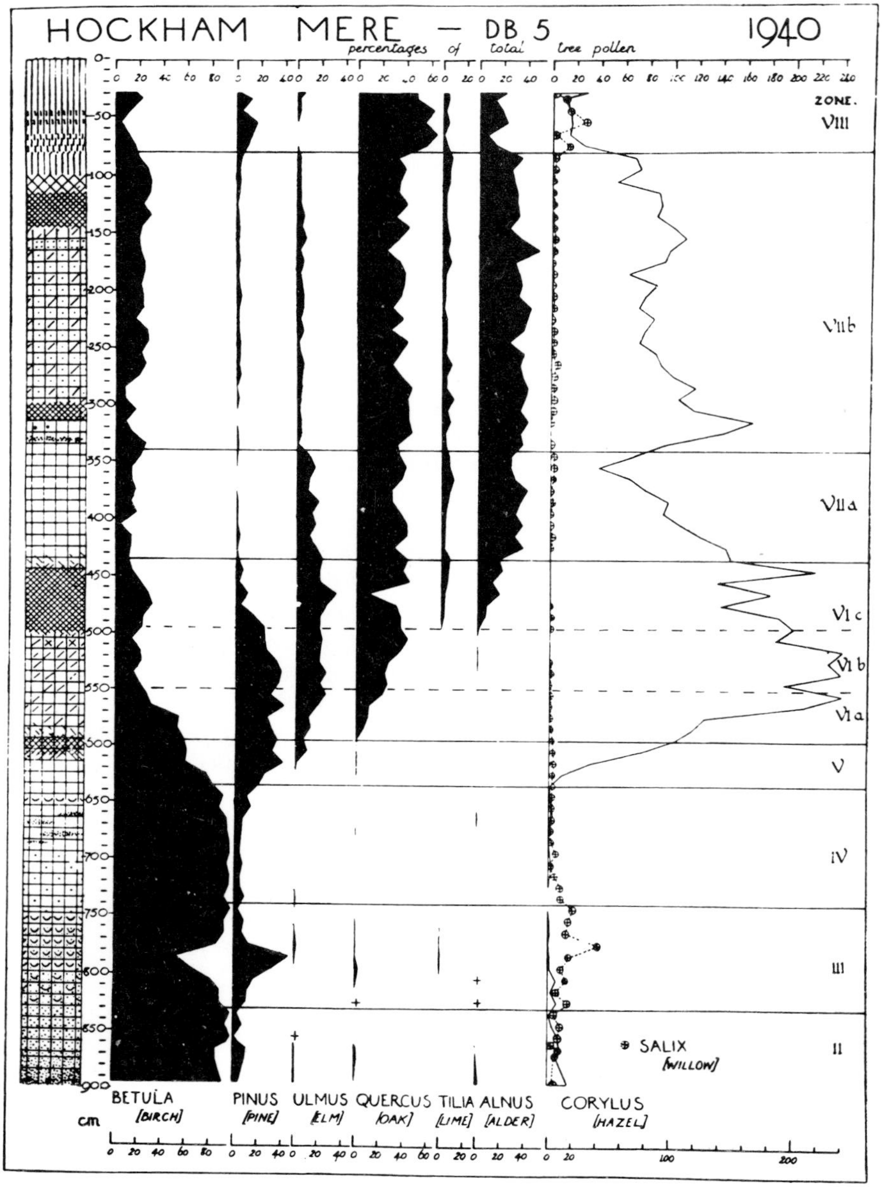

Fig. 1.1 The postglacial tree pollen sequence from Hockham Mere, Norfolk. (From Godwin, 1956)

was broad-leaved and closely similar to that found on the Continental mainland. Floristically it was dominated by oak, with lesser proportions of lime and elm, the latter more particularly on base-rich soils (Fig. 1.1). Pollen spectra of the forest of this period also show characteristically high values of alder pollen. This raises the question of the status of alder in the general forest cover of the countryside at that time. It has been argued that this high representation reflects the wetness of the Atlantic climate, while others suggest that it merely results from the fact that peat bog and lake sites, the main sources of the pollen evidence, by their very nature occur in wet bottomlands where alder is likely to have been co-dominant. On the other hand, alder occurs in oakwoods under higher rainfall conditions (McVean, 1953) and my own experiments on the growth of hardwoods on upland heaths (Dimbleby, 1958) have shown it to be one of the most vigorous growers even with a rainfall below 750mm per annum. Moreover, it frequently figures prominently in soil pollen analyses, which do not have any particular topographical bias. I will return to the possible significance of this shortly.

Another characteristic woodland species of this period is hazel. We tend to think of it as a shrub or understory species, but when it is allowed to grow without coppicing it can reach the canopy, a fact which may explain its consistent representation in the pollen diagrams; had it been only an understory species it would only have flowered lightly and therefore been poorly represented in the pollen spectrum. Holly and field maple are other species to which the same may apply, but in England they are more characteristic of later periods. Towards the end of the Atlantic period light-demanding trees such as ash appeared consistently but at low frequency, and birch, another light-demander which had been dominant early in the postglacial period, continued to show a steady representation in the pollen diagrams.

A vast expanse of unbroken forest has ecological characteristics largely of its own making. The forest canopy determines the micro-climate beneath it; this takes the form of ironing out the extreme fluctuations of the general climate. The direct insolation of summer does not reach the forest floor, nor do the lowest temperatures of the winter frosts. The protection from wind is another very marked feature; consequently the air remains relatively humid at all times. These factors are much less marked once the forest is opened up and in our present landscape of broken blocks of woodland it is rare to find conditions where they even approximate to what must have obtained in the primeval forest. The behaviour of alder, referred to above, may be a direct reflection of changes in the microclimate. The equable high humidity would be conducive to a constantly moist soil, so allowing a moisture-sensitive species to persist throughout the forest, whereas today it only finds such conditions in association with permanent ground water.

As mentioned above, the soils of the primeval forest would have had a long time to mature, over 2000 years being within the same climatic period (Zone VIIa). Our knowledge of these soils is generally inferential, for most of them have been so drastically altered by subsequent land use that their original condition is difficult to determine. It can be shown from a study of soils associated with archaeological sites that many of the soils which today are some form of podzol were originally brown earths, with a relatively high nutrient status and a soil fauna which included surface-casting species of earthworms (Dimbleby, 1965; Dimbleby and Bradley 1975; Case *et al.*, 1969). On the other hand there is direct evidence that along the edges of the Fens the soils of the Atlantic forests were forest podzols (Valentine, 1973); these soils are presumably more comparable with the forest soils of southern Scandinavia than with the man-made heathland podzols which have such low fertility (see below).

The forest itself played a part in determining and maintaining the nutrient status of the soil. The dominant species, being broad-leaved, would tend to form mull humus (Handley, 1954) associated, as we have seen, with brown earths in many places. The active fauna and microflora would ensure the release into circulation of the bulk of the nutrients contained in the litter falling from the trees. Where the soil was a podzol we can infer from the species known to have been present (as shown by pollen analyses) that the nutrient status was high here too; this being so it may be concluded that the humus was of a moder or duff type in which biological activity is much greater than in the mor or raw humus of very acid heathland podzols.

The forest trees also exerted an important influence on the nutrient status of the soil through the action of deep roots. It can be shown that even on base-poor soils the deeper roots are able to extract nutrients from the subsoil to such an extent that the root sap may actually be alkaline (Table 1.1) (Dimbleby, 1952a). This injection of nutrients into the solum tends to counteract the losses through leaching, particularly under high rainfall. Nevertheless, Iversen (1969) has produced evidence that there may be a slow depletion of nutrients even under the primeval forest, and that this shows itself first on the

Table 1.1   (from Dimbleby, 1952a)

Concentration of nutrients in sap from deep and
shallow roots of birch (p.p.m.) — July, 1950

Nutrient	Deep roots	Shallow roots
Ca	77	25
Mg	55	21
Na	14	4
K	75	70
Fe	2.2	0.5
Mn	5	0
P	7	30
N (ammoniacal)	2	36
pH	7.56	4.87

poorer soils where trees which require a nutrient-rich soil are gradually replaced by less demanding species. It is reasonable to assume that in the earlier part of the postglacial period there was much less difference between rich and poor soils than we see today, but if Iversen is correct it would mean that such soils were already diverging even before man played a significant part. Soils on calcareous parent materials probably never display this trend at all. We may therefore envisage a mosaic of forest soils, probably none being very poor, but differing enough in fertility to produce a mosaic of forest communities across the country.

Finally, among the ecological factors of the primeval forest environment, mention must be made of the water regime, particularly in the soil. Here again it must be admitted that what can be said is based on inference rather than on direct evidence. Reference has already been made to the effect of the canopy in maintaining constantly humid conditions at ground level, and it has already been pointed out that the soils would be humus-rich, in many cases with mull humus which has a high water-holding capacity. In such circumstances stream flow is relatively even; water is released gradually from the humus layers, infiltration is promoted, and the movement of water above or below ground is retarded by obstructions, so reducing rapid flow and lowering flood crests, whilst in low-water periods flow is prolonged (Kittredge, 1948). Furthermore, under these conditions the streams are clear and there is little eroded material in suspension. The streams run freely, and though there may be interference with the flow by fallen trees or even by beaver dams, in general the stream-sides do not become peaty.

The effect of Mesolithic man

We have already seen that pre-agricultural man had the tools for forest destruction, but despite this, the scale of his influence remained small. Doubtless this was because of his small numbers and the fact that he did not have the same driving need to clear the forest that his agricultural successors had. Nevertheless closer attention to this critical period in pollen analyses has shown that there is often a detectable phase of clearings, if not of clearance, marked by the appearance of light-demanding herbs, grasses and bracken (Simmons, 1969). Pollen analyses of archaeological sites of this period amplify this picture. In some cases there is no apparent change in the forest cover associated with the occupation site (e.g. Dimbleby, 1963), but in others the effect is very marked (Dimbleby, 1960; Keef *et al.*, 1965). In such cases not only does there seem to have been total clearance locally, but this condition persisted and was accompanied by acidification and podzolisation of the original deciduous forest soil. This observation is important because it relates to the effect of clearance *per se*. Clearance was probably for fuel, or even accidental, rather than for any particular land use. Nevertheless, the indirect evidence of animal husbandry already referred to, perhaps involving the red deer, could conceivably have some connection with clearance episodes. The evidence is still ambiguous.

The impact of prehistoric agriculture

While Mesolithic people had some detectable effect on the landscape it was insignificant compared with that of agricultural man. Here clearance was made with the intention of using the cleared land. It is therefore difficult to distinguish between the effects of clearance alone and the effects of the land use which followed immediately afterwards. For our present purpose the distinction is, perhaps, academic.

Iversen (1941) was the first pollen analyst to demonstrate the effects of Neolithic agriculture in pollen diagrams from peat bogs. He detected a decrease in the representation of tree pollen and an increase in light-demanding grasses and weeds of farmland. At the same time cereal pollen appeared, proving that arable farming was being practised. A plant characteristic of these episodes was ribwort plantain (*Plantago lanceolata*), which Iversen saw as an indicator of abandoned cultivation, and he was able to demonstrate in his pollen sequences the phases of woodland regrowth, pioneered by birch or hazel. He was also able to show that at this level the pollen preparations contained finely divided charcoal, presumably originating from the use of fire in clearance. To this primary clearance he gave the name *landnam* or land taking.

Before going on to consider the continuing impact of agriculture, mention must be made of another phenomenon which Iversen observed – the so-called elm decline. Throughout the Atlantic period elm pollen had been running at 10% or more of the total tree pollen, but at the point in question it dropped suddenly to about half this value and usually did not recover (see Fig. 1.1). This is now recognised as a widespread phenomenon and is taken as the criterion of division between the Atlantic and the following Sub-boreal period. Iversen, Godwin (1956) and others believed that the only explanation for such a widespread change was climatic, though we now know that the date of the elm decline ranges over several hundred years. But it has also been pointed out that the elm was an important tree to man, being particularly acceptable as a fodder plant for his animals; this suggests that anthropogenic factors may be involved in the elm decline (Troels-Smith, 1960). The question is too complex to pursue here, but it is significant that lime underwent a similar decline at various periods which are clearly correlated with anthropogenic factors. Today we see a widespread and sudden elm decline actually happening, but it is not possible at this stage to say whether disease could have played a part in the elm decline of the early Neolithic. It is apparent, however, that man could and did affect the distribution of the high forest trees as well as of the lower life forms of plants.

The *landnam* clearances are often referred to as small temporary clearances, and as such they would hardly disrupt the microclimate of the forest matrix as a whole. They were cultivated as swiddens and then abandoned, soon to be swallowed up in regrowth. Nevertheless, within the areas of the clearings themselves there would have been large microclimatic effects. The control of ground level humidity by the canopy would have been much reduced, exposing the crops to a fluctuating relative humidity. Temperature would also range much more widely and one outcome of this might be that the summer insolation would accelerate microbiological activity and therefore the breakdown of the humus. This could have a temporary beneficial effect, followed by a chronic depression of the level of soil humus. The rate of soil genesis is so slow that it seems unlikely that clearings of a few years' duration, followed by regrowth, would have any detectable effect on the process. The availability of plant nutrients, however, would have shown marked changes. These would arise from the so-called assart effect; that is, the release of nutrients from the decay of roots and rootlets that were killed when the trees were removed. In killing these roots, of course, not only is their richness made available to the crop but their root competition is removed. This temporary availability of nutrients is still exploited today in the forest meadows of Sweden.

The transition from the small temporary clearances to extensive clearance has been studied particularly by Turner (1965). She showed that extensive clearance reached different places at different times and by different routes, but that the transition from high forest to virtual treelessness was sometimes achieved by the early Iron Age (e.g. Wales) or the early centuries of our era (e.g. southern Scotland). Questions of land use arise here, of course, and the picture is not always clear. Though the primary clearance, whether Neolithic or Bronze Age, frequently produced evidence of cereal cultivation, it seems likely that clearance for pasture was often even more important, and perhaps the only practice at higher altitudes. Pollen evidence of herb-rich grasslands comes from both calcareous and non-basic sites in these prehistoric times.

While it is my brief in this chapter to deal with changes brought about by forest clearance, I must take the story well beyond the actual act of clearance in order to encompass those effects which are initiated by forest clearance but which do not manifest themselves in a form we can recognise until centuries later; for instance, soil profile development, nutrient depletion or changes in the water regime.

Studies of palaeosols buried beneath prehistoric earthworks have shown that on base-poor soils, in contrast to the types of soil that apparently existed in Atlantic times, some form of strongly leached

B*

soil develops, and this change seems to have taken place relatively rapidly. For instance, on the North York Moors, where man made temporary clearances probably not much before 1800 B.C. (excepting Mesolithic clearings), strongly leached horizons were appearing in the soil profiles in the middle Bronze Age, some 400-500 years later (Dimbleby, 1962). Here in fact we do not know when extensive clearance was achieved, but it seems likely that the soils were already well podzolised before that state was reached.

A number of factors contributed to this change: the use of fire and removal of soil resources in the form of crops, animals and fuel, but perhaps above all the intensified leaching which was no longer counteracted by the base-raising action of the deep roots. In other words, prolonged clearance alone, in the absence of manurial additions to the soil, would bring about a change to a more acidic, strongly leached type of soil and therefore one poorer in available nutrients. I get into trouble for calling this degradation, but you see what I mean.

Alongside these changes would come changes in the humus layers of the soils and particularly in their biology. Surface-casting species of earthworms are intolerant of acid conditions and disappear, though evidence of their former presence may persist, as already indicated. This brings about changes in the soil structure, and eventually the humus type changes from mull to mor, often associated with a change in vegetation type from a grass-dominated type to one dominated by the ericoid plants, though it should be made clear that the soil change can precede the vegetation change.

The other major factor affected by extensive clearance is the soil water regime. Recent work by Moore (1975) has drawn attention to the fact that the onset of blanket peat formation can frequently be correlated in part at any rate with human activity, and it seems likely that changes in soil structure, as well as changes in the transpiration potential of non-forest vegetation, may be the trigger mechanism. E.E. Evans (1975) has pointed out the common experience in Ireland that heavily-grazed pasture becomes wet as infiltration is prevented, and he remarks that the effectiveness of wind as a drying agent depends on the size of the clearing. In grazed clearings of limited size, therefore, the soil could become wet and run-off increase; indeed Simmons *et al.*, (1975) have evidence on the North York Moors of the inwash of silt into mires from clearances that would have been in a forest matrix. Pennington (1975) comments on the increased run-off and erosion, together with a rise in ground-water levels, contemporary with the Neolithic clearances in the Lake District, but she refers to these changes as 'natural'. It must not be forgotten that the water regime could also be drastically affected even on porous and calcareous bedrock such as the chalk. Evans and Valentine (1974) have demonstrated scarp slope erosion in the Chiltern Hills apparently associated with primary forest clearance. Later on, after extensive clearance of the chalk slopes, there was massive erosion under the influence of intensified arable agriculture in Iron Age and Romano-British times (Evans, J.G., 1966)

Continuing trends

There is surprisingly little evidence of any reversal of the trends set in motion by deforestation and primitive land use, though it can be shown that restorative ecosystems exist in nature and can sometimes be established (Dimbleby, 1952b). Man has kept up his pressure on the land even though it can no longer be used for its original purpose. At the time of small temporary clearances the slash-and-burn technique allowed the regrowth of woodland, but even here the regrowth could vary according to the habitat. In Ireland, upland sites progressively lost their power to regenerate, in contrast to lowland

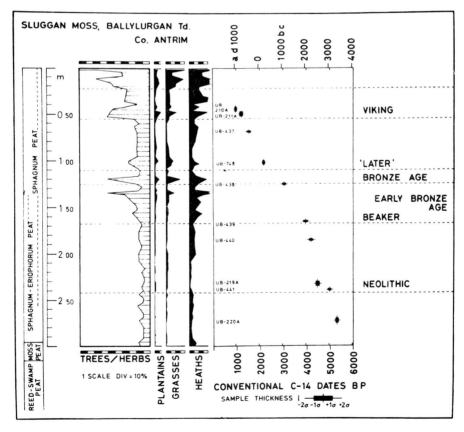

Fig. 1.2 Clearance and regeneration phases at an upland site in N. Ireland. (From Smith, 1975)

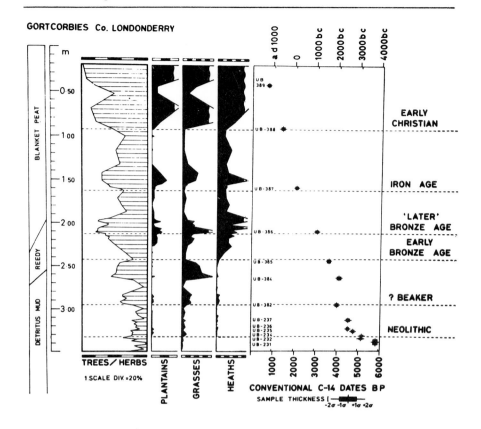

Fig. 1.3 Clearance and regeneration phases at a lowland site in N. Ireland. (From Smith, 1975)

sites which were still showing effective regrowth well into historic times (Figs. 1.2 and 1.3) (Smith, 1975). Neolithic man was able to adapt his agricultural practices to the environmental conditions he met or created. He generally cleared freely-draining upland sites, though some of our river gravels were also intensively used at this time. It is interesting to note that the Neolithic equivalent of lazybeds has been discovered beneath the blanket peat in Ireland (Evans, E.E., 1975), showing the adaptibility of these people in the face of uncompromising environmental conditions. At a later date, the lynchets of Celtic fields may be seen as a comparable adjustment, in this case to trap eroding topsoil, though not all experts would agree with this interpretation.

Sometimes the trends initiated by deforestation ultimately proved fatal. The eventual failure of agriculture on soils now covered by moorland or heathland is a good example (Fig. 1.4). Latterly man has still attempted to extract profit from these lands by adjusting his

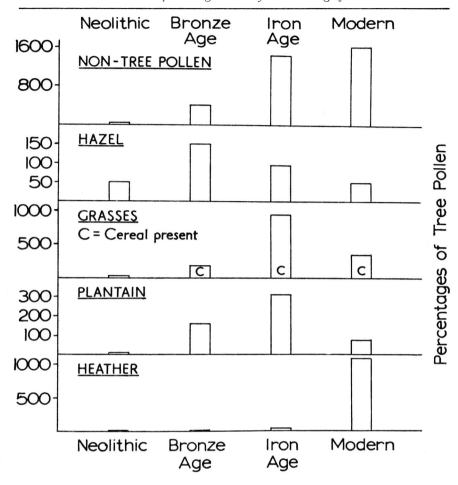

POLLEN ANALYSES OF BURIED SURFACES
GREAT AYTON MOOR, YORKS. N.R.

Fig. 1.4 Percentages of selected pollen types from surfaces of different ages on one area of moorland

practices – sheep-rearing, forestry, as well as various forms of game exploitation – to the now much reduced fertility. I leave aside here the question of any possible influence of climatic change. I do not believe that it is a *primary* cause of site deterioration, but it is outside the scope of this chapter to argue the case here.

Conclusion

Throughout the course of this chapter it must have been repeatedly apparent that many of our present land-use problems are directly referable to the ecological changes brought about by the deforestation of our landscape. Having removed the protective cover of the forest, we are now faced with problems of exposure to wind and storm, desiccation in dry seasons and such factors as frost action in winter. These vary in their intensity, of course, and in some cases can be useful (e.g. the effect of frost in killing weeds and in breaking down clay clods), but whether useful or not we have to accept them in order to benefit from the direct insolation that our crops need.

Some of the soils we have today, apart from the effects of manipulation by later agricultural practices, still have the marks of prehistoric man's activities. The widespread occurrence of various forms of leached soil can often be traced back to this period and they still provide problems for more modern methods of land use. Similarly the shallowness of soils on chalk and limestone limit the use of the land by modern agriculture or forestry.

While soils derived from calcareous parent materials are probably little or no less rich in nutrients than their pre-agricultural counterparts, those on other parent materials certainly are. The attempts to maintain the fertility level of hungry acid soils show how far the ecosystem has changed from the condition in the mixed deciduous woodland that was there originally.

Soil structure and soil water go hand in hand and here too we have connected problems today. Peatlands are still of very limited use, and excessive wetness still limits the value of much land in the north and west. Heavy clay soils (which for reasons of space I have had to exclude from this chapter) can maintain good soil structure under grass, but even here the water table may be higher than it would have been under the forest canopy. At the other extreme, freely-drained soils can experience drought conditions even in our moist summers.

In making these observations I am not making value judgments about man's use of the land either in early times or later; indeed, as I have already suggested, he had no choice but to clear the land. It is important to realise, however, that some of the drastic changes in ecosystems that we have been discussing are directly attributable to the change in the dominant ecological cover, and some of them cannot be reversed unless the forest itself is restored, which is usually impossible. Some of the effects can be mitigated; for instance, nutrient deficiencies can be made good by surface dressings. The others must be accepted as a constraint on the use we can make of the land; in some situations it may even mean that we can no longer continue to exploit the present ecosystems. At least this might force us to rest such land and thus allow regenerative successions to take over.

REFERENCES

Case, H.J., Dimbleby, G.W., Mitchell, G.F., Morrison, M.E.S. and Proudfoot, V.B. (1969). Land use in Goodland townland, Co. Antrim from Neolithic times until today. *Jl R. Soc. Antiquaries of Ireland*, **99**: 39-53.

Dimbleby, G.W. (1952a). The root sap of birch on a podzol. *Pl. Soil*, **4**: 141-53.

Dimbleby, G.W. (1952b). Soil regeneration on the north-east Yorkshire moors. *J. Ecol.*, **40**: 331-41.

Dimbleby, G.W. (1958). Experiments with hardwoods on heathland. *Institute Paper No.* 33. Imperial Forestry Institute, Oxford.

Dimbleby, G.W. (1960). Further excavations at a mesolithic site at Oakhanger, Selborne, Hants. Part II. Fossil pollen and charcoal. *Proc. Prehist. Soc.*, **26**: 255-62.

Dimbleby, G.W. (1962). The development of British heathlands and their soils. *Oxford Forestry Memoirs* No. 23.

Dimbleby, G.W. (1963). Pollen analysis of a mesolithic site at Addington, Kent. *Grana Palynologica*, **4**: 140-8.

Dimbleby, G.W. (1965). Post-glacial changes in soil profiles. *Proc. R. Soc.*, B., **161**: 355-62.

Dimbleby, G.W. and Bradley, R.J. (1975). Evidence of pedogenesis from a Neolithic site at Rackham, Sussex. *J. Archaeol.* Sci., **2**: 179-86.

Evans, E.E. (1975). Highland landscapes: habitat and heritage. *In* Evans, J.G., Limbrey, S. and Cleere, H. (eds.). *The Effect of Man on the Landscape: the Highland Zone.* C.B.A. Research Report No. 11: 1-5.

Evans, J.G. (1966). Late-glacial and post-glacial subaerial deposits at Pitstone, Buckinghamshire. *Proc. Geol. Ass.*, **77**: 347-64.

Evans, J.G. and Valentine, K.W.G. (1974). Ecological changes induced by prehistoric man at Pitstone, Buckinghamshire. *J. Arch. Sci.*, **1**: 343-51.

Godwin, H. (1956). *History of the British Flora.* London, Cambridge University Press.

Handley, W.R.C. (1954). Mull and mor formation in relation to forest soils. *Forestry Commission Research Bull.* No. 23.

Iversen, J. (1941). Landnam i Danmarks Stenalder. En pollenanalytisk undersøgelse over het første Landbrugs Indvirkning paa Vegetationsudviklingen. *Danmarks Geologiska Undersøgelse* R II Nr. 66.

Iversen, J. (1969). Retrogressive development of a forest ecosystem, demonstrated by pollen diagrams from fossil mor. *Oikos Suppl.*, **12**: 35-49.

Keef, P.A.M., Wymer, J.J. and Dimbleby, G.W. (1965). A mesolithic site on Iping Common, Sussex, England. *Proc. Prehist. Soc.*, **31**: 85-92.

Kittredge, J. (1948). *Forest Influences.* New York, McGraw Hill.

Moore, P.D. (1975). Origin of blanket mires. *Nature*, **256**: 267-9.

McVean, D.N. (1953). *Alnus* Mill. *J. Ecol.*, **41**: 447-66.

Oakley, K.P. (1956). Fire as a palaeolithic tool and weapon. *Proc. Prehist. Soc.*, **21**: 36-48.

Pennington, W. (1975). The effect of Neolithic man on the environment in the north-west England, the use of absolute pollen diagrams. *In* Evans, J.G., Limbrey, S. and Cleere, H. (eds.). *The Effect of Man on the Landscape:*

the Highland Zone. C.B.A. Research Report No. 11: 74-86.

Simmons, I.G. (1969). Evidence for vegetation changes associated with Mesolithic man in Britain. *In* Ucko, P.J. and Dimbleby, G.W. (eds.). *The Domestication and Exploitation of Plants and Animals*. London, Duckworth, 110-19.

Simmons, I.G. (1975). The ecological setting of Mesolithic man in the Highland Zone. *In* Evans, J.G., Limbrey, S. and Cleere, H. (eds.). *The Effect of Man on the Landscape: the Highland Zone*. C.B.A. Research Report No. 11: 57-63.

Simmons, I.G., Atherden, M.A., Cundill, P.R. and Jones, R.L. (1975). Inorganic inwash layers in soligenous mires of the North Yorkshire moors. *J. Biogeogr.*, **1**: 49-56.

Simmons, I.G. and Dimbleby, G.W. (1974). The possible role of ivy (*Hedera helix* L.) in the Mesolithic economy of Western Europe. *J. Archaeol. Sci.*, **1**: 291-6.

Smith, A.G. (1975). Neolithic and Bronze Age landscape changes in Northern Ireland. *In* Evans, J.G., Limbrey, S. and Cleere, H. (eds.). *The Effect of Man on the Landscape: the Highland Zone*. C.B.A. Research Report No. 11: 64-74.

Troels-Smith, J. (1960). Ivy, mistletoe and elm: climatic indicators – fodder plants. *Danmarks Geologiska Undersøgelse* R IV, Nr. 4.

Turner, J. (1965). A contribution to the history of forest clearance. *Proc. R. Soc.*, B., **161**: 343-54.

Valentine, K.W.G. (1973). The identification, lateral variation and chronology of three buried paleocatenas in lowland England. University of Reading, *Ph.D. Thesis*.

2. The man-land relationship through time

Harry Thorpe

The preceding chapter has discussed within a broad temporal and spatial context some of the major changes in the natural environment slowly effected by forest clearance associated with the replacement of hunting and collecting by animal husbandry and agriculture. The present chapter traces such changes over three millennia within a specific region, namely the emergent shire of Warwick, based on research by historical geographers, archaeologists, historians and botanists closely connected with the University of Birmingham over the last twenty-five years. It is a case study of the interaction between actual land and actual folk, the emphasis throughout being here on rural conditions, although one would not deny the enormous influence that Birmingham, Coventry and other Warwickshire towns have had on the land-use and landscape of the shire.

At the outset, one would affirm that the greater man's involvement with nature according to his needs and technology at points of time, the greater is the visual impact on landscape linked with the gradual conversion of a once natural landscape into the complex cultural landscape of the present. Whereas within Warwickshire in Neolithic times woodland was a landscape dominant and a rich (but then perhaps, little appreciated) resource, it is today merely a remnant feature, heavily denuded and metamorphosed and only weakly and belatedly reinforced by orderly re-planting of trees of man's own choice. But the fruitful and sensitive soils, long ago exposed as latent resource by the process of clearing, now carry selections of plants meeting a wide range of needs for man and his domesticated animals. In examining the changing man-land relationship through time, visually expressed in landscape, one is closely concerned with soil and what it may bear; with a long period of increasing competition between one element of the biosphere – Man – and other elements of flora and fauna; with human choice and preference at points of time, though often thoughtlessly or selfishly applied; with the deliberate and long continuing destruction of one resource to encourage another;

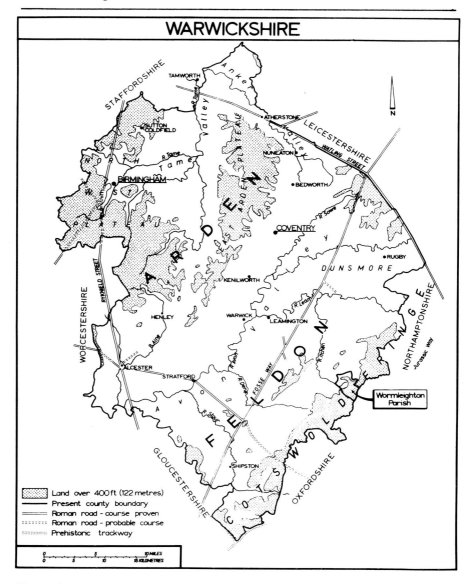

Fig. 2.1 Warwickshire: Relief.

with the incredibly, but perhaps understandably, slow recognition
that there was a compelling need for balance between natural
resource and its use by man, culminating only in very recent years
with schemes for managing our ecosystems in conservation and
planning terms.

Of the physical components of our Warwickshire landscape,
summarised in Figs. 2.1 and 2.2 and fully described elsewhere, relief

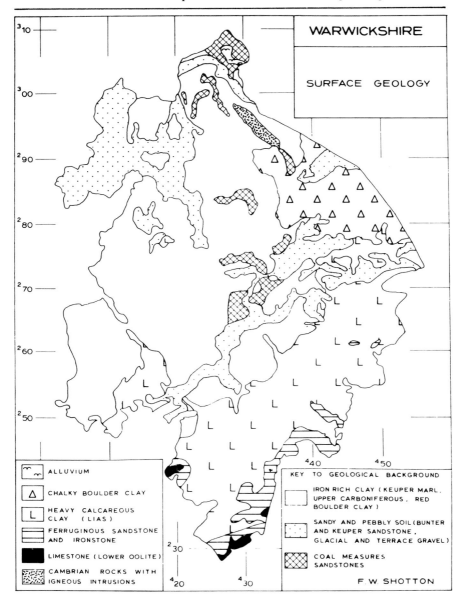

Fig. 2.2 Warwickshire: Surface Geology (Shotton, 1971)

and major drainage lines (one to the Severn, the other to the Trent) have changed little since insularity first crept upon Britain around 5000-7000 B.C. Even more immutable has been its solid geology, passing from Triassic sandstones in the north-west and a horst of Coal Measure sandstones in the north-east, to soft Keuper Marl succeeded south-eastward by heavy lower Lias calcareous clay overlain along the sharp Cotswold scarp by the brown ferruginous middle Lias marlstones giving firm definition to the county's south-eastern boundary (Fig. 2.2). Somewhat less stable were the many drift deposits, particularly the important river terrace materials and the fluvio-glacial sands and gravels prone to leaching especially when cleared. But, in sharp contrast, the pristine biogeographical features were subject to rapid change once incursions into woodland began, accompanied by long, slow, subtle man-induced modifications of soil character and plant life.

How pitiably little do we really know of the floral character of Warwickshire, and many other parts of Britain, during late Mesolithic and early Neolithic times – leading to sweeping assertions (by arguing deterministically from physical conditions to the supposed biogeographical response) that monotonous expanses of damp oakwood (sometimes in pure stands, sometimes mixed with other trees, like elm) covered most of Warwickshire except where reeds and alder flanked the river banks. Certainly, even within the Umberslade area (139/135,715*), where clearing is thought never to have been completed, the numerous rides, the present glades and large amounts of bracken bear little relation to the original woodland of Arden.

But within these extensive forests that at first conferred monotony on Warwickshire's landscape, during early Neolithic times small family groups were pressing along the major river terrace lines and along the drier Cotswold crest, their simple hunting, fishing and collecting cultures making very little impress initially on landscape. Unfortunately, we cannot construct distribution maps to show their itinerant progress; nor do memorials exist to whosoever it was of the great unknowns that first demonstrated empirically that the berries of certain plants, such as *Atropa belladonna*, were best omitted from the dessert course! One may conjecture, too, about the processes of trial and error by which early folk decided which creatures both above and below ground were good to eat, and enquire whether any resources lay neglected, even to this day.

As has been described elsewhere (Thorpe, 1971), these early Neolithic immigrants soon became more closely tied to particular tracts of ground when clearing became a pre-requisite for their first tiny, irregular fields raising summer wheat and barley. The work of the Avon-Severn Valleys Research Project along the river terraces has revealed stockaded enclosures, clay-lined pits that may have carried water for stock, grain storage pits, and elongated religious enclosures of cursus type suggesting a strongly organised social life (Webster and Hobley, 1965). Fodder for their early domestic animals, especially cattle, sheep, pigs and goats, was provided by that puny interloper – grass – accompanied by various weeds (especially plantain) and shrubs that slowly colonised clearings abandoned by shifting

*Map references are to Ordnance Survey, 1/50,000, First Series, sheet numbers.

cultivators galvanised into renewed and extended clearing activity by declining yields. How long was it before the idea dawned that successive cultivation and pastoralism on the same tract of ground were not competitive land-uses but good farming practice? How long

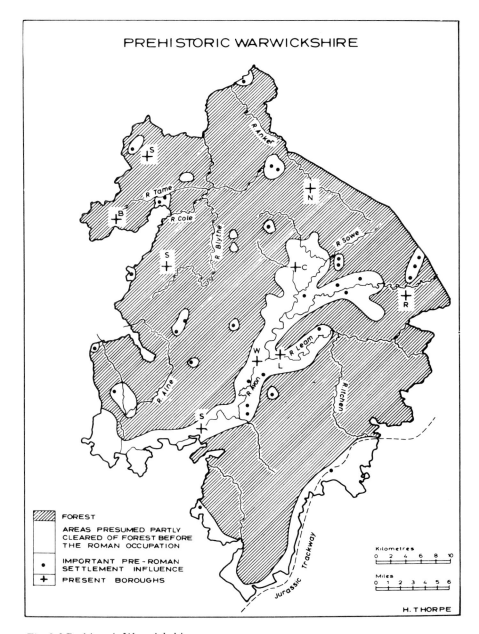

Fig. 2.3 Prehistoric Warwickshire

was it, too, before old abandoned clearings sometimes tumbled down to heath, or bedecked with blackthorn, hawthorn, wild rose, rowan, bramble and holly were again deemed 'natural' landscapes of a more open type ripe once more for the axe or fire? When were these early fields first sharply defined by bank, by ditch or by protecting hedge of thorn and how permanent were the homestead sites?

Throughout Bronze Age and early Iron Age times linear settlement continued to cluster along the Avon terraces, as well as along the Cotswold fringe where the 'cathedral' of the Rollright Stones suggests strong cultural influence along the Jurassic Way (Fig. 2.3) from Megalithic times, culminating in hill forts like Meon Hill (151/176, 453) and Nadbury (151/390, 482) which reflect powerful tribal organisation, strong arable and pastoral economy and active trade in the pre-Roman period. In this upland area ghostly outlines of small rectilinear fields may reflect the impress of small ploughs on the light shallow soils. Elsewhere, on the edge of the great swathe of clearing bordering the Avon, early Iron Age stockaded enclosures, often circular, like that at Beausale (139/247, 701) seem to have served as summer cattle pounds for clustered arable communities strung along the valley. The extent of the area presumed to have been at least partly cleared of forest before the Roman occupation is shown in Fig. 2.3, which has been based on the assumption that deforestation had occurred within a radius of half a mile of all major occupation sites, clusters of significant finds, datable crop-marks and important routeways.

Roman influence within Warwickshire, following the Claudian invasion of A.D. 43, was considerable, reflected in two long straight 'M' roads of the day – Watling Street (later to form the north-eastern boundary of the shire) and the great transverse Fosse of 47 A.D., paralleling the Avon Terrace belt and cunningly sited on the dry scarp foot of the lower Lias limestone (Fig. 2.4). A major effect of the Fosse and its settlements was to extend the main cleared belt well south of the Avon, while along the important tributary roads, salients of clearing and settlement, by fragmenting the woodland into comprehensible blocks, encouraged further regional differentiation. Was the heavy wheeled plough now biting deeply into the cloddy Keuper marls and lower Lias clays, as excavations at Chesterton (151/341, 598) on the Fosse and elsewhere would suggest, engraving long linear patterned ground corrugated by ridge-and-furrow; could one then have recognised alternating field use, associated with autumn-sown and spring-sown crops, rotating fallow and close penning of stock upon it? North of the Avon the forest block of Arden now stood extensive and well defined, while further south continually reinforced settlement momentum held latent resource for further expansion. But one must not overlook the surprising number of kilns for pottery, tiles and glass, linked by long straight roads that have been found in Arden, ranging from Hartshill (140/325, 935) in the north-

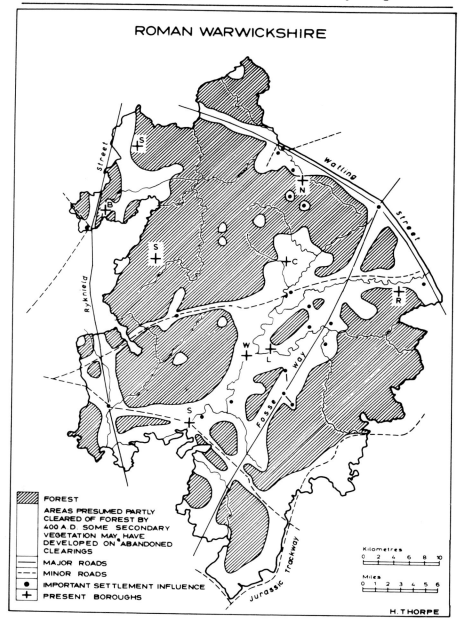

ROMAN WARWICKSHIRE

FOREST

AREAS PRESUMED PARTLY
CLEARED OF FOREST BY
400 A.D. SOME SECONDARY
VEGETATION MAY HAVE
DEVELOPED ON ABANDONED
CLEARINGS

MAJOR ROADS

MINOR ROADS

IMPORTANT SETTLEMENT INFLUENCE

PRESENT BOROUGHS

Kilometres
0 2 4 6 8 10

Miles
0 1 2 3 4 5 6

H. THORPE

Fig. 2.4 Roman Warwickshire

east to Kenilworth and Rowington Green (139/205, 702) further west,
each to be viewed as an oasis of active clearing reflecting its fuel needs.

Of the sub-Roman period in Warwickshire we know very little, but
by about 500 A.D. a triple penetration by Anglo-Saxon colonists had

begun – an Anglian entry via the Trent and Tame, a second Anglian push from the Wash into the upper Avon, reinforced by a Saxon thrust from the south-west along the lower Avon and the Fosse. Significantly, the area of cultural overlap lay in the middle Avon valley

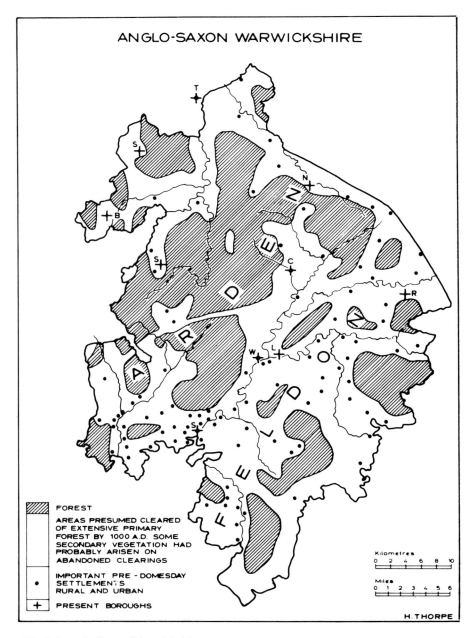

Fig. 2.5 Anglo-Saxon Warwickshire

around Warwick, with a strong concentration of population between the Avon, the Fosse and the Jurassic Way where strong organised nucleated settlements, with extensive open fields worked in aratrally curved strips by large peasant plough-teams, arose partly on long-cleared Romano-British lands and partly within new fellings. So, as Fig. 2.5 shows, came into being the distinctive Feldon (the 'open' or 'open field' land) of south Warwickshire studded with Anglo-Saxon townships with scarcely a place name in *-ley, -worth* or *-field* denoting active clearing among them (Thorpe, 1950). By contract, north of the Avon Terrace belt, penetration of Arden woodland by individual colonists was a slow process accompanied by the rise of scattered farmsteads and small hamlets with distinctive clearing names, like Tanworth (139/113, 705 = 'tanner's clearing') and Henley (151/150, 659), together with many wood names such as Wootton (151/153, 633), Nuthurst (139/146, 720) and Westgrove (151/130, 560). Here the emphasis was generally on individual small fields, worked by a simple plough capable of being drawn by one animal or two, and securely banked and hedged to keep out deer and wild boar. So, compared with the monotonous expanses of forest landscape in Neolithic times, Warwickshire now revealed distinctive man-induced regional characteristics, particularly associated with Feldon, the Avon Terrace belt, Arden and those well-settled areas of the Tame and Anker in the north converging on the old Mercian capital at Tamworth (Fig. 2.5). The settlement pattern of Warwickshire was to be only slightly reinforced in the north-east around Rugby during the Scandinavian period, but Mercian resistance to the Danes saw the identification of Warwick as an Anglo-Saxon burgh and the grouping around it, for the first time, of the administrative unit that we now call the shire.

By the end of Anglo-Saxon and Viking times Warwickshire had received its last bulk contribution of colonial settlement. Norman overlordship came swiftly and remarkably peacefully to Warwickshire villages, hamlets and farmsteads judging by the paucity of defensive works of motte and bailey type. Farming went on apace under Norman bailiffs whose aim was to increase revenue by intensive land-use. It would seem that rabbits were introduced into England from Normandy at this time, initially being bred in captivity as a tasty addition to the menu, but soon escaping to colonise vast areas of woodland and waste and, thereafter, to exert a considerable influence both on peasant food supplies and on smaller plants, herbs and crops until the recent introduction of *myxomatosis* brought drastic changes, the full nature of which we may not yet understand.

That remarkable survey, Domesday Book, provides a detailed, but highly selective, summary of the settlement, population and land-use of the shire enabling us to check our understanding of its emergent character over preceding centuries (Kinvig, 1950, 1971). A comparison of the map of Anglo-Saxon clearing (Fig. 2.5) with that of the distribution of recorded Domesday woodland (Fig. 2.6) suggests

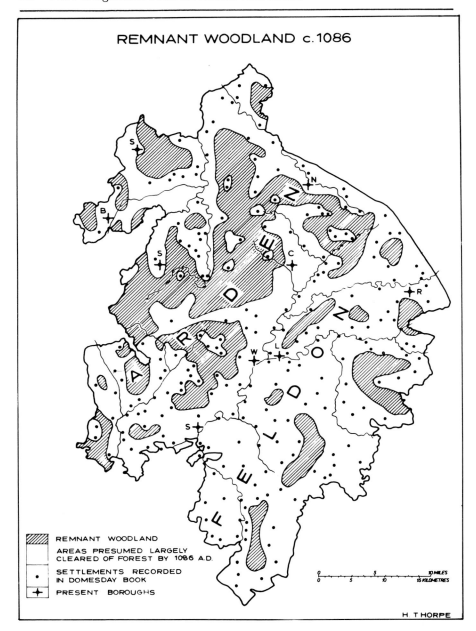

Fig. 2.6 Remnant Woodland c. 1086

that our appraisal of earlier clearing has been reasonably accurate. Moreover, the remaining woodland of 1086 was land still available for clearing, Royal Forest not imposing restraints within Warwickshire. The distribution of recorded vills (Fig. 2.6) accords with the picture that has already emerged of two closely settled and intensively farmed areas – Feldon and the Avon Terrace belt – succeeded northward by thinly-settled, woody Arden except where major valleys of the Alne, Tame and Anker bore greater occupance. Such a picture is further substantiated by Professor R.H. Kinvig's density maps of Warwickshire's Domesday population based on recorded adults, representing some 7000 families, or a likely total population of between 35,000 and 40,000 – no more than that of Leamington today! Actual population density averaged about 55-60 persons per square mile in Feldon, about 40-45 in the Avon Terrace belt, dropping to 20-22 around Birmingham and even less (10-13) in the heart of forested Arden.

An index of the intensity and extent of arable farming is provided by maps of Domesday plough-teams, which highlight the *champion* lands of Feldon some of whose vills mustered between 20 and 40 plough-teams (Kinvig, 1950, 1971). That scarcely any of these vills reported any woodland reaffirms our conclusion that clearing had proceeded so vigorously that no reserves of forest remained. Indeed, in townships carrying a high density of population and very large numbers of plough-teams one wonders whether a fine point of balance had not already been reached between man and animals, on the one hand, and the carrying capacity of the soil in terms of arable and pasture, on the other. In other words, at this level of technology, were diminishing returns on arable land setting in?

Although the Domesday record for Warwickshire does not mention livestock (apart from plough-teams and occasional references to pannage swine), from a variety of evidence one suspects that a considerable number of both cattle and sheep were kept in Feldon vills. Indeed, the very strength of the arable farming system depended on manure as well as on plough power. The ready marketability of dairy produce, meat, hides and wool, as well as grain, would also clearly encourage a well balanced mixed farming system. Evidence for this is provided by some of the hidden facts that emerge from particular comparisons of Domesday data. For example, if one takes the recorded value of Domesday manors and expresses this in terms of value per plough-team, then where one finds a densely populated and well-stocked Feldon manor in which the value per plough-team is very high, although this admittedly may mean that the soils (and one can assess their character, past and present) or the standard of farming was good, it may also indicate that an undisclosed element based on cattle or sheep herding (or on domestic industry, if it existed then) entered into this increased value (Sawyer, 1963).

Meadowland was of even greater value than arable in Medieval times for it provided the important hay crop on which plough-oxen, milch cows and sheep depended for supplementary feed throughout the long winter. Its importance seems to have been particularly great where sheep were concerned (Figs. 2.11 and 2.12). Recorded acres of meadow were high within Feldon and the Avon Terrace belt, but, apart from small acreages in the valleys of the Tame and Blythe, remarkably little was recorded in Arden (Kinvig, 1971). Although it is often suggested that in Norman times most of the hay was derived from alluvial water meadow, one would imagine that by now grassy enclosures, temporarily fenced, had become a familiar feature around the villages contrasting sharply with the ridged-and-furrowed *champion* land beyond. One must not overlook the important effect that long continuing simple technology in the form of the heavy coultered, mould-board plough, drawn by a strong ox-team had on soils and on drainage, reinforced by socio-economic factors related to co-aration and the allocation of selions to particular individuals within the farming community. We have excavated ridges-and-furrows in an attempt to determine whether it was customary after a time for ploughmen to break down ridges into furrows, but the rather limited evidence that we have gained thus far from examinations of soil and sub-soil horizons suggests that ridges-and-furrows remained surprisingly well anchored to the same spot. For example, in the very old Lammas Field of Warwick, that may have been in use from as early as the sixth century, the furrow bottoms made a clear incision in the sub-soil. Of course, some of the ridge-and-furrow seen in the present Warwickshire landscape continued in use as late as the 1860s, but the inscribed patterns themselves may extend back many centuries. Fig. 2.13, based on research by Mr. D.J. Pannett, shows the distribution of ridge-and-furrow in Warwickshire derived partly from aerial surveys undertaken around 1946 and partly from field work (Pannett *et al.*, 1965). Although evidence of such patterned ground may have disappeared from some areas following nineteenth-century inclosure and later changes in ploughing practice, the association of densest distributions with the heavy lower Lias clays of the Feldon is striking (see also Figs. 2.11 and 2.12). Elsewhere it appears only as a weak stipple on the impervious Keuper marls of Arden probably because in general there was little co-aration here, the hamlets and scattered farmsteads employing small individual one-ox ploughs and the like. It is also largely absent from light well-drained river terrace deposits and from expanses of thin stony soil atop drier lower Lias limestone exposures and from the hard middle Lias marlstone outcrops of the Cotswold fringe.

While land-use within the Feldon townships reached temporary maxima, verging on still-stand, both areally and in intensity during the twelfth and thirteenth centuries as revealed by J.B. Harley's study of the Hundred Rolls of 1279 (Harley, 1958), a vigorous colonisation had begun in Arden, particularly on great lay estates like those of the Earl of Warwick and on those of religious bodies such as the Cistercians at Combe (140/404, 798), Merevale (140/294, 978) and Stoneleigh (140/330, 727). Roberts has convincingly traced the rise of many small freemen farmers granted land within the Earls Wood between 1150 and 1350, associated with the establishment of many scattered moated homesteads each set amid a gradually extending pattern of irregular, banked, hedged and ditched fields, often double banked to keep out deer and wild boar (Roberts, 1962, 1965; Bond, 1974). The moat surrounding the homestead similarly served to protect both penned livestock and the kitchen garden from attack or damage at night. These small aquatic features were considerably reinforced in many places by the digging of large fish ponds, such as those at Codbarow near Umberslade (139/138, 708), the size of which in relation to the paucity of local population suggests that fish farming was an economic proposition. Indeed, its known that fish for re-stocking purposes were being transported in barrels on carts at this time. Of equal importance in landscape terms was the growing practice of digging small marl pits in the corners of the irregular fields, partly to provide material for bricks, partly to spread marl on the arable fields and partly to provide water for stock as run-off gradually settled in the impervious hollows, soon to be flanked by meadowsweet, sedge or small trees. This vigorous period of colonisation was accompanied by the springing up of distinctive place-names, such as Earlswood (139/110, 742), Wood End (139/110, 716) and Hazelwood (151/170, 667); by the rise of hamlets on squatting greens, like Green End (140/263, 863); and by the extension of heath and moor names, like Hockley Heath (139/153, 728) and Moorhills (151/193, 671), on abandoned clearings where thin sands and gravels lay atop the marl.

Although the active colonisation of Arden accorded generally with a period of national expansion and relative prosperity that continued up to the Black Death of 1348-9, it would seem that a very fine point of balance between man and land had already been reached in Feldon, accompanied in some densely populated townships by what was virtually economic stagnation soon after Domesday times (Harley, 1958; Thorpe, 1965). This situation was to be re-adjusted not by new technology but by drastic demographic changes associated with the Black Death which decimated many Feldon vills without leading to their complete desolation. As Professor M.W. Beresford has clearly shown (Beresford, 1945/6, 1954), the wholesale abandonment of settlements in Warwickshire did not occur until the fifteenth century, particularly the latter half, but any understanding of the great complex of factors, both physical and human, that led to the depopulation, completely or in part, of some 130 villages and hamlets in Warwickshire alone, most of them lying in Feldon and the Avon Terrace belt – very few in Arden – must begin with the delicate situation following the Black Death. Thus, it should be emphasised that:

1. Initially, the Black Death had a profound effect on the social and economic geography of Feldon by:

(i)   greatly reducing the pressure of man on land, particularly on arable land. In consequence, the resources available for livestock increased.

(ii) leaving some of the lords whose family had fortunately survived the pestilence with a peasant labour force so shrunken that they were unable to cultivate all the arable selions in the open fields or on the demesne. In consequence, grass colonised great expanses of ridge-and-furrow.

(iii) leaving peasants, whose lord had died, in a state of disorganisation and maybe, for a time, of virtual freedom unless a bailiff had promptly taken over on behalf of an absentee inheritor. In consequence, there was for once land to spare and across the grassy selions ran many cattle, sheep and swine.

2. After the Black Death recovery was slow in many areas, partly perhaps because the late fourteenth and early fifteenth century was, according to Flohn (1949/50), Utterström (1955) and Le Roy Ladurie (1973), a period of climatic deterioration, with successions of wet autumns and springs, when the sticky lower Lias clays of the Feldon were hard to plough, and of wet summers with very poor harvests. So grass persisted and even extended on parts of many open fields, and lords, freemen and peasants alike came to appreciate even more the value of livestock products like meat and dairy produce for urban markets, hides and skins for the prosperous leather industries of Birmingham and Coventry and wool for the flourishing national woollen industry with its local textile centre at Coventry, then the fourth largest city.

3. Eventually, ruthless lords saw advantages in hastening a greater conversion of arable to pasture by depopulating whole villages and putting down complete parishes to vast inclosed pastures for sheep and cattle. So a long period of rest came to the corrugated soils of many parts of Feldon, while grassy selions became a landscape dominant across extensive areas.

Thus, whereas the demographic consequences of pestilence initiated a pronounced swing from arable to pasture during the latter half of the fourteenth century, the acceleration of the process during the fifteenth century was the result of a deliberate and fashionable economic policy, adopted on virtually a national scale, by certain powerful landowners and their freemen. The dramatic changes in population, settlement, land-use and landscape are briefly illustrated from within one parish, namely Wormleighton (151/448, 536; see also Fig. 2.1), close to the Cotswold scarp in south-east Warwickshire (Thorpe, 1965, 1975). Atop the large open field parish of 1498 (Fig. 2.7), a lattice of early block enclosure (macro-enclosure) was to be superimposed in 1499, when depopulation struck, gathering parcels of

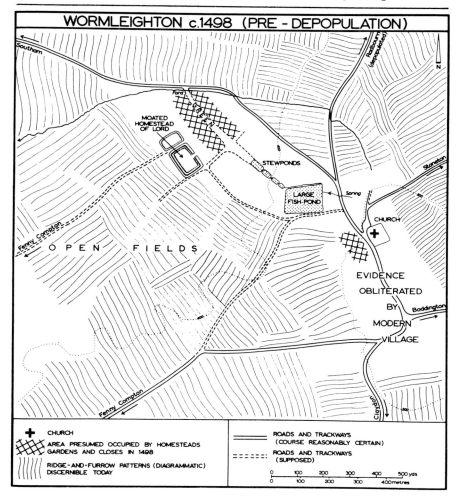

Fig. 2.7 Wormleighton c. 1498 (pre-depopulation)

shotts into great pastoral fields bounded by strong, aratrally curved hedges, double banked and ditched. Thereafter destined to be for long abandoned by the plough, these recuperating lower Lias clay soils were to be heavily manured by cattle, sheep and horses for decades to follow. The aerial view (Fig. 2.11) of 1953 and the explanatory diagram (Fig. 2.12) show the lost village in the valley bottom, the abandoned moated homestead of the lord, a large square fishpond and four small fish breeding tanks (now drained), and the ancient church on the hill (Bond, 1974).

In 1506 a prosperous local freeman butcher-grazier by the name of John Spencer bought the depopulated parish and set about rebuilding the village with a new manor house on the hill. We know a great deal

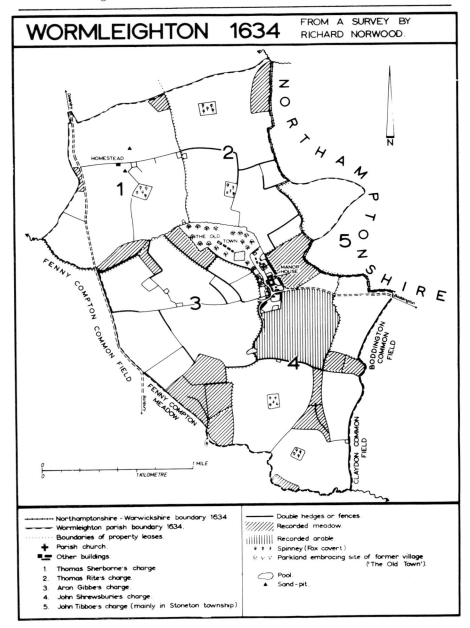

WORMLEIGHTON 1634   FROM A SURVEY BY RICHARD NORWOOD.

·—··—··— Northamptonshire - Warwickshire boundary 1634.
——— Wormleighton parish boundary 1634.
············ Boundaries of property leases.
✝ Parish church.
▪▄ Other buildings.
1.   Thomas Sherborne's charge.
2.   Thomas Rite's charge.
3.   Aron Gibbes's charge.
4.   John Shrewsburie's charge.
5.   John Tibboe's charge (mainly in Stoneton township).

——— Double hedges or fences.
▨▨ Recorded meadow.
||||||| Recorded arable
♦ ♦ ♦ Spinney (Fox covert)
⚶ ⚶ ⚶ Parkland embracing site of former village ('The Old Town').
⬭ Pool.
▲ Sand-pit.

Fig. 2.8 Wormleighton 1634, following depopulation and block enclosure

about his activities, both here and on other large estates that he had acquired. For example, manuscripts and maps in the Muniment Room of Earl Spencer at Althorp provide descriptions of the great field divisions 'double ditched and double hedged' with trees set

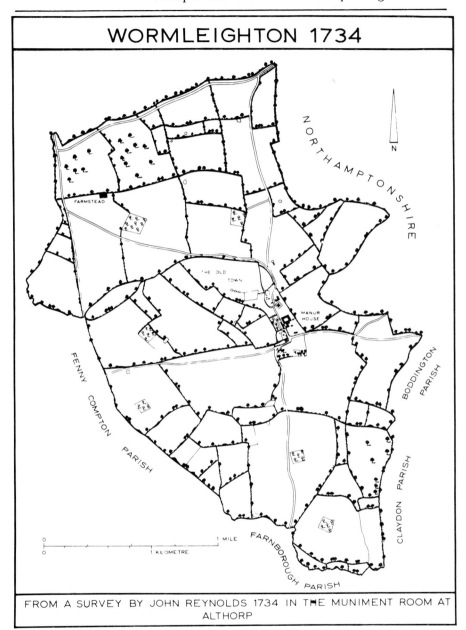

WORMLEIGHTON 1734

FROM A SURVEY BY JOHN REYNOLDS 1734 IN THE MUNIMENT ROOM AT ALTHORP

Fig. 2.9 Wormleighton 1734, showing further enclosure associated with hedges and hedgerow trees

between.* John Spencer mentions that when he first took over the great deforested parish of Wormleighton there was 'no wood nor

*For the sources of all maps and quotations *vide* Thorpe, 1965.

timber growing within 12 or 13 mile', timber here being 'a greater commodity than either corn or grass' so that poor folk had to 'burn the straw that their cattle should live by'. To remedy this he became one of our first conservationists, setting acorns 'both in the hedgerows

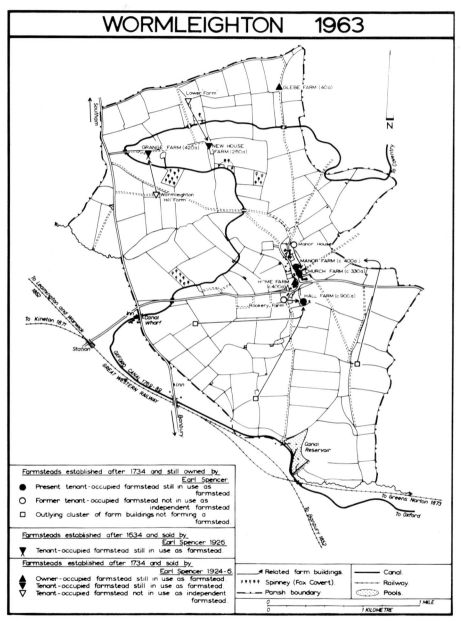

Fig. 2.10 Wormleighton 1963, showing a more advanced stage of field development than the map of 1734 (Fig. 2.9)

and also betwixt the hedges adjoining the old hedges that William Cope (*the depopulator*) made before'. John Spencer spoke the truth, for these great double field boundaries (Figs. 2.8, 2.11 and 2.12) still exist today, and in time one can find the great boles of decayed trees whose dendrochronology suggests an origin about this time. So, after a *champion* existence for almost a thousand years, trees and hedgerow plants, albeit in a thin linear mesh, now reappeared in Feldon, an event of great biogeographical significance. It is clear, too, that in order to provide the heavy hay crops that were required, John Spencer had made a wise use of latent resource by instituting an early system of floating or flooding meadows by leading water from both the large fish pond and the four small tanks across the patterned ground (Figs. 2.11 and 2.12).

Another distinctive landscape form emerged at this time, as great parks and great houses, so clearly shown on early estate maps and on printed maps by Saxton and Speed (Thorpe and Harvey, 1959), arose on depopulated sites and elsewhere, re-introducing stately trees to Warwickshire vistas and restricting deer largely to an ornamental rôle in confined parks. That the parish of Wormleighton was no exception is revealed by a map of 1634 (Fig. 2.8) which shows an emparking of 'Old Town' to provide an appropriate setting for the fine red-brick Tudor house on the hill. But, as Fig. 2.14 shows, Arden still remained well-wooded, a convenient source of timber for domestic fuel, charcoal and construction, the sporadic pattern of its great parks being related more to that of castles, former religious houses and space for gracious living than to late medieval depopulation. By 1634, the Lords Spencer, as they had now become, had further subdivided the great fields of Wormleighton, leasing land in four compact farm blocks to whoever was now rash enough to try to revive the pastoral boom, or again seek a return from grain; setting aside, too, small fox coverts, plantations and pheasantries to meet the needs of hunting and shooting (Fig. 2.8) and thereby re-introducing, albeit very belatedly, oases of semi-natural landscape.

With the gradual decline in wool prices and growing opposition to depopulation during the sixteenth century, there was a revival of grain production in many areas as part of a return to a more balanced mixed farming economy. By about 1600, too, some of the remaining open-field parishes of south Warwickshire were beginning to agitate for the enclosure of *champion* land and its subdivision into small fields for continuing arable use. But in many other Feldon townships the grazing tradition that had sprung up after depopulation continued strongly right through to this century – even until as late as the 1960s. The introduction of root crops, rotations, special grasses, improved plant varieties and animal breeds, better machines and drainage methods further highlighted the benefits of micro-enclosure for those parishes still remaining 'open'. During the eighteenth century continuing enclosure (Tate, 1943-44) by Private Acts, and later by the

Fig. 2.11 Oblique aerial photograph of the parish of Wormleighton (3 May 1953) looking north-west, showing the old church of Wormleighton and a cluster of cottages on the hill-top (bottom left); earthworks of the deserted medieval village and rectangular moated homestead near the canal (1769-89); a great square fish pond with four small fish-breeding tanks (now drained); old water channels leading from the fishponds into the valley below; remains of the great double hedgerows set up soon after 1499; ridge-and-furrow patterns of former arable land-use in the fields around the past and present settlements (see Fig. 2.12). (Photo: University of Cambridge; Crown Copyright reserved)

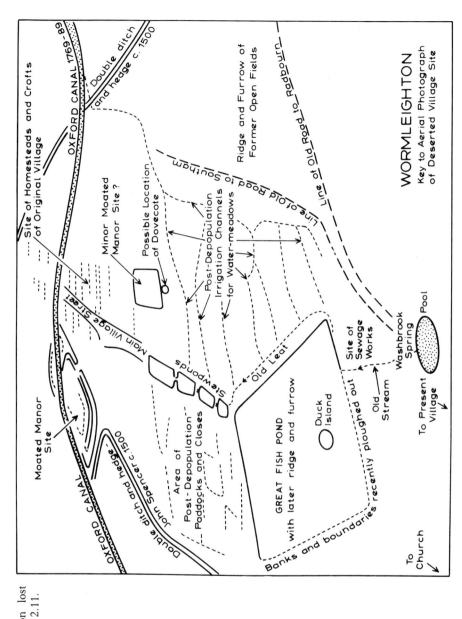

Fig. 2.12 Wormleighton lost village site: key to Fig. 2.11.

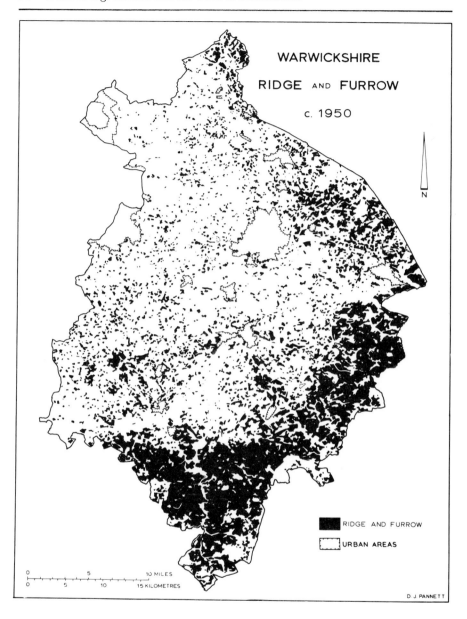

Fig. 2.13 Warwickshire: distribution of ridge-and-furrow c. 1950

General Enclosure Acts of 1801 and 1845, further parcellated the open fields of Feldon (and those around such thriving villages as Tanworth in Arden, 139/113, 705) so that, as seen in 1963, the mixed-farming field pattern of Wormleighton (Fig. 2.10) closely accorded with that of non-depopulated Feldon vills. Even more so, Feldon, with its

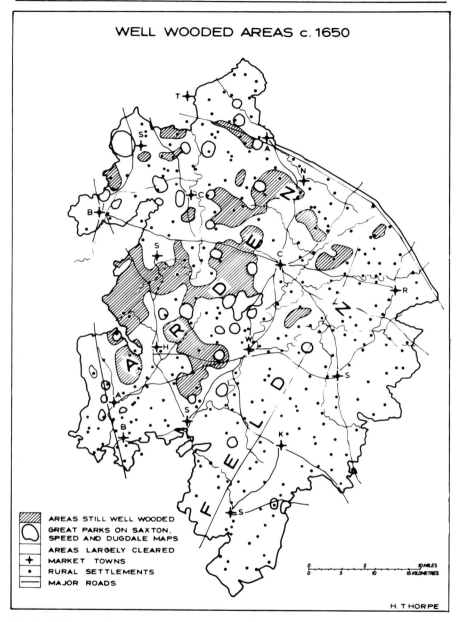

WELL WOODED AREAS c. 1650

AREAS STILL WELL WOODED
GREAT PARKS ON SAXTON,
SPEED AND DUGDALE MAPS
AREAS LARGELY CLEARED
MARKET TOWNS
RURAL SETTLEMENTS
MAJOR ROADS

H. T HORPE

Fig. 2.14 Warwickshire: well-wooded areas c. 1650

rectilinear, tree-strewn hedge patterns (Figs. 2.9 and 2.10) came
superficially to resemble woody Arden again – in its leafy lattice
particularly, though the irregular shapes and sizes of Arden fields and
their stout overgrown hedges and older hedgerow trees still bore the
unmistakeable imprint of piecemeal clearing from very long ago.

The sharp definition of the verges of fieldways and country roads
that followed enclosure, together with the development of turnpike
roads, improvements to the early 'main road' framework and, later,
the coming of 'M' roads encouraged the rise of distinctive ruderal

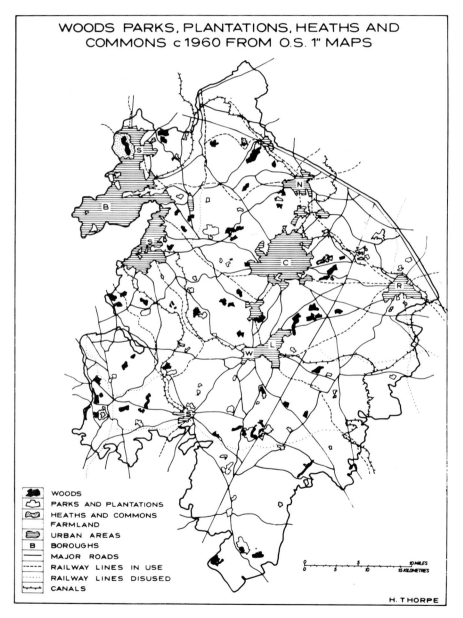

WOODS PARKS, PLANTATIONS, HEATHS AND
COMMONS c 1960 FROM O.S. 1" MAPS

WOODS
PARKS AND PLANTATIONS
HEATHS AND COMMONS
FARMLAND
URBAN AREAS
B   BOROUGHS
MAJOR ROADS
RAILWAY LINES IN USE
RAILWAY LINES DISUSED
CANALS

H. THORPE

Fig. 2.15 Warwickshire: distribution of woods, parks, plantations, heaths and
commons c. 1960

habitats now undergoing subtle transformation from the action of mechanical hedge cutters, petrol and diesel fumes, winter salt splash and summer weed sprays. Similarly, the addition of a canal network (Fig. 2.5), rapidly following the opening of the important Birmingham Canal in 1769, encouraged the spread of a thin arterial tracery of aquatic plants well beyond the main river banks and marl hole verges. The introduction of canal reservoirs, too, like those at Earlswood (139/113, 742) and Rotton Park (139/043, 868), and of other pools for drinking water like that on the river Tame at Aston (139/092, 902), brought back large water bodies to the landscape, the like of which had not been seen since the demise of the great fishponds of medieval times and the later incorporation of ornamental lakes in some of the great parks. Yet again, the coming of the railways, with the opening of the Grand Junction line from Birmingham to Warrington in 1837, brought in a thin spidery web of trackway ruderals many of which have undergone a rapid change of floristic character since Beechingisation (Fig. 2.15). Civil and military airfield construction made further inroads into farmland, though interesting reversions have occurred where Second World War runways, as at Honiley (139/230, 732), have been abandoned or released for agricultural purposes. But by far the greatest inroad on farm land has resulted from the natural growth of long established towns and the rise of new and expanded towns, so that, as Table 2.1 shows, 26.5% of Warwickshire in 1970 was built-up and agriculturally unproductive except for the presence of urban allotments, municipal parks and home gardens. Attitudes towards Birmingham's 'Green Belt' have also tended to soften in recent years as urban population pressure has mounted, while the paucity of proposed Areas of Outstanding Natural Beauty within the county must be considered not so much a reflection on the scenic potential of the shire, as an indictment of man's cavalier

Table 2.1 Warwickshire Estimated Acreages, 1970
(1887 figures in parentheses)*

Land use	Acres		%	
Forest and woodland	16 479	[16 659]	2.6	[2.9]
Arable (including temporary grass)	268 760	[196 740]	43.2	[34.7]
Permanent grass	165 346		26.5	
Rough grazing	5 505	[308 689]	0.9	[54.6]
Orchards	1 937		0.3	
Built-up area and land agriculturally unproductive	165 148	[44 370]	26.5	[7.8]
Total area of Warwickshire (including Birmingham, Coventry and Solihull C.B.s)	623 175	[566 458]	100.0	[100.0]

*From Bagnall, J.E., *The Flora of Warwickshire*, 1891.

treatment of Warwickshire's natural assets over the years.

In the following table the figures in parentheses show that in 1887 only 7.8% of the shire was built-up and agriculturally unproductive. In view of the great loss of land to urban uses that has occurred during the ensuing nine decades, it is perhaps surprising that the description 'Leafy Warwickshire' is still so often applied to the county today. Woodland – cut, re-cut, regenerated and planted – now covers only 2.6% of the area (Fig. 2.15), arable and grass together occupying 70.6%. Much of the 'woody look' within the shire derives from Arden Forest remnants north of the Avon, and from the tree-strewn hedgerows associated with enclosure processes of very varied date and circumstance north and south of the river. But the generally insignificant part played by solid geology in the landscape's character over much of the shire should not be overlooked, for hard rock suitable for stone wall construction forms only very restricted outcrops in Warwickshire though the extensive marls and clays have left their impress in the bricks and tiles of many half-timbered homesteads. Nor must one overlook the importance of social and economic factors when seeking to explain the distribution of the numerous great parks (Figs. 2.14 and 2.15) which considerably reinforce the leafy look in many parishes, both north and south of the Avon, though by no means all the fine trees are regenerated remnants of the once extensive native forests as the conifers and intrusive Sequoias gracing Umberslade Park remind us.

Since the Second World War a new breed of vigorous arable farmers has taken advantage of the accumulated fertility of the long rested pastures of many Feldon parishes, such as Hodnell (151/424, 574) and Upper and Lower Radbourne (151/444, 576), which had continued to remain strongly pastoral since fifteenth-century depopulation first struck. Their great diesel tractors have ruthlessly peneplanated ingrained ridge-and-furrow, breaching the field boundaries of early block enclosure, so creating again in many areas a landscape of vast open field sweeping over an entire parish, obliterating even the ghostly outlines of the former village. A few men and a few machines now do the work of what was once a whole active, integrated village community, producing large grain surpluses to market elsewhere. Except for faint zebra bands of alternating grey and brown the strips, the curvilinear ridges-and-furrows have gone. A new balance is said to have been achieved between minority man, powerful machine, special crop variety, irrigation, industrially produced nutrients and sprays, field drains and the good earth itself so susceptible to man-induced changes. Yet during the wet autumn and spring of 1960/61, when farmers were unable to plough and sow the heavy lower Lias clays of the Feldon, the *Manchester Guardian* for 14 March, 1961 speculated as to whether Warwickshire was destined yet again to become a grassy shire! Lessons learned from our studies in historical geography continually reveal that the delicate balance between man and nature has to be achieved within a complex of physical, biogeographical, social, economic and even political factors. Far-reaching chain reactions can so easily be triggered off by slight adjustments at merely one or two points within this complex. Little wonder that one must continually ask how real is the present state of supposed 'balance' within parts of our restless shire – and for how long is it likely to persist?

REFERENCES

Beresford, M.W. (1945/6). The deserted villages of Warwickshire. *Trans. Bgham, Arch. Soc.*, **66**: 49-106.

Beresford, M.W. (1954). *The Lost Village of England*. Lutterworth Press, pp. 445.

Bond, C.J. (1974). Deserted medieval villages in Warwickshire: a review of the field evidence. *Trans. Bgham. Arch. Soc.*, **86**: 85-112.

Flohn, H. (1949/50). Klimaschwankungen im Mittelalter und ihre Historischgeographische Bedeutung. *Ber. Deut. Landeskunde*, **7**.

Harley, J.B. (1958). Population trends and agricultural developments from the Warwickshire Hundred Rolls of 1279. *Econ. Hist. Rev.*, **11**: 8-18.

Kinvig, R.H. (1950). The Birmingham district in Domesday times. *In Birmingham and its Regional Setting: A Scientific Survey*. Birmingham, 113-34. (Figure 26 shows the distribution of Domesday ploughteams within the shire. Population densities are presented in Figure 27.)

Kinvig, R.H. (1971). Warwickshire. *In* Darby, H.C. and Terrett, I.B. (eds.). *The Domesday Geography of Midland England*. Cambridge, Cambridge University Press, 273-312.

Le Roy Ladurie, E. (1973). *Times of Feast, Times of Famine: A History of Climate Since the Year 1000*. London.

Pannett, D.J., Mead, W.R. and Harrison, M.J. (1965). A midland ridge-and-furrow map. *Geogr. J.*, **131**: 366-9. (I am indebted to Mr. Pannett for allowing me to include his map of the distribution of ridge-and-furrow in Warwickshire as Figure 2.13 of this chapter.).

Roberts, B.K. (1962). Moated sites. *Amat. Hist.*, Winter 1962: 34-8.

Roberts, B.K. (1965). Settlement, land-use and population in the western portion of the Forest of Arden, Warwickshire, between 1086 and 1350. University of Birmingham, Ph.D. Thesis.

Sawyer, P.H. (1963). Review of: Darby, H.C. and Campbell, E.M.J. The Domesday Geography of South-East England. *Econ. Hist. Rev.*, **16**: 155-7.

Shotton, F.W. (1971). Geology and soils. *In* Cadbury, D.A., Hawkes, J.G. and Readett, R.C. (eds.). *A Computer-Mapped Flora. A Study of the County of Warwickshire*. London, Academic Press, 16-19. (I am indebted to Professor Shotton for kindly allowing me to include his map of surface geology as Figure 2.2 in the present chapter.)

Tate, W.E. (1943-44). Enclosure acts and awards relating to Warwickshire. *Trans. Bgham. Arch. Soc.*, **65**: 45-104.

Thorpe, H. (1950). The growth of settlement before the Norman Conquest. *In Birmingham and its Regional Setting: A Scientific Survey*. Birmingham, 87-112. (See especially Figures 22 and 23.)

Thorpe, H. (1965). The lord and the landscape, illustrated through the changing fortunes of a Warwickshire parish, Wormleighton. *Trans. Bgham. Arch. Soc.*, **80**: 38-77.

Thorpe, H. (1971). Historical geography: the evolution of settlement and land use. *In* Cadbury, D.A., Hawkes, J.G. and Readett, R.C. (eds.). *A Computer-Mapped Flora. A Study of the County of Warwickshire*. London, Academic Press, 20-44.

Thorpe, H. (1975). Air, ground, document. *In Aerial Reconnaissance in Archaeology*. Council for British Archaeology, Research Report No. 12: 141-53.

Thorpe, H. and Harvey, P.D.A. (1959). *The Printed Maps of Warwickshire, 1576-1900*. Warwick, Warwick County Occasional Series 1, pp. 279.

Utterström, G. (1955). Climatic variations and population problems in early modern history. *Scand. Econ. Hist. Rev.*, **3**: 3-47.

Warwick, G.T. (1971). The physical background. *In* Cadbury, D.A., Hawkes, J.G. and Readett, R.C. (eds.). *A Computer-Mapped Flora. A Study of the County of Warwickshire*. London, Academic Press, 4-12.

Webster, G. and Hobley, B. (1965). Aerial reconnaissance over the Warwickshire Avon. *Archaeol. J.*, **121**: 1-22. (This includes a distribution map, a selection of large-scale plans and a summary of the character of each site.)

Note: Table 2.1 and Figs. 2.3, 2.4, 2.5, 2.6, 2.14 and 2.15 reproduced from author's chapter in Cadbury, D.A., Hawkes, J.G. and Readett, R.C. (eds.), *A Computer-Mapped Flora. A Study of the County of Warwickshire*, through the courtesy of Academic Press.

3. On the complex nature of man-animal relationships from the Pleistocene to early agricultural societies

Don Brothwell

There is no doubt that human populations, during their evolution, have considerably influenced the survival, biology and health of many animal species, particularly those which had food value. It is therefore pertinent to give some consideration to the complex of man-animal relationships through time as a part of the perspective of change seen in the world's natural environment. Even a survey of recent historic times provides plenty of examples of the impact – often seriously detrimental – of human communities on other species. During the last two hundred years, the rate of extinction possibly equals one species or variety of mammal every year, and as many again may be currently threatened with extinction. Deprivation of habitat or food, overkilling, and even the introduction of other competitive mammals by man (for example, dogs, goats, even the European hare and grey squirrel) are some of the facts for which we must accept responsibility. But all this has a long history and, in order to view the present soberly and correctly, it is a valuable exercise to look back into prehistory, even though there are still more questions than answers concerning the complex changing mosaic of earlier man-animal relationships.

First of all, and as this is part of a centenary celebration, let me go back and view the attitudes of about a century ago. Under the stimulus of naturalists such as Darwin, Haeckel, Huxley and a few others man began to be seen in evolutionary and simple ecological terms. Moreover, such biologists were sensitive to the varying degrees to which human groups imposed themselves on other species at a destructive selective and breeding level. Darwin's (1868) classic publication for instance on *The Variation of Animals and Plants under Domestication* is not only concerned with artificial selection by man, but emphasises variation and questions of relationship with wild populations. Another side to man-animal relationships was illustrated by Carter (1874), when he described the skull of a wild urus, *Bos primigenius*, brought down by a polished stone implement which had shattered on impact and remained partly buried in the skull bones.

The appearance of ancient mammal bones at both industrial and archaeological sites in fact raised constantly this question of 'wild' versus 'domestic' and, even at this time, the complexities of the problem were not overlooked. During the 1870s, for instance, both Rütimeyer (1878) and Wilckens (1876) were concerned with the variation and micro-evolution of early European bovids, and were debating whether a wild Pleistocene form of the small-horned *Bos longifrons* mainly contributed to the emergence of some modern cattle varieties. This was rather a progressive idea, and even today there is resistance to the possibility of more than the giant *primigenius* form occurring in the upper Pleistocene of Europe, even though there is some cave art and osteological evidence to support this alternative view.

A few years later, other zoologists were exploring this question of the influence of man on other animal species around him and were considering, for instance, the possibility that more than one species of *Canis* gave rise to domestic dogs. Without knowledge of population genetics, it was nevertheless realised that changes in these earlier mammal stocks were not the result of intensive selective breeding, but more likely to be the result of far less directed micro-evolutionary processes.

So our Victorian colleagues were fairly astute in their thinking and observations, and indeed were more understanding of earlier man-animal relationships – especially as regards the history of agriculture and domestication – than perhaps some who have worked on these same questions during the past few decades. They were, however, under one important disadvantage in having a very inadequate time scale. Absolute dating, especially as a result of radiocarbon and potassium-argon techniques, has extended our evolutionary history ten-fold on earlier estimates. This does not change our impact on the world around us, but at least we now know that we have been a nuisance in various ecosystems for far longer than originally thought.

So, to begin at the beginning, the emergence of our own line, the hominids, extends over four to five million years. Between about a million and two million years ago, there is fossil evidence from dental variation and associated faunal remains at hominid sites, suggesting that these small, so-called australopithecines were experimenting with diets and increasing their animal protein intake. Some prehistorians would also argue that related to this earliest hunting and collecting phase was the development of a so-called osteodontokeratic culture – that is, bone, teeth and horn were food by-products which were already being used in some form of basic tool-using culture. With even simple stone tools, they became more powerful predators. Very tentatively, one might see their position in relation to other contempory organisms in the foodweb diagram constructed on available evidence by Cox, Healey and Moore (1973) (Fig. 3.1).

Somewhat better evidence for established hunting has been gained from Middle Pleistocene sites associated with an evolving hominid form called *Homo erectus*, and it is relevant that by this time range (circa 1,000,000-300,000 years ago) these early humans had migrated widely in the Old World, and probably extended in family or small tribal groups over much of Africa, habitable parts of Europe, southern Asia and as far east as Java. This extensive spread, it might be argued, was an indication of the adaptive success of the evolving hominids,

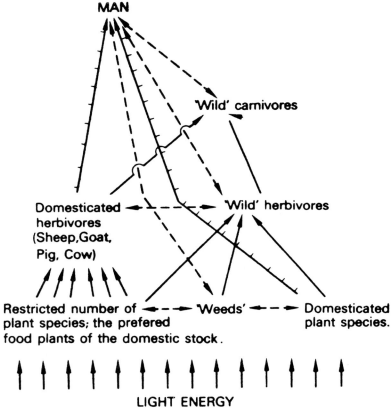

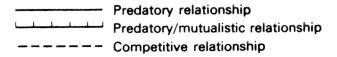

LIGHT ENERGY

This scheme assumes man's complete dependance on domestic animals and plants. This extreme situation will have developed gradually through agricultural history.

——————— Predatory relationship

└─┴─┴─┴─┴─┘ Predatory/mutualistic relationship

— — — — — — Competitive relationship

Fig. 3.1 Foodweb diagrams contrasting the situation for the australopithecine hominids and for human groups in an early agricultural phase. From Cox, Healey and Moore (1973). See over.

with continuing population increase and probably a related drive to
search further territories for game. We know nothing precisely about
the hunting policies, taboos or preferences of these people, but there is
little doubt that they continued in their omnivorous way, exploiting
fire now, and perhaps where larger herbivores permitted,
considerably increasing their meat intake in proportion to other
elements of their diet.

By early upper Pleistocene times, regional populations of *Homo
erectus* had evolved into a number of distinctive, more advanced

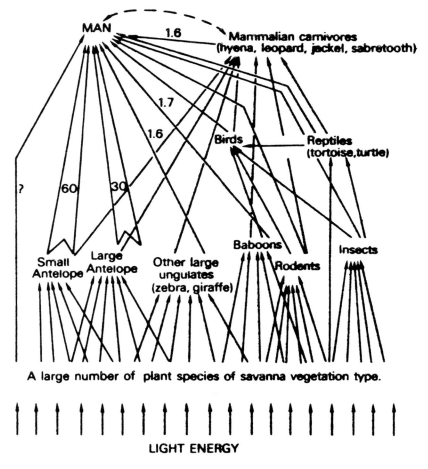

A large number of plant species of savanna vegetation type.

LIGHT ENERGY

The figures given beside certain of the lines leading to man
represent the percentage of bones of that particular animal
found in association with an Australopithecine occupation
site in southern Africa. It is likely that man's precise food
requirements varied with local conditions, availability
of game, etc.

Fig 3.1 (continued)

varieties, the most successful one, our own species *H. sapiens sapiens*, apparently replacing all other forms by about 30,000 years ago. Within the next 10 to 15,000 years these advanced Palaeolithic people, perhaps numbering two or three million, continued to extend their range, probably in relation to food needs and subtle population pressures, and had extended into the Americas. The progressive and highly successful nature of these Palaeolithic groups during the last 20,000 years of the Pleistocene is, I think, extremely important to a proper appraisal of the impact of these now world-spread human groups on other animal communities.

It was, of course, during these times that many species of large herbivores became extinct. The trimming away of this megafauna is impressive (Fig. 3.2), and possible causes have been discussed at length (Martin, 1958; Martin and Wright, 1967; Reed, 1970). The losses appear to be most pronounced in the New World, with 24 genera affected, less so in Eurasia, while southern Asia and the sub-Sahara were far less affected. It is not of course possible to determine precisely when the various species became extinct, but one can at least construct a sequence of change when various species seemed to have been particularly threatened. It can be rightly argued that the extinctions fall at a time of various late Pleistocene environmental changes, and I would not wish to argue that climatic and vegetational changes were not important factors. But the extinction of various species of large food animals in about 30 separate genera amounts to

GLOBAL EXTINCTION PATTERN

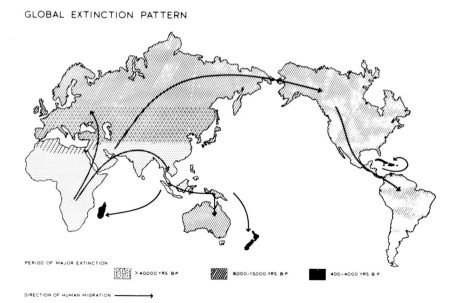

PERIOD OF MAJOR EXTINCTION

▒ >40,000 YRS B P   ▨ 8,000-13,000 YRS B P   ■ 400-4000 YRS B P

DIRECTION OF HUMAN MIGRATION ——————→

Fig. 3.2 The possible sequence of late Pleistocene vertebrate extinctions. After Martin and Wright (1967)

biological carelessness unless one calls in human intervention as the final critical factor. Perhaps a suitable close-up of a small part of this more widespread process is recorded by McNeish (1971) in his work on the early human communities of the Tehuacán Valley in Mexico. Late Pleistocene climatic changes resulted in the diminution of grassland and water holes there, with an expansion of thorn and cactus forests on to the valley slopes. Mammal extinctions ranged from such 'herd' animals as horse and antelope to mammoth and mastodon, and while this could be related to grassland shrinkage and other vegetational changes, 'overkill' techniques on the part of the human microbands in relation to diminishing mammalian numbers would have guaranteed the end.

One might view this late Pleistocene phase then as a clearing-away period from a faunal point of view, and I might add, for all their advanced hunting knowledge and techniques, it may have been a time when some human communities found themselves in an economic slump. I shall return to this period briefly again, but let us just complete our outline through to agricultural times. There seems little doubt, from the evidence of early urban sites that, whatever vegetational and faunal changes took place at the close of the Pleistocene period, human population numbers must have been maintained and then eventually increased. The so-called Neolithic phase, initiated about 10,000 years ago, saw man busy altering his own demography, living partly in villages and even towns, and developing agricultural techniques for the increasing protection and control of certain mammal populations. Dependance on man probably increased at this time in various species, the resulting foodweb being of a very different kind to that of the early Pleistocene hominids (Fig. 3.1). The simplicity of this picture, however, is really related to the needs of archaeologists to attempt palaeoeconomic reconstructions, and fails to show the actual complex nature of the interaction of man with other species which inevitably came into closer contact with him as human numbers and distribution increased, the megafauna dwindled and patterns of vegetation became modified. This was a period of considerable adaptive change, biologically and socially, for human communities, but it is clear that one variable began to get out of hand, and by early historic times world population size for man was probably in the order of one hundred million.

When considering this major change to animal husbandry and the consequent extensive exploitation of an increasing number of animal species during postglacial times, it is now usual to outline the changes in a rather standardised form. Just as one can pinpoint and plot out the centres of, say, earthquake activity, so the considered areas of origin of domestic species may be plotted out (Fig. 3.3). A more tentative scheme can alternatively be given in which the distribution of wild ancestral populations are seen in relation to these early man-

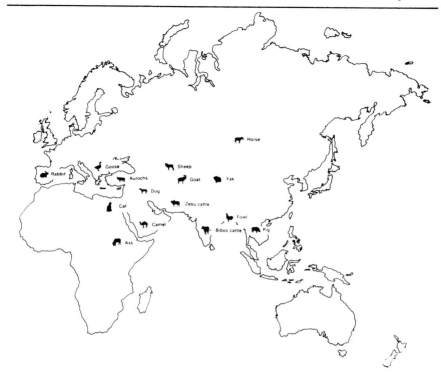

Fig. 3.3 The origins of certain Old World domestic animals in relation to possible areas of domestication according to some authorities.

controlled groups. If time rather than space is the dimension to be considered, then we get a sequence of positions for different species depending on the earliest evidence thought to indicate a domestic variety (Fig. 3.4a). This is a little more satisfactory in that it attempts to show the gradual control of different species over time, but fails to emphasize the highly uncertain knowledge of the variable transitional periods from wild to highly controlled groups for the different species (Fig. 3.4b). However, these schemes fail to recognise the possible recurring attempts on the part of human groups even back into the Pleistocene to increase their dominance in these man-animal relationships, or of the probability that closer man-animal relationships occurred in the past with species now seen only as wild populations. Probably because of their ability to record facts, rather than because they are a special case in the past, we know, for instance, that in certain early Egyptian societies the mongoose, cheetah, gazelle, ibex and even the hyaena were brought under control.

The attempt to see basic patterns in these changes in man-animal relationships is initially a good one, but the time has arrived for some critical evaluation of the really complex nature of such relationships in

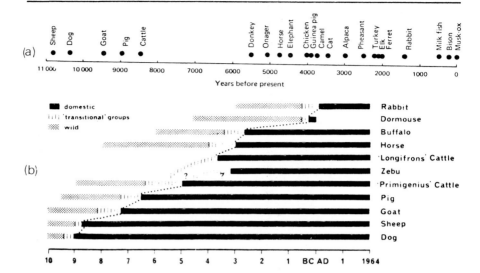

Fig. 3.4 Two ways of considering the history of animal domestication in relation to time: a) by the approximate positioning of the earliest dated evidence in a time sequence, b) by a more elaborate viewing of the transition from wild to domestic through time.

the past, especially those which have led to the transformation of species into fully domestic varieties (Brothwell, 1975). To begin with, there is reason to challenge the value of separating animal relationships with man into the oversimplifying 'wild' and 'domestic' categories. The term 'domestication' has been all to often used to imply one simple process, but in fact it is various grades of relationship in which humans have varying degrees of control over the reproduction and genetic composition of the animal group. The factors which have led to increasing man-animal contacts include food needs and the elaboration of rituals in which animals have a part to play, for riding and transportation, as well as the development of degrees of mutual dependence (Isaac, 1970).

Such links have probably evolved out of processes found in both human and non-human exploitation patterns. Characteristics such as tractability, docility, strong herding instinct and a large capacity for milk production have been named as of special importance, but it is debatable whether real selection for them has occurred in prehistory. Changes in fitness probably occurred following the later stages of all closer man-animal relations, with adaptation to the captive and more restricted environment resulting in various gene pool changes (Hafez, 1968). In many respects, however, it seems debatable whether in the earlier stages of increased contact (and before trends were established which modified the animals in some distinctive way beyond that seen in the wild) one could distinguish any changes from those seen in wild stocks. Moreover, what small scale bone differences might have occurred are likely to be extremely difficult to interpret. Gene pool characteristics resulting from founder effect in an early domestic stock need not be distinguishable from a genetic bottle-neck in a wild population – the result of disease, famine or local migration. Modifications to growth due to malnutrition should produce similar bone changes in both the wild and man-controlled groups. The claim that the histology of bone from wild species is different to that in highly domestic kinds (Daly, Perkins and Drew, 1973) sounds biologically improbable and is not without critics (Watson, 1975).

Out of all the literature published by zoologists, archaeologists and others there have probably emerged as many fallacies as facts about changes in man-animal relationships through time. To begin with, there is the fallacy that the identification of the earliest dated bones of a domestic form of a particular species is an indication of the real antiquity of the domestication process in it. The fact is, however, that finds in deposits are phenomena of chance and may thus misrepresent the truth. Perhaps the canids could be used to illustrate this point. Current views on the distribution of wild or feral canids and the domestication of dogs run as follows.

During historic times, wild members of the genus *Canis* have had a wide distribution, with wolves extending through Europe and Asia into the New World, jackals being located in parts of Africa, the dingo in Australia and the coyote in regions of the United States. Today the spread of these species is greatly restricted by human activity, but sufficient is known of these wild populations for us to be able to appreciate how extraordinarily variable domestic dogs are in comparison to each other. In weight alone, adults of different varieties of dog very from 4 to 160 pounds, and there are considerable differences in physical proportions, coat colour and so on. Nevertheless, as regards the distinguishing features of early dogs, the criteria used to separate them from wolf are by no means well worked out (Clutton-Brock, 1969; Herre and Röhrs, 1971).

It is generally argued that dogs have a unified common ancestry, being domesticated from wolves in a single area over 10,000 years ago. From this restricted beginning, it is assumed that considerable numbers of varieties formed over the next few millennia, and there is no doubt – as seen for example in the tomb illustrations of Beni Hassan in Egypt – that some communities could have produced their own miniature Crufts dog show. In terms of dated finds of early dog, the list is short but widespread – perhaps as early as 12,000 years ago in the Palegawra Cave, Iraq (Turnbull and Reed, 1974), about 7,500 B.C. in Yorkshire (Star Carr) and Denmark (Degerbøl, 1961), with other specimens of about the same dates from Turkey (Lawrence, 1967) and Kurdistan (Reed, 1969). Epipalaeolithic dog from Romania may be earlier (Bolomey, 1973) but radio-carbon dates are awaited. Of slight embarrassment to those who wish to see dogs emerging from the early societies from south-west Asia is the fact that one of the earliest dogs is that belonging to an Amerindian community living about 8,400 B.C. in Idaho. However, there is general feeling that the New World dogs have an Old World origin, joining the palaeoindians in their movement across the Bering Strait. Olsen (1974) questions whether China may hold the answer to this problem and it is interesting that late Pleistocene cave deposits in Japan have produced canids which are distinguishable from the typical wolf of the area (Shikama and Okafuji, 1958). Significantly, both wolf and hunter in the later Pleistocene were probably to a considerable extent occupying the same ecological niches and may at times have been active competitors. In this situation of two dominant predators, it seems to me highly likely that advanced Palaeolithic hunters in more than one area would have seized the initiative to control some members of the wolf population and used them in hunting. There is no time to develop this further here, but it tends to be forgotten in the argument that it was the Palaeolithic hunters and not the early agriculturalists who would have found value in controlling some members of local wolf populations, and this could have extended well back in time. Perhaps it is significant that a small canid is represented with hominid and large mammal remains at Swanscombe, representing a community living about a quarter of a million years ago. Pidoplichko (1969) also reports an association of late Pleistocene 'dog' or wolf with a large mammal assembledge in the Ukraine and there is also a claim of dog at a German Magdalenian cave site (Musil, 1970). So there are grounds for questioning the value of relying solely on skeletal evidence without considering other factors, especially as they would strongly suggest a Pleistocene antiquity for dog micro-evolution.

It would be out of place to elaborate on the various other fallacies in similar detail. Indeed some are research topics in themselves. For instance, do skeletal changes always occur as part of domestication? This question is highly relevant to a proper understanding of, for instance, the emergence of the horse in relation to human societies. To me, the late date of about 3,000 B.C. for the control of this species does not make sense if one considers the wide availability of late Pleistocene horses and the fact that horse behaviour clearly indicates that it is an ideal animal for *early* and not *late* control by man.

Finally, at a very different level of animal organisation, there is the question of health and parasitism. It has been rather taken for granted that, other than the possibility of changing nutritional levels as a result of climatic or vegetational changes or overgrazing, there would be nothing of special health note in animal populations from the Pleistocene to farming times. I am quite sure that this is wrong and that patterns of health and parasitism may have changed noticeably. In particular, restricted breeding and breed differentiation could have encouraged the increase of disease frequencies usually found in wild

Table 3.1   A comparison of the incidence of salmonellosis in modern byre-
tied and loose-housed cattle   (Data from Richardson, A. and
Watson, W.A., *Brit. Vet. J.*, 127: 173-83)

Cows per herd	Percentage of herds with salmonellosis	
	Byre herds	Loose-housed herds
11 to 20	0.9	0
21 to 39	1.2	11.5
40 to 69	6.3	20.8
70 to 99	7.7	34.2
100 to 199	12.1	100

populations. For instance, the frequency of the nervous disorder 'swayback' in lambs can vary by 40% in different breeds. Similarly, mean tick counts can vary between related bovids. The nature and standard of husbandry can also influence the animal's ability to withstand disease. Considering byre versus loose-housed herds, definite frequency differences in *Salmonella* infection can be demonstrated (Table 3.1). These are not statistics purely relevant to modern groups; they should equally be an indication of possible differential micro-evolution which could have occurred in earlier regional animals stocks being increasingly controlled by man. With careful investigation, some of these diseases may be found to have left evidence for interpretation. Brucellosis, with its attendant abortion problem, was surely more of a health threat in closely herded early agricultural stocks and, from the evidence of a possible case of brucellosis arthritis in a Bronze Age man from Jericho (Brothwell, 1965), the infection was a direct problem even to human communities. Similarly, tapeworm parasites could have been far more of a health problem in early agricultural societies than prior to this time. During the latter part of the nineteenth century in Iceland, the authorities clamped down on dog keeping because it was found that the majority were infested with *Echinococcus*, which was a health threat to the human population as well (Annandale, 1905). Positive archaeological evidence of this type of situation was revealed in a Norse cemetary excavation I undertook in the Orkney islands a few years ago. In about 2% of the adults in this community, calcified hydatid cysts in the region of the liver provided clear evidence of a much boosted helminth load in this locality. In the future we can expect more evidence of this animal group in view of the fact that the parasite eggs can be resistant to decay and remain in coprolites for many centuries (Pike, 1967).

I have not mentioned the possible changes in relationship which may have occurred between man and micro-organisms since the Pleistocene. This is perhaps an exotic field to work in, but some progress has been made. Let me exemplify by reference to possible changes which have occurred in the treponematoses, a group which

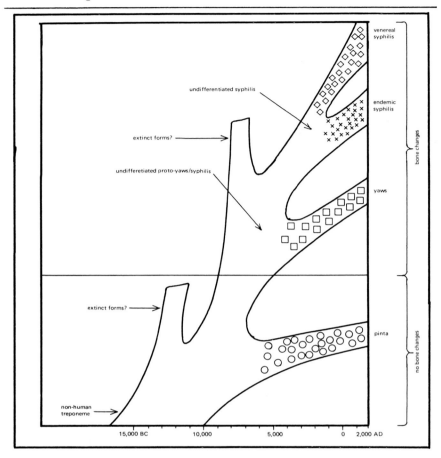

Fig. 3.5 Four variants of the treponeme – a bacteria-like organism which causes syphilis – which probably evolved from a common ancestor in perhaps 15,000 B.C. Only venereal syphilis is normally spread by sexual intercourse. Endemic syphilis, yaws and pinta can be spread by normal contact. Pinta causes infection restricted to the soft tissues, the others result in inflammation which affects bones leaving changes clearly recognisable in ancient skeletons.

includes syphilis and yaws. The variation in this species (*Treponema pallidum*) may well be the result of adaptive changes since the latter part of the Pleistocene, related to its association with man in different environmental circumstances, both climatic and cultural. A tentative evolutionary scheme for this group is seen in Figure 3.5, with a non-bone-changing variety giving rise to. the bone-destructive diseases yaws and endemic syphilis (Hackett, 1967). The final jump to venereal syphilis probably did not take place until well into historic times, possibly the result of a shunting of endemic syphilis into new climatic and cultural zones, and especially into Europe. More than once man has been considerably involved in influencing other species, but in this case there was feed-back with a vengeance. So the notorious French malady, venereal syphilis, turns out to be an excellent example of the long-term extent of human influences on the species around him! But the treponematoses are not the only group of diseases which could, of course, be given as an example here. The movement and success of other micro-organisms were equally linked to human population increase and activity. Bruce-Schwatt (1965) has discussed the history of malaria, where the cycle of events leading to the significant infection of human communities could well have been influenced in some areas by forest clearance and early irrigation schemes. Yet again, the 'success' of tuberculosis in man could well have been related to increasing contact with bovids following the development of husbandry, as well as factors of human population density, hygiene and nutrition.

The conclusions which might be drawn from this brief survey of man-animal relationships in the past are as follows. The impact of man on a wide range of animal species has been considerable – through at least the latter part of the Pleistocene and into Holocene times. We have probably contributed to the extinction of many other species, even during prehistory, and are still doing so. The so-called 'domestication' of certain animals possibly began in the Pleistocene, but was probably greatly accelerated by the occurrence of critical human population thresholds in relation to postglacial environmental changes. The proper evaluation of modern domestic animal varieties, their diversity and the wealth of genetic variation seen in them, should take into account their long histories. Finally, we should view man-animal relationships not only from the point of view of human exploitation for food and other needs, but also from the point of view of micro-organisms associated with man. Here again, changing human populations and cultures have been intimately linked with survivorship potential in a variety of infectious diseases.

REFERENCES

Annandale, N. (1905). *The Faroes and Iceland: Studies in Island Life.* Oxford, Clarendon.
Bolomey, A. (1973). The present stage of knowledge of mammal exploitation during the Epipalaeolithic and the earliest Neolithic on the territory of Romania. *In* Motolcsi, J. (ed.). *Domestikationsforschung und Geschichte der Haustiere, Budapest, 1971,* Budapest, Akadémiai Kiadó: 197-203.
Brothwell, D. (1965). The palaeopathology of the EB-MB and Middle Bronze Age remains from Jericho (1957-8 excavations). *In* Kenyon, K.M. (ed.). *Excavations at Jericho, II.* London: 685-93.
Brothwell, D. (1975). Salvaging the term 'domestication' for certain types of man-animal relationship: the possible value of an eight point scoring system. *J. Arch. Sci.,* **2**: 397-400.
Bruce-Schwatt, L.J. (1965). Palaeogenesis and palaeo-epidemiology of

primate malaria. *Bull. Wld. Hlth. Org.*, **32**: 323.

Carter, A. (1874). *Geol. Mag.*, p. 492. (Quoted by Hughes, 1896).

Clutton-Brock, J. (1969). The origins of the dog. *In* Brothwell, D. and Higgs, E. (eds.). *Science in Archaeology*. London, Thames and Hudson, 303-9.

Cox, C.B., Healey, I.N. and Moore, P.D. (1973). *Biogeography. An Ecological and Evolutionary Approach*. Oxford, Blackwell.

Daly, P., Perkins, D. and Drew, I.M. (1973). The effects of domestication on the structure of animal bone. *In* Motolcsi, J. (ed.). *Domestikationsforschung und Geschichte der Haustiere, Budapest, 1971*. Budapest, Akadémiai Kiadó, 157-61.

Darwin, C. (1868). *The Variation of Animals and Plants Under Domestication*. 2 vols. London, Murray.

Degerbøl, M. (1961). On a find of Preboreal domestic dog (*Canis familiaris* L.) from Star Carr, Yorkshire, with remarks on other Mesolithic dogs. *Proc. Prehist. Soc.*, **27**: 35-55.

Hackett, C.J. (1967). The human treponematoses. *In* Brothwell, D. and Sandison, A.T. (eds.). *Diseases in Antiquity: a Survey of the Diseases, Injuries and Surgery of Early Populations*. Thomas, Springfield, 152-69.

Hafez, E.S.E. (ed.) 1968). *Adaptation of Domestic Animals*. Philadelphia, Lea and Febiger.

Herre, W. and Röhrs, M. (1971). Domestikation und Stammesgeschichte. *In* Heberer, G. (ed.) *Die Evolution der Organismen, II/2*. Stuttgart, 29-174.

Hughes, T.M. (1896). The more important breeds of cattle which have been recognized in the British Isles. *Archaeologia*, **55**: 125-58.

Isaac, E. (1970). *Geography of Domestication*. Englewood Cliffs, Prentice-Hall.

Lawrence, B. (1967). Early domestic dogs. *Z. Saugetierk.*, **32**: 44-59.

Lawrence, B. (1968). Antiquity of large dogs in North America. *Tebiwa, J. Idaho State Univ. Mus.*, **11**: 43-9.

Martin, P.S. (1958). Pleistocene ecology and biogeography of North America. *In* Hubbs, C.L. (ed.). *Zoogeography*. Washington, American Association for the Advancement of Science, 375-420.

Martin, P.S. and Wright, H.E. (eds.) (1967). *Pleistocene Extinctions: the Search for a Cause*. New Haven, Yale University Press.

McNeish, R.S. (1971). Speculation about how and why food production and village life developed in the Tehuacán Valley, Mexico. *Archaeology*, **24**: 307-15.

Musil, R. (1970). Domestication of the dog already in the Magdalenian? *Anthropologie*, **8**: 87-8.

Olsen, S.J. (1974). Early domestic dogs in North America and their origins. *J. Field Arch.*, **1**: 343-5.

Pidoplichko, I.G. (1969). [Late Palaeolithic dwellings of mammoth bones in the Ukraine.] *Kiev. A.N. Ukrainskoi SSR Institut Zoologii*. (In Russian)

Pike, A.W. (1967). The recovery of parasite eggs from ancient cesspit and latrine deposits: an approach to the study of early parasite infections. *In* Brothwell, D. and Sandison, A.T. (eds.). *Diseases in Antiquity: a Survey of the Diseases, Injuries and Surgery of Early Populations*. Thomas, Springfield, 184-8.

Reed, C.A. (1969). The pattern of animal domestication in the prehistoric Near East. In Ucko, P.J. and Dimbleby, G.W. (eds.). *The Domestication and Exploitation of Plants and Animals*. London, Duckworth, 361-80.

Reed, C.A. (1970). Extinction of mammalian megafauna in the Old World Late Quaternary. *Biosci.*, **20**: 284-8.

Rütimeyer, L. (1878). Results of the investigation of animal remains from the lake dwellings. *In* Keller, F. (ed.). *The Lake Dwellings of Switzerland and Other Parts of Europe.* London, 537-44.

Shikama, T. and Okafuji, G. (1958). Quaternary cave and fissure deposits and their fossils in Akiyosi district, Yamaguti Prefecture. *Sci. Rep. Yokohama Nat. Univ., Sect. II, Biol.-Geol. Sci.*, **7**: 43-103.

Turnbull, P.F. and Reed, C.A. (1974). The fauna from the terminal Pleistocene of Palegawra Cave, a Zarzian occupation site in Northeastern Iraq. *Fieldiana, Anthrop.*, **63**: 81-146.

Watson, J.P.N. (1975). Domestication and bone structure in sheep and goats. *J. Arch. Sci.*, **2**: 375-83.

Wilckens, M. (1876). *Naturforscher Verein.* Quoted by T.M. Hughes, 1896.

4. *The environmental impact of traditional and modern agricultural systems*

David R. Harris

In Western society the farmer is conventionally thought of as battling against nature to wrest a living from the soil. The ecological view, on the other hand, conceives of agriculture as an integral part of the environment in which it is practised. Thus agricultural systems are not only economic entities but also distinctive types of man-modified ecosystems. They can be classified in many ways, but it is illuminating to analyse them in relation to two variables: the type of energy on which they depend, and the diversity of plants and animals that they incorporate.

In modern or neotechnic agricultural systems – such as plantation agriculture, commercial grain farming, and commercial livestock ranching – power from combustible fuels, as provided principally by the internal combustion engine, constitutes the main source of energy. In contrast, traditional or palaeotechnic systems – such as shifting or swidden cultivation, wet-padi farming, and nomadic pastoralism – depend on human and animal labour. This fundamental difference in the energy input into agriculture of modern and traditional societies is epitomized in the Western imagination by the visual contrast between, say, the American farmer riding high on his mechanical monster, the combine harvester, and the Asian peasant stooping low to thrust her bundle of rice seedlings into the mud of the flooded padi field.

The second variable is the degree of biotic diversity of the agricultural systems themselves. Just as natural ecosystems can be graded from complex or generalised systems, such as the tropical rain forest, to relatively simple or specialised systems, such as the boreal coniferous forest or the tundra, so too can agricultural systems. Neotechnic systems of the modern world are specialised in the sense that species diversity is low and production concentrates upon raising maximum numbers of optimum sized crops and domestic animals of a few preferred species. Expressed more conventionally, such systems tend towards monocultures. On the other hand, palaeotechnic systems of the traditional world are more generalised in that they usually incorporate greater biotic diversity and characteristically raise more complex assemblages of plant and animal species, each of which is represented by relatively fewer individuals. In other words, they tend to be more polycultural than neotechnic systems.

Not all palaeotechnic systems are polycultures. Some, such as wet-padi farming and nomadic pastoralism, are dependent on a limited range of crops and livestock and have evolved special techniques for raising them and for maintaining the productivity of the system; for example, in the case of wet-padi, the continuous regulation of water supply and the controlled application of organic matter, and, in the case of nomadic pastoralism, the seasonal migration of herds together with the regulation of herd size and composition.

Most palaeotechnic systems are, however, more biotically diverse. They raise complex assemblages of crops in functional interdependence and sometimes integrate livestock into the system as both primary consumers and fertilising agents. Shifting or swidden cultivation and house or door-yard gardening are examples of such generalised systems still widely practised in the tropics, while in mid-latitudes traditional mixed farming – which involves the production on the same land of crop combinations of grains, roots, and livestock – represents a somewhat less diverse system which has in modern times become progressively more specialised under the influence of technical innovation and socioeconomic change.

This ecological approach to the analysis of agricultural systems also illuminates the question of their impact on the physical and biotic environments in which they function. Complex natural ecosystems, such as the tropical rain forest, are not only structurally and functionally more diverse but also inherently more stable, in the sense that their plant and animal populations are less liable to major temporal and spatial fluctuations (Woodwell and Smith, 1969) than are those of simpler ecosystems. Because in the complex ecosystems a greater variety of ecological niches is available for species at most trophic levels, and because alternative paths for energy flow and greater genetic diversity exist within such systems, homeostasis is more readily maintained when changes occur among the constituent species, as when organisms are reduced, eliminated, or introduced by man.

This generalisation applies to agricultural systems as well as to natural ecosystems. Thus the contrast that exists between the highly complex and stable tropical rain forest and the simpler and less stable boreal forest finds a parallel on a smaller scale in the contrast between the complexity and stability of a polycultural swidden plot, in which many different species of crops are grown in structural and functional interdependence (Harris, 1971), and the simple, unstable plant community of a monocultural plantation which is characteristically subject to devastating attacks by species-specific pathogens. One has only to think of the catastrophic effects of crop diseases on modern plantation agriculture in areas of former tropical rain forest to appreciate the environmental hazards of replacing a complex natural by a simpler artificial plant community.

This line of thought suggests two contrasted ways in which the advent of agriculture changes natural ecosystems, although in reality this dichotomy represents two extremes along a gradient of ecological disturbance by man. At one extreme agriculture involves the large-scale replacement of the wild biota by domesticated and semi-domesticated organisms, or, in other words, the *transformation* of a natural into a largely artificial ecosystem created and maintained by man. At the other extreme agriculture proceeds by the substitution of selected domesticates for wild species in equivalent ecological niches, or the *manipulation* of the natural ecosystem rather than its replacement.

Thus when agriculture is based on ecosystem-manipulation, as in polycultural swidden plots in tropical forests, it achieves the objective of channeling energy to man through cultivated plants by substituting for wild species in equivalent spatial and functional niches a mixed assemblage of cultivated trees, shrubs, climbers, herbs, and root crops, thus simulating the structure and dynamics of the natural ecosystem without wholly or permanently replacing it. On the other hand, agriculture based on ecosystem-transformation, such as traditional wet-padi cultivation and most modern forms of farming, involves the almost total destruction of the pre-existing natural ecosystem and its replacement by an artificial system with quite different structural properties and energy transfers. Clifford Geertz expresses this idea, with reference to Indonesia, when he writes that wet-padi, as opposed to swidden cultivation, involves not 'the imitation of a tropical forest, but the fabrication of an aquarium' (Geertz, 1963: 31).

The dichotomy between ecosystem-manipulation and ecosystem-transformation represents not only two extremes in the degree of ecological change induced by agriculture but also a temporal progression from earlier to later systems of agricultural production. In a general sense the evolution of agriculture through the prehistoric and historic past can be seen as involving a progressive shift from ecosystem-manipulation to ecosystem-transformation, accompanied by intensification of the environmental impact of agricultural processes. Some of the broad implications of this generalisation are explored in the remainder of the paper, while Harry Thorpe's contribution to this volume provides a specific, local illustration of the general theme.

The development by human societies of the ecologically specialised agricultural systems which depend on ecosystem-transformation, and which today provide most of the world's food supplies, has occupied several millennia. The initial selection of the relatively small range of highly productive crops and domestic animals which such systems incorporate, as well as the origins of the civilisations which depend on them, date back at least five thousand years in parts of Southwestern and Eastern Asia, in Mesoamerica, and very probably – though not yet demonstrable archaeologically – in parts of South America and Africa south of the Sahara. The replacement, in historic times, of tropical forests by wet-padi pond fields and by plantations of sugar cane, bananas, cacao, and rubber, of temperate woodlands and grasslands by wheat farms and cattle ranches, or of desert shrublands by irrigated oases of cotton and alfalfa, represents the ultimate outcome of secular processes of ecological, genetic, and cultural selection and adjustment that have their origins deep in prehistory. Before such specialised agricultural systems emerged, cultivation and animal husbandry proceeded by ecosystem-manipulation. By this means, for example, fruit-bearing tree crops and tuberous root crops were progressively substituted for wild tree species, lianes, and herbs in the tropical forests of Southeast Asia, Africa, and the Americas; small-grained cereal crops and domestic sheep and goats multiplied in place of wild grasses and herbivores in the woodlands and grasslands of prehistoric Southwest Asia; and free-ranging pigs and cattle spread at the expense of wild scavengers and browsers in the forests of prehistoric Europe.

During the many millennia of ecosystem-manipulation that preceded the emergence of specialised agriculture, the environmental impact of man's subsistence activities remained relatively slight, although considerable changes were brought about in the distribution, composition, and structure of plant and animal communities, particularly through the use of fire, and soils were also modified, as Geoffrey Dimbleby's contribution to this volume shows with respect to Britain. With the development and spread of generalised palaeotechnic systems of agriculture, particularly swidden cultivation, environmental modification intensified. The most immediate effect was an increase in forest clearance. Non-agricultural hunter-gatherer populations do, and did in the past, clear vegetation to facilitate food procurement, but once swidden cultivation became an established system of food production the extent and rate of forest clearance increased substantially. Initially cultivators are likely to have selected sites in less heavily vegetated areas where natural or human agency prevented the establishment of closed-canopy forest, as along unstable stream courses or in areas disturbed by frequent hunting and gathering. But as swidden cultivation came to be more widely adopted as a subsistence strategy – in response to population increase and/or other factors – areas of closed-canopy forest began to be cleared.

The long-term environmental effects of swidden cultivation vary greatly in relation both to the capacity for regeneration of the ecosystem and to the duration and frequency of the cycles of clearance, cultivation, and forest regrowth, which themselves relate to the distribution and density of the human population. Thus in lightly populated areas of tropical rain forest, such as the upper Orinoco basin, forest regeneration is so rapid and the density of cultivators per unit area of forest so relatively slight, that swidden cultivation appears to have had only minor long-term effects on the rain-forest ecosystem, despite having been practised there for many centuries (Harris, 1971). This situation exemplifies what I have elsewhere called the stable mode of swidden cultivation (Harris, 1972). Conversely, in ecosystems where forest regenerates more slowly, as in environments where plant growth is checked seasonally by lack of moisture or low temperatures, swidden cultivation can manifest itself in an unstable or pioneering mode that is capable of profoundly modifying the local ecosystem, even when human population densities remain low. Thus the broadleaf deciduous forest of temperate Europe was more susceptible to impoverishment through persistent swidden cultivation (Dimbleby, this volume) than are humid tropical forests, although the fact that soils tend to be more fertile in temperate than in tropical areas partly compensates for the limitation on plant growth imposed by low winter temperatures.

Climatic and edaphic factors are not the only ecological variables that affect the susceptibility of forest ecosystems to disturbance by swidden cultivation. Variation in the crops raised, and in the presence or absence of grazing and browsing livestock, also conditions its environmental impact. In particular, the contrast between those swidden systems in which seed crops and vegetatively reproduced crops respectively predominate invites comment. In swidden plots in which vegetatively reproduced plants are the principal crops, as traditionally they are in many parts of the humid and sub-humid tropics, plant diversity tends to be greater, plant stratification more intricate, and the canopy of vegetation more completely closed than in plots dominated by cereals and other herbaceous seed crops. The former represent more complex and more stable ecosystems than the latter, and this tendency is accentuated by the fact that opportunities for soil erosion are reduced because the soil surface is more completely and more continuously shielded from insolation, raindrop impact, and wind, by the plant cover.

Vegetatively reproduced, carbohydrate-rich crops such as bananas, breadfruit, yams, manioc, taro, and sweet potato also make lower demands on soil fertility than cereals such as maize, wheat, and rice which yield considerable amounts of protein as well as starch. When the cereal farmer harvests his crop he removes from the system a greater proportion of available nutrients than when the root-crop cultivator digs up his tubers, corms, or rhizomes. Other factors being equal, declining yields become apparent sooner in cereal plots, and for this reason, as well as because their open-canopy structure renders them more liable to weed invasion and soil erosion, they tend to be

D

cultivated for shorter periods than plots devoted to vegetatively reproduced root and tree crops.

Swidden systems based on cereal crops, such as traditional maize cultivation in the Americas, sorghum and millet cultivation in Africa, and upland rice and millet cultivation in Asia, thus not only have a greater capacity to modify the environment in which they are practised but are also less stable ecologically than root- and tree-crop systems and more liable to have to expand territorially. In other words they tend toward the pioneering mode of swidden cultivation. On ecological grounds therefore one can infer that cereal-based systems will tend to spread more rapidly and more widely than root- and tree-crop systems – particularly as the former also provide a more self-sufficient diet – and this process is in fact traceable in the early agricultural history of many regions of the world.

One such region is temperate Europe, where the relatively rapid occupation of the wooded and forested areas by prehistoric cultivators (Ammerman and Cavalli-Sforza, 1973) suggests that frequent relocation of clearings and associated settlements was necessary. These pioneering swidden farmers depended mainly on wheat, barley, and other seed plants (Godwin, 1965) which, in the absence of fertiliser other than the ash and the above- and below-ground organic debris derived from forest clearance together with the droppings of free-ranging livestock, made relatively heavy demands on soil fertility. Furthermore, cattle, goats, and sheep retarded the regeneration of woody plants by browsing on abandoned plots as well as in woodlands, and thereby accelerated the conversion of forest into grassland and other secondary plant communities.

Thus the common assumption that swidden cultivation has had little or no lasting effect on the environments in which it was – and still is – practised requires modification (Bennett, 1973). The very fact that it proceeds, initially at least, by ecosystem-manipulation implies this, and the assumption is true in comparison with the more drastic changes associated with ecosystem-transforming agricultural systems. But if account is taken of the ubiquity of swidden cultivation as a traditional agricultural technique, practised over several millennia in ecosystems ranging from the equatorial rain forest to the boreal forests of northern Eurasia, its widespread environmental impact must be acknowledged.

With the development of more specialised agricultural systems, in prehistoric and historic times, the impact of agriculture on the land and on wild plants and animals became more intense and more enduring. Such systems are characterised by more continuous and intensive use of the land and they therefore depend on techniques to maintain soil fertility over the cultivated area. These techniques relate to either or both of two main processes: direct soil enrichment by the addition of organic and mineral fertilisers, and the regulation of water supplies. In the tropics most palaeotechnic specialised systems have achieved this continuity and intensification of agricultural production primarily by techniques of hydraulic cultivation, such as wet-padi farming (Geertz, 1963), dry-land irrigation in its various manifestations (Stamp, 1961), and forms of drained-field agriculture (Armillas, 1971; Denevan, 1970; Denevan and Turner, 1974; Wilken, 1969); whereas in the temperate zone specialised palaeotechnic agriculture has depended more on soil enrichment through the use of plant and animal fertilisers, as exemplified by the traditional mixed grain-livestock farming systems of Europe.

The development and spread in the last two hundred years of more highly specialised neotechnic systems in and beyond Europe has accentuated this contrast between tropical and temperate agriculture. This is evident particularly in the concentration on capital-intensive irrigation schemes that is so marked a feature of agricultural development in many tropical countries, and in the ever increasing investment in fertilisers that has accompanied the modernisation of agriculture in the temperate lands of Eurasia, Australasia, and the Americas.

The accelerating shift from palaeotechnic to neotechnic agriculture that has occurred this century, both in temperate and in tropical areas, has been paralleled by a corresponding diversification of the ways in which agriculture affects both the biotic and the abiotic environment. Whereas in earlier centuries the environmental effects of cultivation and animal husbandry were largely restricted to the exploited area and its nearer environs, the effects of modern agriculture are more pervasive. The latter cannot be discussed comprehensively here, but in conclusion three categories of environmental change may be mentioned which illustrate the increasingly hazardous ecological consequences of modern agricultural development.

The first of these is the modification of wild plant and animal communities. This process represents the continuation of a trend discernible throughout the history of agriculture, but its pace has quickened and its scale broadened with modernisation. Change usually results in a decrease in ecological diversity. Frequently it leads to habitat destruction and to reductions in the wild biota, as Max Hooper's discussion in this volume of recent changes in English woodlands and hedgerows demonstrates; but agricultural development may also bring about unexpected increases in the populations of advantaged species, as the history of – for example – recent plant invasions in the American Southwest clearly shows (Harris, 1966).

The second category of environmental change is the alteration of hydrological systems as a direct or indirect consequence of agriculture. This too has a venerable history; for example, irrigation canals were in use in eastern Iraq over 7000 years ago (Oates, 1972: 303) and large-scale artificial drainage of swamp land for cultivation is now known to date back 5500 years in the highlands of Papua New Guinea (Golson, 1975). But it is the modern construction of large barrage dams across major rivers for the development of irrigation and hydroelectric power that has brought the greatest environmental (and social) problems in its wake (Scudder, 1973). These are too well known to require enumeration, but habitat destruction by flooding and siltation upstream, and increased salinisation on cultivated lands downstream, are among the most common hazards. Less significant on a world scale, but locally damaging, are environmental changes resulting from modern agricultural drainage works, such as the loss of soil by wind erosion that has followed the lowering of the regional water table in parts of East Anglia.

The third category of change concerns the agricultural crops and livestock themselves and brings us back to the theme of increasing specialisation through time. As palaeotechnic systems of cultivation and animal husbandry have been progressively replaced by neotechnic systems – first in the European homeland of the modern agricultural revolution, next in temperate lands overseas, and most recently in the tropical lands of the Third World – so has the range of domestic biota on which agriculture depends narrowed. The price of modernisation is too often the elimination of valuable varietal diversity and a lowering of an agricultural system's ability to withstand environmental stresses such as disease and drought. The threat to the genetic resources of crop plants inherent in agricultural modernisation is now widely recognised; and, as Erna Bennett and Otto Frankel point out in their contributions to this volume, the obstacles in the way of an effective programme of genetic conservation are now more socioeconomic and political than scientific.

The value of maintaining crop and livestock diversity is apparent to anyone who undertakes field work among traditional agriculturalists in the less modernised parts of the world. Indeed, to me the sight of regimented fields of hybrid corn or sorghum on the Great Plains of North America contrasts depressingly with the harmonious disorder of tropical swidden plots and door-yard gardens. The North American scene symbolises the modern commitment to specialisation for efficiency. That way lies the minimisation of costs and the maximisation of profits, but at the expense of dangerously narrowing the ecological basis of world food production. The problem we face now is how to resolve the conflict of interests between specialisation for short-term economic efficiency and diversification for long-term ecological survival.

REFERENCES

Armillas, P. (1971). Gardens on swamps. *Science*, **174**: 653-61.
Ammerman, A.J. and Cavalli-Sforza, L.L. (1973). A population model for

the diffusion of early farming in Europe. *In* Renfrew, C. (ed.). *The Explanation of Culture Change. Models in Prehistory.* London, Duckworth, 343-57.

Bennett, J.W. (1973). Ecosystemic effects of extensive agriculture. *A. Rev. Anthrop.*, **2**: 36-45.

Denevan, W.M. (1970). Aboriginal drained-field cultivation in the Americas. *Science*, **169**: 647-54.

Denevan, W.M. and Turner, B.L. (1974). Forms, functions and associations of raised fields in the Old World tropics. *J. Trop. Geogr.*, **39**: 24-33.

Geertz, C. (1963). *Agricultural Involution. The Process of Ecological Change in Indonesia.* Berkeley and Los Angeles, University of California Press.

Godwin, H. (1965). The beginnings of agriculture in North-West Europe. *In* Hutchinson, J.B. (ed.). *Essays on Crop Plant Evolution.* Cambridge, Cambridge University Press, 1-22.

Golson, J. (1975). No room at the top: agricultural intensification in the New Guinea Highlands. *In* Allen, J., Golson, J. and Jones, R. (eds.). *Sunda and Sahul: Prehistoric Studies in Island Southeast Asia, Melanesia and Australia.* London, Academic Press. (In press).

Harris, D.R. (1966). Recent plant invasions in the arid and semi-arid Southwest of the United States. *Ann. Ass. Am. Geogr.*, **56**: 408-22.

Harris, D.R. (1971). The ecology of swidden cultivation in the upper Orinoco rain forest, Venezuela. *Geogr. Rev.*, **61**: 475-95.

Harris, D.R. (1972). Swidden systems and settlement. *In* Ucko, P.J., Tringham, R. and Dimbleby, G.W. (eds.). *Man, Settlement and Urbanism.* London, Duckworth, 245-62.

Oates, J. (1972). Prehistoric settlement patterns in Mesopotamia. *In* Ucko, P.J., Tringham, R. and Dimbleby, G.W. (eds.). *Man, Settlement and Urbanism.* London, Duckworth, 299-310.

Scudder, T. (1973). The human ecology of big projects: river basin development and resettlement. *A. Rev. Anthrop.*, **2**: 45-55.

Stamp, L.D. (ed.) (1961). *A History of Land Use in Arid Regions.* Arid Zone Research 17. Paris, Unesco.

Wilken, G.C. (1969). Drained-field agriculture: an intensive farming system in Tlaxcala, Mexico. *Geogr. Rev.*, **59**: 215-41.

Woodwell, G.M. and Smith, H.H. (eds.) (1969). *Diversity and Stability in Ecological Systems.* Brookhaven Symposia on Biology 22. Brookhaven, National Laboratory, Biology Department.

SUMMARY OF DISCUSSION IN PART I

The discussion to this part of the conference developed as a very useful background to the later sessions. It was felt to be essential to know something of the original state of the land in which man started to exert his influence. In this way the various processes of change could be better evaluated.

In that part of the discussion dealing with Dimbleby's paper it was pointed out that alder (*Alnus glutinosa*) seemed to be a particularly useful coloniser of poor ironstone lands where top-soil had been eroded after intensive early cultivation. Hutchinson considered that this might have been due to its ability to fix atmospheric nitrogen through the bacterial nodules on its roots; it had been planted in a number of places with poor acid water-logged soils and on old ironstone workings as well as in china clay reclamation schemes on sand.

A discussion on the tendency of conifers to produce poor acid soil conditions followed, and it was suggested that birch and alder might be used as soil-improving species in place of or admixed with conifers. Points were also made on the different buffering qualities of 'acid rain' from industrial smoke as contrasted with the acidity resulting from conifer plantations, the latter on the whole being considered much more effective.

In reply to a question, Thorpe agreed that the Black Death in the forested Arden region of Warwickshire was not by any means so severe as it was in the more open Feldon area. This was due partly to the isolation of Arden villages and the small amount of trading with cities where infection was intense, and also to the fact that in areas with big livestock populations nutrition was better and for this reason the disease was not so severe; finally, considerable difficulty was encountered by rats in spreading through forested areas. Records of the quick replacement of parish priests in Felden, sometimes at the rate of three a year, spoke for itself.

A lengthy discussion developed from Brothwell's paper on animal domestication which cannot be given here in great detail through lack of space. In reply to Waddington, he stated that although some evidence pointed to the use (and presumably domestication) of the dog before that of sheep, goats or cattle, the evidence available was not sufficient for one to be at all certain. The dog *may* have been associated with man since the Pleistocene however.

Several speakers commented on man's extreme conservatism in the matter of domesticated animals, which is particularly noticeable in Africa, as Finlayson pointed out. The only domestic animals there are the pig, goat and cattle, which are of northern origin, which is strange when one considers the extreme richness of the native fauna. Brothwell made the point, which was generally agreed with, that once a group of animals had been domesticated this seemed to block off other possibilities. The sound archaeological principle of conservatism was what one speaker described it as, whilst Russell considered that certain animals were domesticated in Asia because of the strongly contrasting winter and summer, though Brothwell had reservations about this explanation.

The matter of conservatism in the domestication of animals was taken up by Bennett, who pointed out that this was true for plants also: once the stimulus to domestication was satisfied the tendency to search elsewhere for other possible domesticates was considerably reduced. David Harris felt that there was very little domestication of animals anywhere outside south-west Asia, with the partial exception of llamas and turkeys in the New World. He suggested that this might have been related to the progressive degradation of environments through arable farming in the former area, resulting in the closer association of the grazing animals with man because of the destruction of their grazing areas. On this hypothesis, animal domestication would have developed later than that of plants – a view with which many would disagree. Harris further made the point that in other parts of the world where the modification of the environment was less intense such a domestication of the local mammalian fauna did not take place.

The problem of when reindeer domestication took place was raised by Thorpe. Brothwell felt that this subject had been rather neglected by archaeologists. Frankel pointed out from this example the important differences between animals associated with and used by man and those which were truly domesticated. He believed that reindeer had never been truly domesticated in fact, since it had never undergone selection by man. The genetic component was more important perhaps than the environmental one.

A lively discussion also revolved around David Harris's paper. In reply to a question by Ulbricht on the possibility of developing mixed cropping as highly efficient production systems, Harris agreed and continued by saying how depressing it was to find western-trained agricultural developers enthusiastically advocating western cash crop systems without any regard to traditional practices. He stressed the need, echoed by other participants, of persuading the governments of newly-emerged tropical countries to re-evaluate their traditional systems of agriculture before discarding them completely. Bennett agreed, and wondered whether more attention ought not to be paid to ecosystems than to the almost mythical objectives of higher yields at all costs. FAO had a great responsibility here, she felt, though Frankel believed that the pressures came mainly from the people themselves, of which the 'cargo cult' was a significant expression.

Reservations on this were expressed by Harris, who felt that attitudes of pride ought to be reinforced in the local traditional agricultural practices which had developed over thousands of years, no doubt as a response to the environmental conditions of the region, and that education should not run counter to this.

Some differences of opinion were expressed on the fragility of forest ecosystems. Harris felt that the deciduous temperate forest cover was fragile, although Keay thought that Thorpe's descriptions of Warwickshire proved the opposite, and in reply Harris pointed out the very high rates of regeneration in the tropics under swidden cultivation, even though the northern temperate soils have the greater fertility. Thorpe and Russell, and Harris himself, felt that there were many factors involved. Forest regeneration could take place rapidly with a conveniently close seed source but not so easily when forests are clear-felled over very wide areas. Human population densities were an important factor here, as Keay pointed out.

PART II
NATURE CONSERVATION AND
RURAL LAND USE

5. The balance of rural land use*

Michael Gane

Land is a complex resource which varies greatly in character, productivity and accessibility from place to place. It is used in a variety of ways and nearly always there are alternative ways of utilising any particular piece of it. Sometimes the use for one purpose, e.g. urban development, rules out other uses such as agriculture or forestry; in other situations multiple use is possible, as in the case of heather moorland used for both grouse shooting and hill grazing.

The existence of alternatives and the range of possibilities for multiple use provide the basis for a pattern of usage which, at any point in time, is a temporary reconciliation of different conflicting bids for land. The pattern is a compromise solution for land allocation and the compromise may be described as the *balance of land use*. This balance is dynamic because the relative strengths of competing demands for land and its fitness for different purposes change over time. The balance is also influenced by the way in which conflicts of demand are resolved by society. Market forces operating under laissez faire conditions can provide a solution to the problem of land allocation, but it is not a solution which is socially acceptable, at least in present-day Britain. Therefore, the balance results from an interplay of economic pressures, fiscal measures, legal constraints and the system of planning and development control which has been imposed.

This chapter is concerned with rural land use and how the balance of rural use is changing; urban land falls outside the terms of reference. However, the division between urban and rural is becoming increasingly blurred in Britain. Whereas an increasing share of the population now derives its livelihood from employment in urban areas while the numbers working in agriculture and forestry have shrunk, a growing proportion prefer to live in rural surroundings, commuting to

* The views expressed in this chapter are those of the author and do not represent the official policy of the Nature Conservancy Council.

work daily. Urban dwellers, now so much more mobile than they were half a century ago, look to the rural areas to provide informal recreation and an outlet for increased leisure. Therefore, the balance of rural land use cannot be considered in isolation; it is greatly influenced by urban needs and urban pressures.

The balance concept can be applied in different ways. In the past, changes in the balance of primary land use in Britain have been analysed. Now, reinterpretation is necessary because rural land management is being increasingly influenced by social concerns, including scenic beauty, informal recreation and nature conservation. The chapter goes on to suggest a new application, which consists of analysing land by area according to its quality in relation to different objectives of management; i.e. to derive a *balance of rural land quality*. One dimension of this balance is nature conservation, which is clearly deteriorating and will therefore need to be considered in depth in view of its importance.

The balance of primary uses

Land has usually been classified according to three primary uses – agriculture (in its various forms), forest and woodland, and urban development. Estimates of the way the primary use pattern has changed in England and Wales during the century have been made by Best (1968), who has carefully interpreted the available statistics. Agriculture accounted for nearly 80% (11.9 million ha) and forest and woodland nearly 7% of the land area in 1960. The latter category was estimated to have increased by about 0.4% (from 6.4 to 6.8%) during the preceding decade (Best and Coppock, 1962) and the conversion of agricultural land (mostly rough grazing) to forestry continued during the following ten years at a rate in excess of 5,000 hectares per annum. (Best, 1975, pers. comm.). Coppock (1968) has estimated that the total area under woodland in Great Britain increased by nearly a quarter between 1938 and 1968, due largely to the extensive afforestation with conifers that has taken place in upland areas. Agriculture has also given way to urban development. By 1960, urban development covered 10.7% of England and Wales, having doubled in extent since the beginning of this century.

These shifts in the primary use of land and the rural balance between agriculture and forestry tell us only part of the story. There are other uses, i.e. other purposes of land management, which are not revealed. Primary uses have been distinguished in the statistics by the predominant form of vegetative cover, arable, pasture or trees as the case may be. But the vegetation does not necessarily provide a reliable guide to the primary purpose for which land is managed. Agricultural and forest production are still the predominant aims over very large areas, but increasingly their pursuit is being tempered or constrained by other land management objectives of new kinds. In a few cases the new objectives have become paramount and are creating new forms of primary land use.

New categories of land use have emerged which are associated with increased mobility and the growth of demand for informal recreation, changing public attitudes to the preservation of scenic beauty and the national heritage, and a more widespread interest in nature conservation. Since 1949 (when the National Parks Commission was established), 10 National Parks have been created with a total area of 1.36 million ha (9% of England and Wales). By 1968 there were 31 Areas of Outstanding Natural Beauty (AONB) covering a further 950,000 ha (6%) (National Parks Commission, 1968) and there are now many miles of Heritage Coast. National Nature Reserves, growing in number all the time, at present cover 283,000 ha spread amongst 140 Reserves in Britain, and in addition the Nature Conservancy Council has notified 3,525 Sites of Special Scientific Interest (SSSI) with a total area of 1.23 million ha. These considerable areas are not all; to them should be added the land controlled by various voluntary bodies. The National Trust now protects upwards of 2,300 properties with an area of more than 190,000 ha (National Trust, 1973), while in the nature conservation field, the Society for the Promotion of Nature Reserves and the County Trusts manage more than 800 reserves (over 24,000 ha) in the United Kingdom (Society for the Promotion of Nature Reserves, 1974) and the Royal Society for the Protection of Birds looks after over 56 reserves (15,390 ha).

These new categories of use overlap the divisions of the primary classification. National Parks and Nature Reserves contain arable, pasture and woodland but land management in them is influenced to a lesser or greater degree by the new social purposes. The creation of a National Park is meaningless unless it enables the scenic quality of the area to be maintained and informal recreation needs catered for. Nature Reserves are set aside for the express purpose of conserving flora and fauna, physiographic features and geological interest. To allow for these, the balance of primary land use requires reinterpretation in terms of management objectives; changes in the *balance of land management* need to be recorded. The pursuit of the old primary objectives is being constrained in some instances, in others multiple use management is being developed, and there are circumstances (notably in Nature Reserves) when agriculture and forestry are only used incidentally, as tools of management, to achieve conservation aims.

The extent to which it proves possible to shift the balance in the socially desired direction without, at the same time, taking the land into some form of public ownership is one of the most interesting features of the contemporary rural scene in Britain. National Parks here are unlike National Parks in other countries and do not even fit the definition of them which was adopted for international purposes at the IUCN Conference at Delhi in 1969, because the land in them is not controlled by the State. 60% (by area) of the National Nature Reserves in Britain have been created by agreements with the landowners, compared with 26% which have been acquired by purchase and only 14% which are leased. In the wider countryside, the Nature Conservancy Council can, within limits, compensate the owner of an SSSI for his financial sacrifice in maintaining its scientific interest by agreement under S.15 of the Countryside Act, 1968, and the Countryside Commission negotiates and pays for the creation of long distance paths such as the Pennine Way.

An owner's right to use his land in whatever way he wishes is also influenced through specific land designations which carry weight when planning decisions are being made by local authorities. AONBs and SSSIs are examples, and it is worth noting that a landowner has no power to prevent the creation of these. In the case of SSSIs, the Nature Conservancy Council is charged with the statutory duty of notifying these sites to local authorities, who must inform the Council of all planning applications which affect them, thereby giving an opportunity for objections to be raised. However, changes in the way land is used for agriculture and forestry generally fall outside the scope of formal planning controls, so that the importance of SSSIs as an influence on land use is limited, although owners may benefit through becoming eligible for financial assistance by means of S.15 agreements as previously mentioned and possibly, where the Treasury so decides, for relief from Capital Transfer Tax.

The balance of rural land quality

Analysis of the changing balance, whether measured by areas classified according to their primary use or according to land management objectives, still provides us with an incomplete assessment. The analysis is superficial in both senses of the word and tells us nothing about the fitness of the land for the purposes to which it is put. There has been a revolution in public concern for the quality of our environment in recent years (Wilson, 1971) and land is one of the most important components of the rural environment. Therefore, there is also a need for qualitative assessment to find out whether degradation or improvement is occurring, and to link it to the changes in use already described. We should envisage a *balance of rural land quality* as well as a balance of rural land use. Both are dynamic balances and they are closely inter-related.

The balance of rural land quality is difficult to define precisely and gives rise to problems from which the estimates of primary use do not suffer. In spite of the inadequacies of existing land statistics (which are well known and have been frequently deplored in Britain), the

Table 5.1   Aspects of rural land quality

Qualitative dimension	Features to be assessed
1. Agriculture	Fitness of land resource for agricultural production
2. Forestry	Fitness of land resource for forestry production
3. Water	Capacity of land to supply, store and drain water to acceptable standard of purity
4. Landscape	Aesthetic quality of the countryside
5. Informal recreation	Capacity of countryside to support informal recreation
6. Nature conservation	Capacity of countryside to sustain wildlife and other features of nature conservation interest

recording of areas by their uses is relatively straightforward. Not so with the recording of areas by their quality. Qualitative assessment is linked with the purposes of management because land used in one way may become less suitable for use in another, and, in relation to the latter use, suffers a deterioration in fitness or quality. Therefore, the balance of quality is multidimensional and has as many dimensions as there are categories of land use. Within each dimension it should provide a summary of the areas in each quality class or grade and show how those areas are growing or shrinking. Overall, the balance should tell us how human activities are affecting the capability of land, as a resource, to satisfy human needs. An analytical framework for this has not yet been developed and only tentative suggestions about its main features are possible at this stage, as shown in Table 5.1.

Each dimension generates its own special problems of assessment. A grading system needs to be devised for each, with the following desirable characteristics:

(a) sensitivity to the feature to be assessed
(b) ease of survey and monitoring
(c) comprehensiveness so that it is not unduly affected by local changes
(d) comparability of results with other countries and regions of the world

Each feature must be assessed in the most appropriate way but some degree of subjectivity is unavoidable with the grading of all of them, because value judgements are involved. However, it is vital that the value judgements be laid on a sound basis of factual information derived from objective survey and be made explicit. There is also the difficulty of how to combine the gradings for the separate features into a single composite assessment of rural land quality, if the features are judged not to be of equal importance and their relative weights are expected to change over time.

With agriculture, for example, it is necessary to measure changes in the capacity of land to produce crops and livestock as distinct from measuring agricultural production. The latter fluctuates from year to year according to the weather and can be altered by increasing the input of other resources – more labour, fertilisers, farm machinery, etc. The Agricultural Land Classification for England and Wales, therefore, comes to mind. This divides all land into five grades based on 'versatility as determined by physical characteristics' (Rushton, 1975) and •particular areas are only likely to need regrading when their productivity is changed permanently due to say drainage or conversion to other use.

Even though it is not yet possible to measure alterations in the balance of rural land quality, some indication of the qualitative changes which are occurring in Britain can be obtained by considering each of the six dimensions in turn:

1. Agriculture is problematical and it is not clear whether the fitness of land for this purpose is changing significantly in either direction; probably not, because improvements in fertility in some areas (e.g. due to drainage) are being offset by losses where farm land is put to other uses which render it unfit for agriculture.
2. Forestry has benefited due to afforestation in upland areas, although there may have been some deterioration due to soil changes where broadleaved woodlands have been converted to conifers.
3. Water is a complex feature. Some aquafers are being pumped down, while water storage capacity increases with new reservoir construction. The quality of the water resource has undoubtedly declined in particular areas, such as the Norfolk Broads, and although there are fears of widespread changes induced by agricultural fertilizers enriching the nutrient status of streams, a few grossly polluted sections of our river systems have been cleaned up sufficiently to allow fish to return. The net result is probably adverse however.
4. The Countryside Commission's recent publication 'New Agricultural Landscapes' (Westmacott and Worthington, 1974) reveals significant losses of landscape features such as hedges, copses and marshy areas, and extensive replacement of permanent pasture by arable in a number of representative areas in England. These changes, and the visual and olfactory impact of modern farming, amount to extensive deterioration in many people's eyes.
5. Informal recreation capacity is also suffering because the ever-growing number of people flocking to the countryside,

particularly the National Parks and other 'honey pot' areas, are endangering the peace and enjoyment which visitors seek (Department of the Environment, 1974). Land management methods to increase visitor carrying capacity are in their infancy, although very interesting possibilities exist.

6. Nature conservation gives the greatest cause for concern. Our natural heritage is subject to ever increasing pressures and continuing attrition. Characteristic assemblages of wildlife, which were often created by the farmer's activities in the past, are now being depleted by the impact of advances in agricultural technology which favour monocultures and suppress species diversity in the interests of farming efficiency. Crops of conifers in place of broadleaved woodland substitute different ecological habitats which generally support a less rich flora and fauna. Land drainage is catastrophic for plants and animals, particularly the invertebrates, which live in ponds and marshes. Mineral exploitation and industrial development can destroy physiographic features and the nature conservation interest of areas which, to the uninitiated, appear to be worthless wasteland. Human pressure from recreational activities degrades and despoils erodable habitats, such as coastal sand dunes, and disturbs the wildlife of less fragile systems over much larger areas of the countryside. The assault, founded on ecological incomprehension, comes from every direction and, if continued, must inevitably lead to environmental impoverishment which is the more serious because it is often irreversible.

Nature conservation quality

It is evident that the balance of rural land quality is being most seriously upset by deterioration in the nature conservation dimension. This makes it desirable to consider ways in which changes in nature conservation quality might be more precisely analysed or measured. In Britain, two distinct approaches to qualitative grading have been used, the first for classifying sites according to their importance for nature conservation, and the second to enable the wider countryside to be assessed, according to its nature conservation significance, for planning purposes. Neither approach is aimed at measuring large scale changes in environmental quality, but they are useful starting points and illustrate the inherent difficulty of the task.

During the last decade, an account of sites of special importance to nature conservation has been compiled. This is known as the Nature Conservation Review (NCR), which is expected to be published during 1976. The basis of the NCR is the selection of a representative sample of all major natural and semi-natural ecosystems in Britain.

Four grades of sites have been distinguished, all of which merit notification as SSSIs:-

Grade I   Sites of international or national importance. These are the best examples of each type of habitat that are known.
Grade II   Close substitutes for Grade I of nearly equivalent scientific merit.
Grade III   Sites of high regional importance.
Grade IV   Sites of local significance.

Only 'elite' sites, i.e. those in Grades I and II, are eligible for inclusion in the National Nature Reserve series which the Nature Conservancy Council is building up. Most land falls outside these four grades and either possesses some conservation value (farmland, road verges, parkland, etc.) or virtually none (land covered by buildings and man-made surfaces). However, a serious shortcoming, from the point of view of nature conservation quality assessment, is that the NCR deals only with the flora and fauna; it excludes consideration of sites of physiographic and geological interest, which are being covered by a separate survey.

Site assessment has been based on ten criteria:

1. Extent – the importance of a site tends to increase with area and safeguarding requires a minimum 'viable unit'.
2. Diversity – the numbers of both communities and species.
3. Naturalness – the degree of modification which has occurred; often the richness of a site is related to its history and the amount of disturbance which has taken place.
4. Rarity – rare communities have received more attention than rare species.
5. Fragility – sensitivity to adverse conditions.
6. Typicalness – all major ecosystems should be represented, however widespread or common they may be.
7. Recorded history – sites gain in value if there are long standing scientific records for them.
8. Position in ecological/geographical unit – contiguity with other sites may assist management to sustain a site's scientific interest.
9. Potential value – sites may be capable of restoration where they have deteriorated, or used to recreate an ecosystem which has been destroyed.
10. Intrinsic appeal – containing distinctive species such as colourful butterflies.

It is obvious from this list that, although careful scientific investigation provides a basis of fact, the grading of sites calls for judgement and weighing up the relative importance of the various criteria. It is highly subjective, however expert the assessors may be, and leaves room for differences of opinion amongst assessors from time to time. For this reason it is open to criticism, although the criticism will only become significant if (or when) an objective method of grading is devised, capable of measuring satisfactorily the features in the ten criteria which the majority of ecologists acknowledge to be important.

Ecological evaluation in the countryside generally has been discussed by Goldsmith (1975) who describes a method used on a transect from the Wye Valley to the Black Mountains in 1972. This was based on four parameters – extent, rarity, species diversity of plants and of animals – which were combined, unweighted, into an Index of Ecological Value. Tubbs and Blackwood (1971) have devised a method, used for planning purposes in Hampshire, which is based on mapping 'ecological zones'. Each zone is assigned a value according to specified criteria. The criteria are subjective, but the system seems to produce consistent results. It may be thought that consistency and simplicity are more important than subjectivity in practice, at least at the present stage, and therefore the Tubbs/Blackwood system or something similar has much to commend it.

Nature conservation and the balance of land use

Putting aside the problems of assessing quality, in conclusion it is worth briefly reviewing the practical measures being taken in Britain to check the deterioration of the rural environment from a nature conservation point of view. The Nature Conservancy Council is the statutory body responsible for nature conservation and is therefore endeavouring, with the limited resources at its disposal, to maintain or enhance land quality in this respect. It is supported by a vigorous voluntary movement throughout the country, with which it enjoys a close and beneficial relationship. Action which affects the balance of rural land use is being taken by the nature conservation movement as a whole. Activity is principally directed at the safeguarding of sites and conservation in the wider countryside. The latter is pursued through the provision of advice and representations to government departments, local authorities, public corporations and private landowners.

Site conservation may have a small direct effect on the primary balance because land which becomes a nature reserve ceases to be managed primarily for agricultural or forestry purposes. In theory this is true, although in practice the effect is often minimal as the owner of the land continues to manage it much as before, foregoing 'improvements', such as drainage and fertilisers, which would be inimical to wildlife although they would also increase productivity.

However, no more than 0.6% of Britain is National or Local Nature Reserve and if all Grade I sites in the NCR became reserves, this percentage would only rise to 2.1. The impact on the primary balance is therefore relatively small. At the same time, in qualitative terms, attrition of 'key sites' which are not safeguarded continues, usually in a manner that escapes public attention. Changes in land use are frequently prevented by the refusal of planning permission on SSSIs, sometimes after appeal and public inquiry, but SSSI status is certainly no guarantee of immunity and many sites are destroyed in ways that are not subject to planning approval.

In the wider countryside, as much influence as possible is being brought to bear on the planning process at all levels. This undoubtedly helps to channel industrial and other developments away from the more valuable and vulnerable areas. In favourable situations it can lead to positive steps to encourage wildlife by improved land management, as in some Country Parks. But generally the posture is defensive and, because most of what happens on farms is not affected by planning, the efforts of conservationists can only meet with limited success.

If circumstances do not change, it seems inevitable that the balance of rural land quality must continue to deteriorate, at least along its wildlife dimension. Not only are sites of particular importance being destroyed but also wildlife in rural areas generally receives very little protection through the planning process. A serious attempt at measurement of the qualitative changes taking place is urgently needed to show the rate at which they are occurring. The fact of deterioration is not in doubt but there is insufficient evidence to determine the desirable scope and scale of remedial action. Furthermore, qualitative measurement along the other dimensions and elucidation of what is happening to the balance of land quality in its entirety is desirable because remedial action in one direction must inevitably influence what happens in others. Perhaps by developing qualitative assessments of this type we can move towards the goal of a coherent land use policy for Britain as a whole.

REFERENCES

Best, R.H. (1968). Competition for land between rural and urban uses. *In* Institute of British Geographers. *Land Use and Resources – Studies in Applied Geography*. London, Special Publication no. 1, Chapter 6.

Best, R.H. and Coppock, J.T. (1962). *The Changing Use of Land in Britain*. London, Faber, Chapter 10.

Coppock, J.T. (1968). Changes in rural land use in Great Britain. *In* Institute of British Geographers. *Land Use and Resources – Studies in Applied Geography*. London, Special Publication no. 1, Chapter 8.

Department of the Environment (1974). *Report of the National Park Policies Review Committee*. London, HMSO.

Goldsmith, F.B. (1975). *Ecological Evaluation.* Paper given to the Institute of British Geographers Conference, January 1975.

National Parks Commission (1968). 18th Annual Report. HMSO, House of Commons Paper 63.

National Trust (1973). *Properties of the National Trust: January 1973.* London, National Trust.

Rushton, P.L. (1975). The agricultural land classification of England and Wales. *ADAS Quart. Rev.,* **16**: 125-30.

Society for the Promotion of Nature Reserves. (1974). *Conservation Review No. 7.* Nettleham, Lincs., SPNR.

Tubbs, C.R. and Blackwood, J.W. (1971). Ecological evaluation of land for planning purposes. *Biol. Cons.,* **3**: 169-72.

Westmacott, R. and Worthington, T. (1974). *New Agricultural Landscapes.* Cheltenham, Countryside Commission.

Wilson, T.W. (1971). *International Environmental Action.* New York, Dunellan Publishing Co.

6. Changes in the landscape of woodland and hedgerow

Max D. Hooper

I intend to interpret the title of this chapter by speaking of woodland and hedgerow in the lowlands of Britain. In the context of this volume I shall refer mainly to changes over the last century.

What I have to say will be divided into three parts, each successive one a little more speculative. The first I believe to be wholly true. It concerns the known facts of the changes. Secondly, I want briefly to refer to the causes of such changes. This too, I think, will be the truth but perhaps less near the whole truth. And finally, I want to discuss the consequences of change. In this area the data are few and not always quite what the research scientists would desire. I shall try to be objective but my personal feelings may show through the threadbare cloth of scientific knowledge to reveal a false pattern.

What are the changes? The changes are of two types, quantitative and qualitative. Both hedgerows and woodlands have changed in extent and in kind.

Hedgerow changes are predominantly changes in extent. For perhaps 75 years since 1875 there were virtually no such changes. It is true that Coppock (1958) found a few cases of very small losses in specific parishes. I can counter this (Pollard, Hooper and Moore, 1974) with evidence for a similar small number of minor increases. Readjustments were always being made here and there but only after the 2nd World War did hedgerow removal begin on an increasing scale and attract increasing attention. My own estimate, based on studies of old aerial photographs, is that between 1945 and 1970 the annual rate of removal over England and Wales was 5,000 miles and I know of no other objective study which alters that conclusion. It is true that you may see other figures in the literature. These are not necessarily wrong but may refer to different time periods. My figure of 5,000 miles removed per annum disguises a quite striking variation in rate with time. Removal began quite slowly after the war, gradually increased during the 1950s (perhaps stimulated by the introduction of grant aid in 1957) and appears to have reached a peak in the first half of the 1960s – a peak from which it has since declined.

As well as this temporal variation in rate there is spatial variation to contend with. Of the 5,000 miles average loss it appears that most was from half a dozen counties in eastern England – an area of 6 million acres out of a total of about 25 million acres of hedgerow landscape.

Now it must be remembered that the distribution of hedgerows has never been uniform throughout the land. In 1945 Norfolk might have a dozen miles of hedgerow on a square mile of land, Warwickshire 15 miles and Devon 30 miles. Most hedges have gone from those areas which had least to begin with. Norfolk, for example, in the period 1946-1972 lost half its total mileage of hedgerow (Baird and Tarrant, 1973) while east Leicestershire lost less than 10% (Pollard, Hooper and Moore, 1974).

Taking England and Wales as a whole it seems that the average annual rate is a little less than 1% so that overall about a quarter of the hedges have disappeared in the last 30 years.

Similar figures are available for the extent of woodlands, notably from the Forestry Commission Census figures. In terms of extent, woodland has increased almost continuously over the last century. I say almost continuously since there was a slight fall during the First World War:

Date	Acres woodland/England only
1871	1,314,316
1887	1,518,321
1905	1,683,324
1924	1,630,987
1939	1,809,800
1947	1,865,046
1967	2,199,400

Now again one could subdivide such figures in various ways – in terms of space and time as I have indicated for hedgerows if one wished. The Forestry Commission (1952, 1970) in their analyses subdivide such figures into woodland types – High Forest, Coppice, Scrub, etc. and give data on species composition. These bring out the well known swing to conifer away from broadleaved woodlands and, what is becoming more frequently discussed in conservation circles, the decline in coppice management. I myself think that two further trends need noting – the growing concentration of woodlands on less productive lands and what appears to be an increasing frequency of small woodland blocks. Data to support these two trends are sparse but I would commend to you George Peterken's study of Rockingham Forest (Peterken and Harding, 1974).

Now the answer to the question of what causes such changes depends upon the level of answer required. To carry simplicity and semantic encapsulation to their uttermost limits one could just say 'economics'. That is too simple, even if it be the whole truth, and not to expand it a little would remove certain complicating factors from the discussion of the consequences of change.

Take hedgerows as an example. The concentration of removal in the eastern counties at once pinpoints the arable sector of English agriculture. Here fewer and fewer animals have been kept over the last 30 years and such animals as are still kept are intensive stock. In such circumstances hedges have no function. They take up land and they are alive so if they are not to continue to take up more and more land they must be trimmed. Hence hedges are removed to make the land available for a profitable crop and to save the expense of regular trimming. The cause is economic but is it the economics of hedges or arable farming that is the root cause? There is also a complication in the consequences – how does one separate the results of hedgerow removal *per se* from the results of changes in cropping pattern of the fields the hedges once surrounded?

Similar arguments could be adduced in relation to the four types of change in woodlands. In all, economics takes its place. In the case of the change of coppice to scrub or promotion to high forest, we can see economic forces at work. The demand for coppice products has fallen – no bakers or maltsters demanding faggots, fewer hurdles, fewer thatchers, fewer hedges laid. But the way that coppice develops will depend upon the economic interests of the estate in which it lies. In one case it may be developed to high forest because the estate has a forestry enterprise, in yet another case game birds may be thought of as a crop and the coppice becomes scrub, unmanaged in a forester's sense but perhaps heavily keepered. Are the consequences a result of the lack of coppicing, or the result of the new management?

These complicating factors are all too often forgotten when gathering data to assess consequences, and the situation is further bedevilled by the behaviour of the organisms in which the conservationist is interested. Or perhaps better, it is bedevilled by our ignorance of the behaviour of these organisms.

Take birds and hedges. Birds nest in hedges; hedges are being removed so birds must also be removed. This seems a logical sequence and one might be tempted to say that as an average of 5,000 miles of hedgerow was removed each year in the period 1946-1970 and an average mile's length of hedgerow held, on average, 25 nests then as a consequence of hedgerow removal a quarter of a million birds were made homeless each year.

Such arithmetic is fallacious. On no one sample area of farmland that I have investigated has every single hedge been removed, so it would be possible that hedgerow removal had no effect – all the birds that formerly nested in twelve miles of hedge might now nest in the remaining 2 or 3 miles – if birds could telescope their nesting territories. I have some data (Hooper, 1970) which suggest this could happen to some extent but that there is a limit of about 7-8 miles of hedge to 1 square mile at which bird diversity and population numbers begin to fall. Put into ecologists' jargon one might say that above 8 miles/sq mile the population of birds was not limited by competition for nesting sites but below 7 it was. This too is not entirely satisfactory as a generalisation. Hedges differ and the precise point at which a decline sets in may depend upon which specific hedge is removed first and there is some evidence that the best bird hedges are the least likely to be removed (Hooper, 1974).

On top of this the conservationist must take into account that for those individual species of bird that have been investigated most intensively (Murton and Westwood, 1974) it appears that the hedge is a suboptimal habitat. I can perhaps best illustrate this by reference to some work my colleague John Parslow did on the Blackbirds on a farm near Peterborough. On this farm there were considerable numbers of Blackbirds nesting from year to year and yet these Blackbirds produced insufficient young to compensate for adult mortality. The numbers were made up, each year, by immigration of the surplus production of individuals from nearby woodlands. Hence it appears that what happens on the farm is less important than what happens in the woodland for the perpetuation of Blackbirds through time. The presence of hedgerows merely spreads the surplus out and so makes the bird more obvious.

While there is very little evidence to support it (and what I have just said should illustrate the pitfalls of pure logic) it does seem logical that as the flora and fauna of hedges is very largely of woodland origin the same sort of overall picture might be true for insects, mammals, and the plants as well as the birds.

For those concerned with conservation this line of argument forces a very careful consideration of the changes in woodland and their consequences. Of the four changes that I have mentioned, the last one – the increasing frequency of small woods is of most interest. It seems to me that these small woods dotted about the landscape are just like islands in the sea – islands in a sea of arable. Now the number of organisms on a natural island is predictable from a simple rule

$$\text{the No. of species} = CA^K$$

where C is a constant – the number of species on one unit of area (which, of course, depends upon whether one is dealing with trees, mosses or birds, woodland or grassland, and whether one is working in square metres or acres) – A is the area and K depends upon the degree of isolation of the island but commonly appears to be around 0.3 for real oceanic islands and 0.18 for areas with some degree of continuity. In short, by creating inland islands the intensification of agriculture is producing the sorts of pressures which exist on small oceanic islands: – the pressures of inbreeding, genetic drift, instability and high probabilities of extinction. Can we confidently predict the fate of the Dodo for many species?

A general theory dealing with this sort of situation has been put forward by MacArthur and Wilson (1967) and more detail added recently by Terborgh (1974) and by Diamond (1972 and 1976). These recent developments suggest that if a large continuous area is broken up into small pieces then the number of species on any individual piece will relax to a new equilibrium. The rate at which this relaxation takes place depends upon the area and number of species present. The more species originally present and the smaller the area of this newly created island the faster the species disappear from it.

The evidence that Diamond and Terborgh put forward concerns birds on oceanic islands but there is some evidence that plants in woods behave in the same way. Some years ago I investigated the species-area relationships of a limited range of vascular plants in two sets of woods in Northamptonshire and Cambridgeshire (Hooper, 1971). My original interpretation was that differences in K in the formula $S = CA^K$ were related to the differing patterns of separation in the two sets. However, the American work makes an alternative approach possible. Assume, as does Terborgh, that the separations are sufficient to prevent all recolonisation, and as one set of woods has been isolated since 1770 and the other since about 1270 A.D., make a further assumption that each set is representative of the general state of woodlands at two points in time 500 years apart. Then rates of species loss and Terborgh's extinction coefficient, can be calculated for a range of woodland areas from the regressions of species on area, and Terborgh's equations. If this is done it is found that it is related to area for plant species in woodland 'islands' in the same way as Terborgh found for birds on real islands. This supports Terborgh's model of the rate of species loss, provided the assumptions are valid. In this instance they are at least reasonable. The species of plants recorded were characteristic woodland species with limited powers of dispersal; all the woods are Oak – Ash – Hazel woodland on calcareous boulder clay, managed for a large part of their history as coppice with standards.

If Terborgh's model is correct, conservationists may take heart from the fact that woods appear to lose plant species at rates which differ little over a wide range of areas. Over 500 years all the woods from 4 to 128 hectares (10 to 320 acres) have lost some 20 to 25 species. The important questions are whether it is always the same species which are lost most quickly and, if so, have these species ecological characteristics in common? If they have then small woodlands may not suffer from the expected disadvantages of small size – provided they are managed in such a way as to take account of the characteristics the species have in common.

Are these changes reversible? This depends upon precisely what specific change you have in mind. If you think of an ancient forest now subdivided into many small woods – any one of these woods may have lost several species which we could put back by replanting – to be followed by management for those species – in this case, then the answer is that the change is reversible.

On the other hand if the woodland were removed entirely and the land used for cropping could we recreate the woodland system? The answer here may be yes or no according to your view and your time scale – yes if the time scale is a century and to you a wood is just a place with trees, but no if you time scale is shorter or if you want the full range of species that we now see in an ancient wood. This would take a thousand years.

REFERENCES

Baird, W.W. and Tarrant, J.R. (1973). *Hedgerow Destruction in Norfolk 1946-1970.* University of East Anglia.
Coppock, J.T. (1958). Changes in farm and field boundaries in the 19th century. *Amateur Historian*, **3**: 292-8.
Cowie, J.D. (1972). *Rates of Hedgerow Removal.* Leeds, MAFF.
Diamond, J.G. (1972). Biogeographic kinetics. *Proc. natn. Acad. Sci. U.S.A.*, **69**: 3199-203).
Diamond, J.D. (1976). Reclamation and differential extinction on land bridge islands. Proc. 16th Int. Ornith. Congr. (In press).
Forestry Commission (1952). *Census of Woodlands 1947-1949.* HMSO.
Forestry Commission (1970). *Census of Woodlands 1965-1967.* HMSO.
Hooper, M.D. (1970). Hedges and birds. *Birds*, **3**: 114-17.
Hooper, M.D. (1971). The size and surroundings of Nature Reserves. *In* Duffey, E. and Watt, A.S. (eds.). *The Scientific Management of Animal and Plant Communities for Conservation.* Oxford, Blackwell, 555-61.
Hooper, M.D. (1974). Hedgerow removal. *Biologist*, **21**: 81-6.
MacArthur, R.H. and Wilson, E.O. (1967). *The Theory of Island Biogeography.* Princeton.
Murton, R.K. and Westwood, N.J. (1974). Some effects of agricultural changes on the English avifauna. *Br. Birds*, **67**: 41-69.
Peterken, G.F. and Harding, P.T. (1974). Recent changes in the conservation value of woodlands in Rockingham Forest. *Forestry*, **47**: 109-28.
Pollard, E., Hooper, M.D. and Moore, N.W. (1974). *Hedges.* London, Collins, pp. 256.
Teather, E.K. (1970). The hedgerow: an analysis of a changing landscape feature. *Geography*, **55**: 146-55.
Terborgh, J. (1974). Preservation of natural diversity: the problem of extinction-prone species. *Biosci.*, **24**: 715-22.

7. Practical conservation and land use management: the case of modern agriculture

John Davidson

This chapter deals with the impact of modern farming on the landscape in three types of geographical area, the rural/urban fringe, lowland agricultural zones and the scenic uplands.

'Conservation' in conventional terminology is taken to mean the 'wise use' of resources. In the context of landscape, it implies notions of purposeful action rather than a policy of laissez faire, the positive use of resources rather than their preservation in a museum-like way, the *enhancement* of values by creative action and renewal, living on *interest* rather than capital and the maintenance of a 'sustained yield'. Conservation demands long term rather than short term decisions and it is concerned with the inter-relationship between different rural resources on the supposition that the value to society of the whole fabric of the countryside may be greater than the sum of its parts.

In relation to landscape conservation policies, we are concerned with three issues:

1. protection of unique landscapes with special archaeological and visual characteristics which we seek to retain;
2. repair of landscapes spoiled by dereliction in various forms;
3. establishing new landscapes and ensuring their continued survival in a self-sustaining way.

Therefore, a whole range of philosophical and political issues is concerned with the judgements to be made about the definition of quality in landscape, the priority to be given to protecting the best compared with repairing the worst and the purposes for which landscape conservation is undertaken – who benefits and what kinds of satisfaction they derive. Of equal importance are the practical measures that can be used to achieve conservation objectives in agricultural regions.

The picture is one of separate systems pursuing single purpose goals without a great deal of reference and interaction. Each would claim that they had conservation aims for their particular resource. The Nature Conservancy Council is seeking to conserve wildlife, the water industry is concerned with conservation of water supplies and the Forestry Commission is helping to conserve the nation's stock of timber.

The activities of all these resource planning systems impinge upon landscape conservation. However, the two systems which have perhaps the greatest impact are the agricultural planning system and the statutory Town and Country Planning system.

The agricultural planning system has been concerned with the protection of agricultural land against urban development and other changes of use, achieving this aim by working closely with the statutory planning system. The main purposes of agricultural planning, however, have been to produce food cheaply, now more efficiently, for the nation and to ensure that farmers have adequate incomes. The system consists of a Government department with advisory wings which has sought to influence farmers and landowners by grants, fiscal policies, advice and education. Farmers themselves, aided by their own organisations the NFU and the CLA, are the executive agents of this system.

In operating this planning system there are obviously many landscape implications. There have been changes in the type of agriculture so that arable land has increased and pasture declined. Hedges and hedgerow trees have been removed to make way for bigger machines; land has been drained to bring it into cultivation or increase the output from it. These changes are well known, partly as a result of a study by Westmacott and Worthington (1974) sponsored by the Countryside Commission, which documented the landscape changes in seven areas of lowland England. The main findings of the consultants were in many ways predictable, in some surprising.

The consultants probed the attitudes of farmers on landscape and wildlife conservation and concluded that farmers believed that a functional landscape which reflects modern, efficient agriculture is visually pleasing. With this notion are strongly held traditional views of and about the farming community that farmers automatically pursue conservation policies and that the future of the landscape is safe in their hands; to a lesser extent they claim that it may also be ecologically satisfactory.

In the future it seems that agriculture will progressively adopt more advanced technical methods and that changes witnessed in the landscapes of eastern England may well spread to the western counties. Certainly Westmacott and Worthington (1974) supported this view and there was evidence that the dairying and livestock areas were likely to undergo equally as radical changes as the arable areas to the east. Some farmers argue that the pace of change will not quicken, others accept this event as inevitable but argue that the visual consequences are no less satisfactory than the landscape that is being replaced. Wide vistas are different to enclosed fields but may give equal satisfaction.

On the definition of conservation given earlier, in the agricultural situation conservation goals are not being pursued. It is largely a single purpose activity concerned with short term measures in response to economic events.

The statutory Town and Country Planning system has been seen as having some responsibility for taking an overview of all resource planning in the countryside. In practice, the ability to secure landscape conservation has been dependent upon two mechanisms:

1. the protection of open countryside from building development by the application of development control measures;
2. additional national designations have helped to protect particular areas of high quality landscape, e.g. in National Parks, Areas of Outstanding Natural Beauty and areas defined in development plans as of great landscape value. Other areas have been defined as Green Belts for planning purposes to prevent the outward spread of towns and cities.

The effect of this system of labelling the countryside has been to cover much of it with protective designations in which development control is extra strict and to make additional resources available for eyesore clearance and other improvements to the landscape. The battery of powers available to the planners includes Tree Preservation Orders, and Article 4 directions, which can make it necessary for applications for planning permission to be submitted which would otherwise have been permitted under the General Development Order.

I have been describing, broadly, the 'old' system of planning which, in the mid-1960s, was found to have weaknesses. It was realised that the conservation of landscape, even in designated areas, could not be achieved through the medium of statutory planning control and that major landscape changes were taking place outside the control of local planning authorities.

A new system of planning, introduced by the 1968 Town and Country Planning Act, in theory improves upon the old one and provides scope for planning authorities to prepare positive policies which apply to particular parts of the countryside and deal with the relationship between physical planning, agriculture and forestry. The new system, however, was not developed with the countryside in mind, although, again in theory, there is no reason why it should not fit the circumstances of the countryside well. In practice, however, the countryside has received low priority and, even in those structure plans which have been published, only cursory attention has been given to countryside conservation issues and it is too early to see any practical results on the ground.

If the planning framework exists, how are we to make it work to

E

achieve landscape conservation objectives in practice? The Commission has been promoting some experimental projects which might point the way to measures applicable in the future. These exercises are concerned with a local level of involvement in the management of private land which is in use for agricultural purposes.

The projects upon which I shall be drawing have been carried out in upland areas (in the Lake District and Snowdonia) and in the urban fringe around Manchester (the Bollin Valley). The approach has been based upon the appointment of project officers with agricultural training and experience operating under the auspices of a local authority and seeking to influence the management decisions of both public and private landowners by various means.

The following general principles emerge from this work:

1. The importance of local authorities employing staff who can understand farming problems and communicate these to local authority chief officers and elected members.
2. The advantage of identifying a tract of countryside and giving responsibility for identifying problems and working out solutions to one individual with a remit which includes a large amount of consultation with the many statutory agencies with fragmented responsibilities. One person with a territorial responsibility can identify the short-comings of bureaucratic methods of working and can at least begin to help remedy these.
3. The importance of acknowledging that parts of the cost of landscape conservation work must be borne by the public purse. In the Lake District, for example, where skilled labour is in short supply for work such as dry stone walling and maintenance of footpaths, the project has been responsible for encouraging the setting up of two or three small business enterprises to do this work. The maintenance of landscape features which are a valued part of the Lake District scene, once undertaken by farmers when they contributed to the functioning of the farm, is now no longer possible without financial assistance. In the Bollin Valley, the damage caused by townspeople who live nearby has been repaired and the costs met by the project – litter has been cleared and volunteers used to manage woodland which would otherwise be left to decay.
4. Practical conservation in these areas has depended entirely upon the good will and support of the farming community. Participation has proved to be the underlying philosophy and nothing has been done without first obtaining the agreement of the occupiers of the land.
5. Farmers, we have found, have difficulty in obtaining advice, even if they wish to pursue conservation practices; the advisory agencies which exist, including the Nature Conservancy Council and the Countryside Commission, have not yet geared

themselves to providing the practical advice which farmers are seeking. Moreover, the Ministry of Agriculture officials can find themselves torn between their own private view and official policy. There is a need for some concerted action at Government level in this area. The Countryside Commission is promoting the concept of 'demonstration farms' where conservation proposals can be put into practice so that they can be inspected by other interested farmers.

This chapter has avoided defining in detail the goals of landscape conservation in intensively farmed regions. It is, however, implicit that an important aspect of a conservation policy should be the retention of features of special scenic, historic or scientific value. Another aspect should be the replacement of vegetation cover, where it has been removed over extensive areas, by trees and shrubs to new alignments and groupings which do not conflict with the needs of modern agriculture. Although it is important that these concepts are discussed further so that society can form a view about the type of future landscape it wishes to see and use, it is also necessary to develop means acceptable to the farming community of achieving results on the ground and this has been the orientation of this chapter. The underlying principle of the Countryside Commission's experimental work is that conservation measures are the responsibility of landowners, public or private, and the Government's role is to assist with technical advice and financial aid. There remains the intriguing task of finding ways of motivating owners towards a conservation approach to management so that the landscape which emerges as a by-product of modern agriculture serves a range of other purposes for the community.

REFERENCE

Westmacott, R. and Worthington, T. (1974). *New Agricultural Landscapes.* Cheltenham, Countryside Commission.

8. Biosphere reserves: the philosophy of conservation

Otto Frankel

In the chapters and reported discussion so far there has emerged a wish to discuss the philosophy of conservation. This is really perhaps what ought to be done in the present chapter because the biosphere concept lies at one end of the scale of conservation, whereas perhaps John Davidson's paper lies at the other.

I want first of all to describe the Biosphere Programme of UNESCO in rather general terms. In the words of Dr. Lloyd Loope, the consultant who now looks after it in the UNESCO office in Paris, it is a 'grand design of nature conservation', which is clearly what it is. It has four main characteristics which distinguish it from nature conservation on a national scale. First, it is world-wide and its objective is to include all the major biomes and their diverse ecosystems. Second, it is to be based on international agreements and mutual obligation, not on formal treaties between governments but on letters of understanding which, one believes, may have at least moral if not legal strength; but in times to come these may grow into legal obligations. Third, it is hoped that at least in the early stages of the biosphere programme, technical and financial co-operation will be made available to developing countries. Fourth, there is to be emphasis on research and on long-term monitoring of environmental and biological changes; it is also to provide sites for any kind of environmental or other research relating to natural communities. It is a rational approach to long-term conservation, though it is probably somewhat idealistic in practical, political terms.

How do Biosphere Reserves fit into the scene of conservation as we know it? I think here I must discuss what one might call the elements of conservation. First, I believe one must regard conservation as dynamic, and we are therefore concerned with the *dynamics* of a system under conservation. Nothing in nature is static, neither the environment nor the biota which are to be the subject of conservation. I suppose this concept is generally acceptable as basic to nature conservation, unless the emphasis is on the preservation of endangered or threatened species, which is essentially a static concept, since the immediate concern is with the prevention of threatened extinction rather than with the long-term survival in a dynamic evolutionary process. The preservation of a threatened species has analogies with the preservation of an historical monument unless or until the species is safely returned to natural conditions. These remarks are not intended to convey that nature reserves have no part to play in the conservation of threatened species, although this is not necessarily a major objective of biosphere reserves. I shall refer again to this aspect.

Second, the dynamics of an ecosystem or a community subject to some form of conservation depend on *man's involvement*, and in particular on the nature and extent of economic utilisation. The preceding contribution, by John Davidson, provided an excellent example of the conservation of landscape quality under land use management. Subject to restraints imposed by an authority, in this case the Countryside Commission, there is scope for changes in management systems in response to the dynamics of technological or economic change. At the other end of the conservation gradient, biosphere reserves are wholly excluded from economic exploitation, at least in the core zone. Management is restricted to measures required for the maintenance of the ecosystem. The dynamics are thus subject to the interactions within the system and to the effects of climatic and other major changes affecting the system as a whole.

The third element of conservation is the *time scale of concern* (Frankel, 1974), the actual or notional period of validity of the legal or administrative provisions for conservation. Time restraints may be imposed by the nature of the conserved system itself; preservation of a beautiful or otherwise significant tree or copse, or of a small remnant of the original vegetation in the midst of a drastically transformed landscape, are limited to the life of the tree or of the dominant species. Here again analogies with historical monuments are patent, but the maintenance or reconstruction of the latter are a good deal easier; in Japan, historical buildings built of wood are periodically rebuilt when decayed or burned down. Thus, even where economic exploitation is altogether excluded, the nature of the reserve, its size, organisation and maintenance may restrict its durability, as can the intent, the time scale of concern in the strict sense, on the part of the organisation responsible for its establishment and management. I asked one of the chief proponents of nature conservation in Australia, a distinguished poet and a publicist for conservation, what her time scale of concern was, having explained the concept. She said, 'Oh, my life, that of my daughter, and perhaps that of her children.' I think this is typical of the attitudes of many people: the lifetime of people who are now alive or about to be alive. The future is uncertain, and seeing what has happened in the last half-century, can one wonder at a lack of confidence in the long-term effect of our own conservation efforts?

For *domesticates*, i.e. organisms used by man, whether animals or plants, a limited time scale of concern is appropriate. We do not know which domesticated animals, if any, will be used in the future, what crops will be cultivated, less still what characteristics the crops of the future will need to possess. Nor do we know what kinds of variation future biologists will be able to generate. Should it become possible to preserve and restructure DNA, the preservation of existing genotypes would be out of date and unwanted. But for the time being such technologies are not available, and we continue to rely on the range of variation presented by the gene pools of our crop species. There can be no question that these should be preserved, at the very least as a pretty inexpensive evolutionary insurance. In view of the uncertainty of future needs, the notional time scale of concern for domesticates hardly needs to extend beyond the next century or two, subject to revision in the light of future developments.

The end purpose of *nature conservation* is to preserve natural communities with a high degree of integrity, subject to processes which are intrinsic to natural communities in their environment. Conservation can be seen as linking the past, present and future, hence as an endeavour to serve future generations as much as the current one. Accordingly, the notional time scale should be open-ended, the basic philosophy being that man, though indubitably the dominant species, has not only a rational interest, but also an emotional impulse to keep alive a diversity of organisms which are not primarily subject to use and exploitation by his own species, and to let them carry on the process of living and evolving which has given rise to their and his own existence. Indeed, to some of us it may be an abhorrent thought that perhaps in a century or two there may be few organisms around which man either does not use or is unable to destroy; and one may have an acute sense of guilt that it is in the short spell of a generation or two that we have created the momentum for this vast genocide.

Such an 'evolutionary ethic' (Frankel, 1974) may be the philosophical background of long-term conservation in general, and of biosphere reserves in particular, but in essence the *concept of biosphere reserves* is the hard-headed scientific planning and management of examples of natural ecosystems for present and future study and enjoyment by man. It is a concept which attempts to persuade the nations of the world to unite in protecting the major biomes, both terrestrial and coastal, for all time, the intent being that the conservation be in permanence and should not be broken by the exigencies of political or social pressures. In the words of a MAB (Man and Biosphere) task force, 'biosphere reserves will be protected areas of land and coastal environment; together they will constitute a world-wide network, linked by international understanding on purposes, standards and exchange of scientific information. Each biosphere reserve will include one or more of the following categories:

(1) representative examples of natural biomes, which means more than one ecosystem in a biome, (2) unique communities or areas with unusual natural features of exceptional interest; it is recognised that representative areas may also contain unique features, for example one population of a globally rare species, (3) examples of harmonious landscape resulting from traditional patterns of land use, (4) examples of modified or degraded ecosystems capable of being restored to more natural conditions.' Now, 3 and 4 do not fit in to what I have been discussing previously, and these were introduced by ecologists from densely populated countries such as Great Britain, I think very understandably and sensibly. Clearly, many ecosystems which have been greatly modified by man are of aesthetic, historical or scientific significance and provide opportunities for long-term studies of ecological changes under different conditions of management and for the conservation of locally adapted biota.

The definition and inclusion of 'unique areas' caused a good deal of controversy. I quote, without comment, examples which were given: centres of distribution of rare or endangered species; the confluence of different floristic provinces such as the Carpathian mountains; or the particular opportunities for research such as newly formed volcanic islands.

Biosphere reserves must be large enough to safeguard their integrity over long periods of time. They should consist of a substantial inner or 'core' zone which is specially protected, and a 'buffer' zone which should be ecologically consistent with the core, but accessible to a moderate extent of human use compatible with the purposes of the reserve. This may include approved types of research, land use such as grazing or a moderate extent of cropping or forest utilisation, educational activities, and tourism. Indeed, tourism may be essential in contributing funds for the maintenance of reserves.

Both buffer and core zones provide security of tenure, which is an important aspect of all long-term ecological observations and experiments. Such protection is needed for the 'IBP (International Biological Programme) sites' which are still in active use, for the sites used in other programmes of MAB, or for the long-term study of recovery processes in degraded ecosystems. Naturally, such activities are to be confined to the buffer zone. There was a struggle over the admission of research to the core zone, and some of us stuck to it like grim death, against strong objections from our Russian colleagues who wanted access to the core zone to be reduced to the barest minimum; they even wanted a minimum of management which I imagine would not be practicable, for example, in many African reserves. Monitoring, which is to be a major feature of biosphere reserves, could be impossible unless there were access to the core zone where it would have to be conducted on fixed sites over long periods of time.

Research is envisaged at three levels: an understanding of the dynamics of the particular ecosystem, comparisons between ecosystems, and comparisons in time. These require both destructive and non-destructive research. I believe that a minimum of so-called destructive research should be admitted to the core zone – taking core samples, or taking vegetation samples at long intervals can scarcely harm a long-term reserve, and on this basis understanding was reached. In fact, all types of research relevant to nature studies are to be admitted in the buffer zone, and long-term surveys are to be admitted to the core zone. The programme is to be initiated by a survey of the biosphere reserve. There are to be continuous or frequent observations of climatic variables, hydrological variables and pollutant levels, including nuclear radiation; and periodic observations, including soil characteristics and plant and animal characteristics. I believe it would be highly important that population genetic surveys should form part of biological surveys. We have now relatively easy measures of variability in natural populations, and it is highly important that selected organisms in biosphere reserves should be sampled initially, and again at intervals commensurate with the length of their life cycle. This would give us not only the kind of information on longer-term dynamic changes in natural populations which we almost completely lack, but also would provide an invaluable guide to the organisation of nature reserves and their management. It would give us answers to the question 'What is the role of genetic variation in species survival?' I must admit that I have stated dogmatically, and rather effectively in political spheres, that the maintenance of genetic variation is essential for survival, but we have no evidence. It is biological common sense, and no more. We ought to obtain evidence, and we can now attempt to get it.

So this is the concept of the biosphere reserves, and what is the reality? There are hopeful beginnings. Dr Loope tells me that Senegal has just nominated the Sine Saloum area on the coast, about 200 km south of Dakar, as Africa's first biosphere reserve. It contains a wide range of ecosystems, including marine, estuarine, mangrove, and dry forest. There is considerable interest in Indonesia, the Philippines and Malaysia. In Mexico, two reserves have been established in the state of Durango, through the co-operation of the Instituto de Ecología, the government of the State of Durango, and local authorities. Reserva de La Michilía is composed primarily of pine-evergreen oak forests. It is said to have large intact areas and to be rich in fauna. It does have some human habitation outside the 'core area', and socio-ecological studies are planned. Reserva de Mapimí is located in a desert basin north-west of the town of Ceballos. It was established primarily for protection of and research on the desert turtle and other rare desert animals. The Mexicans are working hard to make these reserves a political and economic reality. Meanwhile, scientific investigations commenced this spring, with a study of the food habits of the white-tailed deer in relation to those of cattle. Elaborate and concrete plans for international co-operation already exist. There is much interest in collaboration between personnel at Los Alamos, New Mexico (a future U.S. Biosphere Reserve?, with both desert and pine-oak ecosystems) and Mexican biologists working in the Durango reserves. Numerous foreign scientists, including some from Canada and France, are planning to start research in Durango within a year.

One of the aims of the biosphere reserves concept is that they shall have the assistance, technical and financial, of other nations and that, with the help of UNEP and IUCN, assistance will be forthcoming for nations wishing to establish biosphere reserves but lacking the technical and financial resources to do so. On this will depend the success of the programme in some developing countries. It is of course very likely that developed countries will declare national reserves as biosphere reserves, and some have grand opportunities for doing so, perhaps none more so than Canada and next no doubt the United States. Australia has still great opportunities and one may hope that we shall set up a number of biosphere reserves, although I am not so optimistic that Australia will have the human resources to conduct the research activities that we regard as essential for the proper functioning of biosphere reserves. But if no more than a few biosphere reserves are set up within the next few years, if the programme achieves no more than this, and if some of them are in the hard-pressed wildlife areas of East Africa, it will have been well worth forming.

REFERENCE

Frankel, O.H. (1974). Genetic conservation: our evolutionary responsibility. *Genetics*, **78**: 53-65.

SUMMARY OF DISCUSSION IN PART II

The discussion for this section cannot be related clearly to individual papers. A great deal was said about standards and viewpoints, since these obviously condition the types of landscapes we wish to see. Where economic situations change, the standards and end-products must obviously change also.

Davidson and Gane, speaking about recreation areas, felt that, although some people liked to be separated and to feel screened from each other by woodland belts, others preferred to be sociable and close to one another. What is the philosophy of conservation, Bennett asked, and answered her question by defining it as the prevention of degradation rather than the preservation of an endangered species, be it never so beautiful.

Holdgate expressed a view that too much nonsense was talked about conserving already highly degraded landscapes such as the heather moors which are discussed in the first chapters of this book. Gane's reply was that, although conservation meant different things to different people, he considered it a properly respectable objective to conserve different sites for different reasons. Others, later in the discussion, touched on this by saying that conservation of deflected or sub-climaxes naturally involved careful management, since otherwise they would continue to the climatic climax (as for instance with chalk grassland moving towards forest) in a very few years. So far as the Nature Conservancy was concerned, representative samples of the various habitats existing in this country ought to be conserved, though there was some controversy on the size of such sites. A static as well as a dynamic approach was needed. He also felt that, for the conservation of gene pools, efforts should be made to conserve species, when they were under threat.

Williams and Hooper discussed the problem of herbaceous species survivals, in terms of the theory of conservation of island biota, in isolated woodlands, where micro-evolution might be expected to have taken place over periods of several hundreds of years. Williams saw no evidence of this, but Hooper disagreed.

From this, Hutchinson took the discussion back to hedgerows in which the romantically degraded hedgerows of the 1930s which were magnificent bird refuges but quite useless agriculturally were contrasted with the earlier neatly woven and ditched specimens of value to the farmer but less interesting to the city naturalist. He further made the point that the East Anglian hedges, which were so small as to be of little use to bird or farmer, were those that had been most removed and therefore should be least regretted. Hooper agreed but nevertheless mentioned some interestingly beautiful and species-rich hedges in the Norfolk and Suffolk wood pasture areas which ha' unfortunately also been removed. Aesthetics in the countryside were also mentioned by several contributors, the viewpoints differing partly according to where they had been born and bred.

To the farmer, the hedgerow tree was a nuisance, though to the conservationist it was valuable. Yet, hedges themselves were of value in preserving a flexible approach to farming, and many farmers who had taken hedges out were now regretting it, Hutchinson stated.

McPhane was worried that during the preceding discussion the tacit assumption was that no-one wanted any changes in the countryside. He thought that a time might be near when a revulsion from city life would impel people towards making a living in the country, presumably by means of smallholdings. Davidson agreed that the countryside in Britain could only be preserved in its present form on the assumption that high technology agriculture would continue as at present.

This elicited a comment from Holdgate who pointed out that, if this country were no longer able to import the food it needed from developing countries because their own populations needed it, then we should have to grow it ourselves. So the cosmetics of landscape would disappear or at least become something very different from what we are now used to. Intensive cultivation systems and intensive livestock production would give us something very different from what we inherited from Capability Brown, for instance. With a nation of smallholders, the residual woodlands and wild areas would certainly disappear. At present the farmers look after the land and do so very well indeed, preserving the aesthetic aspects where they can. The point here perhaps is that if the urban community wants more beauty it will have to pay for it.

Davidson was asked at this point to comment on the Countryside Commission's views on the kinds of investment decisions necessary to maintain landscape conservation objectives. A report is under way on this, and it would seem that the hard-pressed farmers might well not be able to comply without financial help from government. He agreed that a new world food situation would inevitably evoke completely new conservation objectives such that it would be impossible to make large increases in food production and to keep the present landscape conservation policy intact at the same time. With all this Frankel agreed, although he pointed out that the countryside of Japan is exceedingly beautiful and yet is highly productive. Standards are dynamic also, and he compared the ephemeral standards of landscape aesthetics with the more enduring ones of nature conservation – to be as natural as possible with the minimum of interference by man.

The more philosophical approach as to whether one ought to conserve anything at all unless it was of direct use was put forward by Bennett and was vehemently disputed by Frankel. Biosphere reserves, for instance, are not extremely space consuming on a world scale. However, in this very destructive era, as Frankel pointed out, should we not feel *concern* for other biota? Should we not demand conservation of ourselves if some other organism was the dominant species? One does not have to grieve over the disappearance of every species to be a good conservationist, and the issues must be looked at in the light of realities. An interesting example of the preservation of an area of the old Danish heaths was mentioned by Thorpe as showing that a nation needed to be reminded of its history and cultural heritage also, the judicious conservation of landscapes illustrating this.

The conservation of landscapes and typical ecosystems as examples of past and present land use practices was thought by Harris to be of legitimate value and Frankel pointed out that very similar discussions to those which had just taken place in these discussions had resulted also from MAB and UNESCO deliberations.

In short, it was generally felt that aesthetic, cultural, historical and practical farming parameters should all be considered when taking decisions on conservational matters. The economics of food production and importation must obviously be taken into account, not only in the developing countries but also in one such as Britain where the landscapes have been predominantly transformed by man's economic activities.

PART III
GENE POOL CONSERVATION
IN AGRICULTURE

9. Threats to crop plant genetic resources

Erna Bennett

It seems to me that no discussion on man and the environment can have meaning if it fails to face up to problems of a social and political character. The tone of a symposium such as this must, inevitably, be social and political, and I feel bound to maintain this tone. Genetic resources are endangered by circumstances that arise from social and political events, and it can only be by action at the same level that the threat can be overcome.

The environmental crisis is the creature of a society and its politics, and as one of the components of the environment genetic resources do not differ fundamentally from any other sort of resources that, through use or misuse, affect the lives and well-being of the members of society. The use and misuse of resources are determined ultimately by political decisions.

Let us look first, however, at what we mean when we speak of genetic resources. Compared with other resources they may seem at first sight to be rather intangible. They reside in living organisms, and therefore are not only in a state of constant change but also are vulnerable to the same environmental dangers as ourselves. Briefly, genetic resources may be described as the total genetic potential of all plants actually or latently useful to man. At present, by far the largest part of genetic resources is that represented by what are known as primitive cultivars.

Man first began to cultivate plants somewhere in the foothills of the Kurdish mountains about ten thousand years ago. In the following millenia, agricultural man migrated to many parts of the then known earth, and often beyond, far from the original home of the plants he cultivated, taking their seeds with him. He settled in humid river valleys and rich alluvial plains, he created oases of cultivation in hostile deserts and penetrated to harsh and forbidding footholds in the highest mountains. In the course of time his crops became adapted to every kind of habitat, and many thousands of races arose, each possessing unique combinations of genes stabilised by adaptive linkage conferring distinct genotypic and phenotypic characteristics.

The aim of agriculture was – and still is – to disturb the environment. The stable plant associations of nature gradually gave way to a patchwork of cultivation which in time came to dominate the landscape of whole regions of the earth. Just as the chemical activity of a substance is enormously enhanced by reduction to colloidal dimensions, so the greatly fragmented patches of cultivation created by early man enhanced the genetic activity of the plants he cultivated and the plants that mingled with them. In the millenia-long melting pot of plant races thus created, genetic exchange between plant races and species took place on a scale never before – or since – possible. The patchwork of cultivation sown by man unleashed an explosion of hybridisation and a flood of evolution that found expression in literally inestimable numbers of new races of cultivated plants and their relatives. The inhabited earth was .the stage, for ten thousand years, for an unrepeatable plant breeding experiment of enormous dimensions. Nowadays, in an age when weedy fields and fragmented cultivation have yielded to wide expanses of uniform cultivars, we cannot hope to repeat this experiment. Its products, the evolutionary consequences of a unique genetic explosion, are the principal component of our genetic resources today. They are highly vulnerable and non-renewable.

Moreover, of the many thousands of species of plants, only a fraction of a percent have been used by man. Of these, not much more than a few score of species have come to constitute man's major crops. But very many as yet uncultivated plant species are known to yield products of importance to man. There thus still awaits us the enormous and who knows how rewarding task of exploring the wild and still unevaluated sector of the plant kingdom. This task has barely begun. Here, too, is a further component of plant genetic resources, a component of unknown dimensions. We need only mention here, in passing, that new techniques, such as somatic hybridisation, can fundamentally alter the picture at any time.

I have said elsewhere (1971) that in terms of man's ecological success the method of food-winning that agriculture represented is strikingly reflected in a marked and rapid population increase. The diagram (Fig. 9.1), based on various estimates of the human population at different times and derived from different sources, shows this quite clearly. The log scale merely accentuates the effect. The first part of the graph is, of course, highly conjectural, but it is worth noting that a ten-fold positive or negative correction is possible without significantly affecting the form of the graph.

We may say, therefore, that following the introduction of agriculture man rapidly became an ecological dominant, and this is reflected in an increase in human numbers. Throughout the agricultural millenia the human condition improved slowly, but steadily, a progress disturbed only by sporadic disasters of temporary

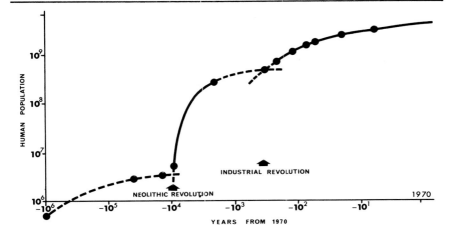

Fig. 9.1 The size of the human population during the last million years.

effect. In the relatively short space of one thousand five hundred years from the first appearance of farming in the valleys of the Tigris and Euphrates, food production had so increased as to stimulate a flourishing trade, the growth of the first urban societies, the construction of great cities and the beginnings of the civilisation of which ours is a part. On our diagram it is not until much later — and now on the basis of much more reliable estimates — that we note a further sharp population increase. This coincides with the industrial revolution and the general spread of towns, and it is in this second great population upsurge that we find ourselves today.

It is so easy these days to see man's effect on his environment in terms of the depletion of energy and resources, of pollution and overcrowding and a steady decline in the quality of the environment — overshadowing the profound but gradual transformation of the earth wrought by agriculture to the extent that very few indeed of the family of man live or have ever lived beyond the protection of a man-made habitat — that it is not surprising that population increase has been picked upon by many as the real cause of our present environmental crisis. Some ten years ago a well-known journal published a paper which argued, with the aid of mathematics, that by a certain day in the twenty-first century we shall have reached a shoulder-to-shoulder density on earth. The literature is heavy with similar forecasts. The 'population explosion' and the 'food-population gap' provide foundation stones for a philosophy of pessimism and a mood of anti-humanism that has become the characteristic of our age.

I believe this philosophy must be challenged, and that scientists by the nature of their work are uniquely in a position to do so. That the human population is increasing is a fact. It is also a fact that two-thirds of our kind are grossly under-nourished, but these facts are a challenge. They must also be the starting point for any rational programme of resource utilisation. But it is not to a defective human element that we must look, or into the depths of a defective human soul, if we are to resolve the environmental crisis, but to other factors, and I suggest that we are surrounded by telling clues as to what these might be.

On the way to attend this symposium I saw tons of tomatoes being destroyed by bulldozers. Many thousands of tons have been so destroyed. In this way an abundant harvest which should be cause for pleasure is made to yield scarcity and high prices instead of food for people who need it. As I am speaking, heavily-laden fruit trees awaken fears of a 'disastrous abundance' rather than satisfaction that the hungry will be fed. In the North American 'granaries of the world' thousands of tons of grain are destroyed or adulterated to prevent their use as human food when yields are 'too high'. Politicians do not like scientists to talk like this, but might not the plant breeder ask, with very good reason, where then is my usefulness when one of the two blades of grass I have made to grow is destroyed because it has no place in the jungle of our economic system and its laws?

Knibbs (1928) and Bernal (1958) have both examined the earth's carrying capacity in terms of an increasing human population, and they present detailed arguments, based on the conditions and possibilities of their day, that the earth could support a four-fold (Knibbs) or a five-fold (Bernal) population increase, using contemporarily available resources and techniques. Since then resources and techniques have vastly improved. So also have crop varieties. Yet even with the large yield increases of the high-yielding varieties of the 'green revolution' man has scarcely begun to tap the genetic potential that genetic resources hold for the future. Two decades of wheat and rice improvement on an unprecedented scale shed but the faintest glimmer on the possibilities of improving all our crops. But can any of us be sure that if we use genetic resources to create higher yields of better crops they will not end up in store, forbidden to be eaten, as is now common in Europe, or destroyed, rather than in the pots of our under privileged fellow-men?

The earth, we are often told, is finite, and its cultivable surface is limited. This is not denied, but even with an increasing population it is, in itself, no cause for concern. To anyone travelling in a fast train the buffers at the end of the line must be a disturbing sight. But we are not in sight of the buffers yet. In spite of this, many who guide public thinking are behaving as if they were. They are also behaving as if we did not know how to stop the train, though in fact we know a great deal about how to stop it. There is even some evidence that the train slows down automatically.

Demographers rarely express concern at the annual growth rates of populations in developed countries, which stand at present at about one percent or less. Family size – without the imposition of external restraints – falls close to or within the limits regarded as satisfactory for population stability. In the underdeveloped world, however, annual growth rates range from 2% to more than 3.5%. This, say demographers and doom-watchers, *is* a cause for concern. But we should look more closely at the nature of these raw statistics.

When we do, we can see that they reflect many very different factors, many of them social. Inter alia, they reflect a falling rate of infant mortality, and the first stages of a struggle to lift the average life expectancy of underprivileged people from something under forty years – as it was in England several centuries ago – to a value still far short of the traditional span of three-score years and ten. When modern medicine operates against a background of poverty and underdevelopment the increased survival to maturity of formerly wretchedly short-lived human beings is bound to be reflected in increases in the annual rate of population growth. When reasonable standards of life-expectancy and living have been attained by the ending of poverty, population increase will level off as it has done already in developed countries. In the meantime I who believe that an infant mortality of almost 30 per thousand in the capital of my own underdeveloped country in the first decades of the present century was iniquitous, cannot now be persuaded that twice that level is not doubly iniquitous in the third world today.

In my own family, and I would venture to say in most of yours, we can see a similar story repeated in miniature. My grandparents shared their parents with more than a dozen sibs of whom four or more died as infants, and my parents theirs with eight or ten of whom one died as a child. I have three sibs, and my own generation has an average of less than two children, no children having been lost in these last two generations. Throughout these four generations there has been a fairly steady but unspectacular increase in well-being. To this we must add the impact not only of modern medicine but also of the behaviour patterns of a developed society. Thus, in this example, we can trace not only a peak in growth rate when old reproductive patterns coincided with new and improved social and medicinal conditions, but also a shift from underdevelopment to development which, with its associated changes in behaviour patterns, seems from the evidence to provide one of our simplest and most effective brakes on population increase.

Since more than two thirds of the human population still live in conditions imposed by underdevelopment, we might usefully look at the pattern of our own transition from underdevelopment. This took place over a period of rather less than four human life-spans, beginning with the miraculous seed that was sown by Abraham Darby in the first few years of the 1700s not very far from where we are now. Darby's industrial innovations, along with many others that were then beginning to come together and cross-fertilise, did not in fact germinate into the industrial revolution until the greater part of a life-span later, but already by the 1770s the industrial revolution was truly on its way.

By the 1840s, a life-span later, industrial productive capacity in one country at least had reached a level such that an economist of the time (Schulz, 1843) estimated that in France 'at the present stage of the development of production an average working period of five hours a day from every person capable of work could suffice for the satisfaction of all the material interests of society.' The replacement of human labour by machine-performed work between 1770 and 1840 yielded a 27-fold increase in industrial productivity. Little more than another life-span later, industrial productive capacity had increased to the point that Lord Leverhulme (1918) felt competent to observe that 'with the means that science has already placed at our disposal, and which are all within our knowledge, we might provide for all the wants of each of us in food, shelter and clothing by *one hour's work per week* for each of us from school age to dotage.'

A lot has happened, perhaps, to modify the uncompromising outlines of Leverhulme's thesis. Non-productive activities absorb slightly more than 40% of the labour force against the 30% of his time. Few of us fancy working till dotage. And I doubt whether his generation regarded post-school education for all beyond the age of twelve as a desirable social ideal. Nevertheless, productivity registered a five-fold increase in the closing decades of the nineteenth century and the first decade of the twentieth. Since then, this fourth human life-span of the industrial revolution has achieved through automation, rationalisation, cybernation – call the process what we will – and the mushrooming growth of cartels, trusts and multinationals, an astonishing 90-fold increase in industrial productivity. We might well wonder why society's potential to feed, clothe and house all its members has not been realised in spite of the well-nigh miraculous increases in social productive capacity made possible by the industrial revolution. Why, instead of the enlargement and the enrichment of the lives of men and women, does the underdeveloped agricultural world starve, and the industrial developed world drown not in industry's benefits but in its effluent?

Not of a population surplus, I have argued. Cordell (1972), speaking of the problems and prospects of the human environment, offers at least the outlines of an answer. Contemporary society, he says, is geared to the wrong objectives. Society's productive machine runs faster and faster not to satisfy existing needs but to create new ones, by advertising, by product change, product proliferation and product obsolescence. When needs are satisfied production is not cut back; rather, new products are created. Real advances in productivity lead not to a decline in prices but to advertising and promotional activities. Man's role is seen to be that of a passive consumer.

Small wonder that such a society should spend more on advertising than on agricultural and medical research combined, or that the solid waste produced annually in the United States, its most typical representative, is sufficient in quantity to build a wall 75 feet wide and 20 feet high along the entire frontier with Canada, or that it costs five billion dollars annually to dispose of it. In such a context the offer of five *million* dollars to a world food programme aimed at the seventy percent of our species who live in the underdeveloped world seems grotesquely out of proportion – a tenth of one percent of a nation's garbage disposal costs for the relief of hunger among underprivileged peoples. Once upon a time we were told of the poor who lived from the crumbs from rich men's tables; now they get crumbs from garbage cans. These are the marks of a society which has become the enemy of man, rather than the expression of his collective will. Even the founders of the Club of Rome have gone on record recently (see Brooks and Andrews, 1974) as questioning the quality of growth, and especially its distribution around the world. 'We know,' they say, 'that the present structure of the world is obsolete.' The same view finds a positive response in a rapidly increasing number of observers.

The pattern of accelerating production has not, until only recently, made itself felt in agriculture. But in the last two decades world yields of the five major cereal crops have doubled, even though systematic exploitation of their genetic potential has barely begun. Yet hunger persists. Poor farmers become poorer and, in the end, migrate to cities that cannot give them work. Rich farmers, with the means to purchase herbicides and fertilisers, become richer on the high-yielding cultivars of the 'green revolution'. At the same time the lower-yielding but genetically diverse varieties of traditional farming – whose variability and adaptability are the indispensible and irreplaceable resource on which future generations will depend for new crops – are unthinkingly destroyed, and herbicide and fertiliser residues pollute the environment, disrupt ecological cycles and kill the microbiota of soils, lakes and rivers. Poor land goes out of cultivation, either as a result of economic pressures or of legislation aimed at curbing 'abundance'. The hungry remain hungry while agricultural productivity increases and unsaleable, but not uneatable, surpluses accumulate. The FAO Committee on Commodity Problems (1970) has warned of the need 'to make realistic estimates of the future growth of demand and to regulate production accordingly – *primarily by pricing policies* – if the emergence of unsaleable surpluses is to be avoided' (my italics). No mention here of population pressures, and no evidence whatever of a reluctantly yielding earth. On the contrary, the danger to man and his resources alike is seen to lie in outworn social and economic patterns that cannot provide food for those that need it, and impede the use of the earth's natural abundance.

Borlaug (1971) said once of the 'green revolution' that it provided not a solution for the problem of hunger, but a breathing space for man. It has been my purpose in speaking as I have to suggest that scientists use this breathing space to take a deep and critical look at the contradictions of a society that is obsolete, rather than to continue to act as if its defects did not exist. Scientists, unfortunately, have been accustomed not to look at the social consequences of their work. In an age in which the time interval that separates research and its application grows constantly less and the distance that once separated the scientist from the citizen has disappeared, there is now less justification than ever for the social isolation of the scientist. He must begin to ask, and to answer, social and political questions. In the old and unlamented days of ivory towers the scientist felt secure in his isolation, and questions of loyalty hardly touched him. Today, whether he likes it or not, the scientist is immersed in the tide of human events and the conflicts of loyalty that torment contemporary society. As a citizen he must make a choice, but as a scientist his choice cannot be detached from his direct and personal involvement in the technical and biological processes that increasingly affect political decisions and charge him with a special responsibility. But to whom is he responsible? Who can claim his loyalty? We have little logical choice but to agree with the view of Ravetz (1971) that the scientist's loyalty and responsibility is to humanity itself, because the scientist is a steward for nature, and guardian of its resources.

The problems we have discussed in this symposium, the threats to resources and the environmental crisis, resulting from a politico-economic system hopelessly outdated by human technological capacity, make a mockery of such documents as the Universal Declaration of Human Rights which affirms the right of all to a standard of living adequate for the health and well-being of every person and his family. Such declarations can have but a hollow ring to the seventy percent of our fellow men who, in the underdeveloped world, provide the bulk of the raw materials for the industrial wealth of the world but themselves are condemned to chronic hunger and unrelieved poverty. At the same time in developed countries, industrial production accelerates helplessly, natural resources are hastened to depletion, and undisposable surpluses – destined for destruction or indefinite storage – accumulate. As we have seen, the productive capacity to meet all the needs of man already exists but the consumer society is unable to mobilise it. 'By its very nature,' says Hutchinson (1975), 'it creates and then exaggerates differences between one man and another that have no foundation in equity.'

Scientists have begun to question the political structures and economic ideas that are now seen to endanger not only world resources but also the human future. More and more their doubts are expressed in terms of a humanist revolt against the anti-humanism and the alienation of contemporary society. 'The root of our disillusion,' says Hutchinson, 'is this. If liberty means licence to exploit any advantage I may have over my neighbour, and to hold on to that advantage as of right, what meaning can I attach to equality, and in what sense can I claim a fraternal relationship with him?'

History repeats itself in curious ways. We may recall that the revolt against established authority and law that roused the world from its medieval sleep in the fourteenth century was led by that merchant class which was to found, and then to dominate for six centuries, the wealth-seeking society against which we revolt today, and that they did so in the name of human values and a civic humanism which, as the Renaissance, left us a cultural inheritance and cultural resources so rich that we still draw from them the greater part of our notions on the nobility of man. Other times, other classes, and the scientist-citizen now holds in his hand the key to a new humanism that can take man beyond the political limits now reached by society. But the key is useless without the courage to use it – the courage to question laws that have not formerly been questioned, and to expose shibboleths that have become articles of faith.

One such article of faith is the notion of 'a world of plenty'. But why a world of plenty? Is not a world of enough a more worthy and meaningful objective? Seneca once said, and it can be said again today, 'The geometrician teaches me to work out the size of my estates, rather than to work out how much a man needs in order to have enough. He teaches me to calculate, instead of teaching me that there is no point whatsoever in that sort of computation, and that a person is none the happier for having estates that tire accountants out. What use is it to me to be able to divide a piece of land into equal parts, if I am unable to divide it with a brother?'

Our message today must surely be the same. Resources there are, and more than sufficient for a 'world of enough for all'. Along with other resources, plant genetic resources open out to us almost endless possibilities of enlarging the life of man. For that we need only a respect for the earth on which we live, and the determination and the courage to create an environment on earth that is worthy of man, whatever the shibboleths we cast aside in the process of realising it.

REFERENCES

Baron, H. (1966). *Crisis of the Early Italian Renaissance: Civic Humanism and Republican Liberty in an Age of Classicism and Tyranny.* Princeton, University Press.

Bennett, E. (1971). The origin and importance of agroecotypes in Southwest Asia. *In* Davis, P.H. *et al.* (eds.). *Plant Life in South-West Asia.* Edinburgh, Botanical Society, 219-34.

Bernal, J.D. (1958). *World Without War.* London, Routledge, Kegan and Paul.

Borlaug, N.E. (1971). *Mankind and Civilization at Another Crossroads.* McDougall Memorial Lecture, FAO Conference, 16th Session, FAO, Rome.

Brooks, D.B. and Andrews, P.W. (1974). Mineral resources, economic growth and world population. *Science*, **185**: 13-19.

Cipolla, C.M. (1974). *The Economic History of World Population*. London, Penguin Books.

Cordell, A.J. (1972). The socio-economics of technological progress. Unpublished lecture in the series 'Human Environment Problems and Prospects', Faculty of Science, Carlton University.

F.A.O. (1970). *Report of the 45th Session of the Committee on Commodity Problems*. Rome, FAO.

Hutchinson, J.G. (1975). *The Challenge of the Third World*. Eddington Memorial Lecture. Cambridge, Cambridge University Press.

Knibbs, G.H. (1928). *The Shadow of the World's Future*. London, Benn.

Leverhulme, Lord. (1918). Foreword. *In* Spooner, H.J. *Wealth from Waste*. London, Routledge.

Mitchell, B.R. (1975). *European Historical Statistics, 1750-1970*. London, Macmillan.

Ravetz, J.R. (1971). Conflicts of loyalty in science. *Nature*, **234**: 20-1.

Schulz, W. (1843). *Die Bewegung der Produktion: eine geschichtlich-statistische Abhandlung*. Zürich.

Seneca. (1969). *Letters from a Stoic*. London, Penguin Books.

United Nations. (1973). *Statistical Yearbook*. New York, Department of Economic and Social Affairs, UNO.

United Nations. (1973). *Yearbook of National Accounts Statistics*. New York, Department of Economic and Social Affairs, UNO.

10. Conservation of crop genetic resources and their wild relatives: an overview*

Otto Frankel

Plant genetic resources of actual or potential use to man can be grouped into five broad categories:

A. The varieties, or cultivars, produced since the advent of scientific plant breeding 100 years ago (the advanced cultivars). For the most part these are selected for uniformity and high performance, requiring some or all of the components of present-day agricultural systems – intensive cultivation, fertilisers, plant protection, irrigation.

B. The varieties of traditional agriculture (the traditional, or primitive cultivars) which had evolved over centuries (or millennia) as a result of migration, introduction and natural selection in the various environments in which crops were cultivated. There is great diversity *between* and also *within* primitive cultivars since their population structure evolved through natural selection to enable the crop to survive the rigours of the climate or attacks by parasites, and thus to provide the low but steady yields essential in subsistence agriculture.

C. Wild and weedy relatives of crop species.

D. Wild species used for food, feed, fibre, timber.

E. Wild species of potential use.

The first category, the *advanced cultivars*, including those which are now obsolete, have been, and continue to be, widely used as resources

*This Chapter has been prepared by Sir Otto Frankel at the request of FAO as a contribution to an overview paper on genetic resources which was commissioned to FAO by UNEP for consideration by the 4th Session of its Governing Council in March 1976. The views expressed here are those of the author and may not necessarily reflect those of the Governing bodies of FAO and UNEP on this matter.

for further breeding. They constitute a highly valuable, but rather limited gene pool because of their uniformity, and because many are related to each other. 'Genetic vulnerability', i.e. epidemics aggravated by genetic homogeneity, is increasingly recognised, the corn leaf blight epidemic of 1970 in the United States having dramatically demonstrated the dangers of extreme genetic homogeneity (Harlan, 1975). Advanced cultivars of most crops are fairly adequately represented in existing collections.

In the last ten years attention has been drawn to the *primitive cultivars*, for two reasons – the wealth in potentially useful genetic variation they contain, an invaluable resource for present and future plant breeders; and the rapid rate at which they are disappearing through being replaced by advanced cultivars. With some exceptions, primitive cultivars are *not* adequately represented in existing collections, for several reasons. First, many large collections placed their main emphasis on selected, pure-bred cultivars. Second, populations collected in the field more often than not were subjected to line selection when entered into a collection, thus greatly reducing their innate genetic variability. Third, most collections with large holdings were maintained by periodic planting-out, exposing the material to 'genetic erosion' arising from natural hybridisation, natural selection, and genetic drift in small populations – in effect greatly infringing the genetic integrity of the sample. In recent years the threat to these invaluable resources caused growing concern, and the need for urgent action to save what still remained in the field was clearly recognised, culminating in recommendations 37-48 carried by the Stockholm Environment Conference.

The use and conservation of *wild plants* of direct or potential value has been considered as deserving less attention, mainly because they were thought to be less threatened; but for many this is no longer the case. Moreover, it is difficult to draw a line between those which are or are not of direct use. Accordingly, the conservation of ecosystems and of endangered species is relevant to the subject of this chapter, especially since new methods of 'genetic engineering' have raised the interest in wild plants as parental material in plant breeding.

In essence, *the problem of the conservation of genetic resources* is to explore and collect the vanishing genetic heritage, and to classify, evaluate, conserve and document the collected material, for the benefit of present and future generations. It resolves itself into the following interacting, yet discrete operations:

1. *Exploration and collecting.* To assemble a significant representation of the cultivars of traditional agriculture (category B) and, according to need, of wild plants in categories C-E, giving priority to those which are threatened or are needed for plant improvement. This will involve extensive collecting in the field, and in many cases calls for urgent action.

2. *Conservation and distribution*. To take steps to have germ plasm in collections made available to users, and to have it maintained under conditions which will safeguard its long-term survival and genetic integrity for the benefit of future generations (categories A-E).

3. *Evaluation*. To stimulate systematic evaluation of collections and to ensure that the resulting information is made widely available for the effective utilisation of genetic material.

4. *Documentation*. To provide a broadly adaptable documentation and information system as the only effective link between all operations and all participants.

5. *Education and training* at various levels as a preparation for the component tasks.

The sections which follow review the present state with regard to each of these operations, examine current activities, and point to needs and gaps calling for action.

The state of genetic resources

General: structure and function

In considering the state of genetic resources in the light of recent developments, one must make a distinction between what one might call structural or organisational developments on one hand, and functional or substantive progress on the other. In general terms it can be stated that considerable advances have been made in recent years in the organisational and technical superstructure and in political and public awareness, but relatively little progress of a substantive kind, i.e. in terms of material collected or of conservation becoming comprehensive.

Here are some of the structural changes which have taken place recently; page numbers refer to fuller discussion below.

(i) Largely in response to the recommendations of the Stockholm Conference, international and national awareness and involvement have greatly increased. The long-standing participation of FAO has been strengthened by increases in staff and by its association with IBPGR (see below). UNESCO and UNEP have become directly involved.

(ii) The Consultative Group on International Agricultural Research (CGIAR) established the International Board for Plant Genetic Resources (IBPGR) to promote genetic resources activities on a global scale, with access to financial support through CGIAR. It had its first meeting in June, 1974.

(iii) The international agricultural research institutes supported by CGIAR have assumed responsibility for establishing large collections and for co-ordinating genetic resources work in a number of major crops.

(iv) National participation is being strengthened in a number of highly important regions, notably in the Near-East and in South-East Asia where regional links are being formed (p. 143).

(v) Scientific and technological problems – in conservation and storage, in exploration, and in evaluation – have been further clarified and a documentation system has successfully passed the pilot stage (p. 139) (see Frankel & Bennett, 1970; Frankel & Hawkes, 1975).

(vi) Specialist education at university level has produced a substantial flow of qualified personnel working in many developing countries, and short training courses and some training pamphlets have been introduced (p. 140).

Against all these impressive advances indicating widespread interest and, at long last, substantial support, the record of actual achievement is not impressive. 'It must be admitted that for all the organisational development, and despite repeated and urgent pleas by the [FAO] Panel of Experts, remarkably little collecting has been done to date,' (Harlan, 1975) i.e. in the decade of campaigning for genetic conservation. Nor have there as yet been definite moves to make collections as safe as we can make them, in spite of widespread agreement on procedures and willingness to join a collaborative conservation network (pp. 142-6).

Now that the organisational foundations have been laid, there is every reason to press on with the work itself, with whatever human and material resources can be brought into action, with a maximum of adaptive commonsense, and as far as possible with a minimum of delay, and of avoidable formalities and potentially restrictive priorities.

Exploration

Land races were generated wherever crops were raised over long periods, but the diversity is greatest in the 'centres of genetic diversity' where crops originated or migrated in the early millennia of the agricultural revolution. But even crops migrating between the hemispheres in the post-Columbian centuries acquired adaptive diversity in their new homes, such as maize in Africa, Asia and Europe, peas in Brazil, beans in South-East and South Asia, and many more. Land races in Europe began to be displaced by plant breeders' selections a hundred years ago, but some European land races introduced into America, Australia and New Zealand survived well into this century, and their eroded remnants can be found in some collections.

In the ancient centres of diversity – the countries surrounding the Mediterranean, South-West, Central, South and South-East and East Asia, Eastern and Western Africa, Mesoamerica, the Andean region and sub-tropical South America – the wealth of genetic variation they contained had been discovered by the great Russian botanist N.I. Vavilov in the 'twenties and 'thirties, and the collections which he and his collaborators assembled probably have not been equalled because much of the material has since disappeared in the field. The gradual advance of modern, selected varieties began to be felt in the years before the war when Harlan and Martini (1936) extended the warning that 'the world's priceless reservoir of germ plasm ... is now being imperilled'. This process became a flood in the early 'fifties, with introduced or locally selected varieties replacing the traditional populations, as part of the spreading of economic development. Replacement was most rapid and wide-spread in annual crops, especially the cereals wheat, rice and maize. But it affected many others – even tree fruits, which led to the replacement of many ancient local fruit varieties in the Near-Eastern countries, Turkey, Iran and Pakistan; and it is still spreading, even into the rain forests in South-East Asia where genetic reservoirs of forest and fruit trees are becoming endangered.

The answer, of course, is not to attempt to stem the tide, but to assemble and preserve a fair representation of the genetic diversity which is vanishing with the traditional forms of agriculture of which the primitive varieties were an integral part. This can be done effectively and economically by collecting samples of crops in the field, in markets, or in other ways. This is relatively simple in the majority of crops since they are reproduced from seeds which can be more or less easily collected and transported, but far more difficult with crops which do not produce seeds and are propagated vegetatively. While such crops present technical problems (Hawkes, 1975; Sykes, 1975) the general principles and methods of plant exploration are worked out (Marshall and Brown, 1975) and generally accepted.

There is, however, a need for discussing *exploration targets*, i.e. the areas and the crops which should receive urgent or early attention. In the past the choice of targets reflected the aims and attitudes of institutions or individual collectors. The objectives were *non-specific*, such as those of the great Russian collecting expeditions under Vavilov whose aim it was to assemble the greatest possible diversity of a great variety of crop species, in all the centres of diversity to which they had access – they were, for example, not admitted to India. Similarly, the collecting expeditions conducted more recently by Japanese workers under Kihara and Yamashita were non-discriminatory, but oriented towards objectives of scientific interest. Alternatively, many of the extensive collections of the U.S. Department of Agriculture were largely '*mission oriented*', as were those of other institutions and nations, i.e. targets were chosen for the purpose of solving specific economic problems, such as resistance to a parasite or even a specific biotype of a parasite, or for some other ecological, agronomic or biological characteristics. Target areas were selected on the basis of previous collections or other relevant information. These are thoroughly useful objectives, as long as the desired characteristic can be recognised, which is rarely the case; or the information is significant, which will be increasingly the case as we assemble, evaluate and document representative germplasm collections. But mission oriented collecting by definition is highly selective and hence contributes relatively little towards countering the threat to the genetic resources of a crop as a whole.

The question of targets and priorities has assumed a new significance with the realisation of the magnitude and urgency of the threat, and with the involvement of international organisations – FAO, UNEP, CGIAR, IBPGR – and the availability of substantial public funds. Clearly, there is a need for guiding principles for the selection of targets and priorities, even though one would wish for flexibility in their administration. Crop and area priorities were examined at three meetings of FAO's Panel of Experts on Plant Exploration and Introduction (FAO 1969, 1970, 1973) and by a group of experts which was convened at Beltsville in 1972 by CGIAR and its Technical Advisory Committee (TAC). While there were minor diversities between the reports of these meetings, there was a large measure of agreement on the crops requiring and deserving attention. Those nominated by at least two of the four examinations are listed in an Appendix (see p. 148). IBPGR re-examined crop priorities at its second meeting in May, 1975. The Board's designation as priority crops included all those previously listed, adding maize, banana and rubber (previously listed at one meeting only) and as new priorities sugarbeet and castor. Clearly there is widespread agreement on priorities, although there are differences of opinion on priority ratings which may at least in part be due to differing criteria for allocating priorities.

Criteria were discussed repeatedly by the FAO Panel of Experts, which tended to regard the extent of threat as the first, and the economic importance of the crop as the second criterion for attention. The size and quality of existing collections were also taken into consideration, the excellent collections of maize, for example, being the reason for excluding the crop from priority rating. The (as yet unpublished) criteria which were discussed by IBPGR at its second meeting do not materially diverge from those of the Panel and the Beltsville group, but add a significant additional criterion – the recognised requirements of plant breeders and research workers for genetic materials. This is a valid criterion, especially valid in the region in which the material originated, and this had been generally recognised. Beyond this point care must be taken that mission orientation does not take priority over genetic salvage and conservation which were the primary motifs for world-wide concern. Two points must be made. The needs of the plant breeders of tomorrow are rarely recognised by those of to-day; if the latter receive prime consideration, the resources the next generation may desperately need may be lost by default. Second, any lengthy consultations and deliberations which tend to delay action must be based on valid grounds indeed.

Delay is certainly not intended by IBPGR. It proposes to promote the early establishment of crop committees which will make recommendations on exploration targets and priorities for a crop or a group of related crops. They are to be associated with the international research institutes responsible for research on the improvement of crop productivity. The committees may provide an active link with institutions and individual scientists in developed as well as developing countries and thus stimulate a broader participation in genetic conservation on the part of the scientific world as a whole than the international organisations have so far succeeded in bringing about. An annual review of the state of genetic resources is to be made by crop committees and by the Board itself, with information to be sought from all relevant sources, especially with regard to emergencies arising from climatic and other changes. The drought in the Sahelian region which imperilled genetic resources of sorghum, millet and other crops, and the termination of the work of the Cotton Research Corporation which made it necessary to find a home for its important collections of germ plasm and breeding stocks, are 'emergency' situations of the kind which it is proposed to meet with appropriate action.

In addition to crop priorities, it is necessary to designate areas in which germ plasm of particular crops is threatened, wanted, or both. Such crop-area priorities had been identified in the reports of the FAO Panel and the Beltsville group which have been quoted above. An attempt to specify more clearly the localities and the nature of the material they contain was made in 1972 (Frankel, 1972) but was only very partially successful. It must be recognised that detailed information on the location of valuable material in the field which could and should be collected is so far no more than sporadic, and this gap in our knowledge is bound to impede and delay systematic collecting activities. It is evident that continuing detailed intelligence about the state and location of material can only come from local sources, especially when the original genetic resources have become rare and scattered, as is the case with the cereals in Near Eastern countries. Assistance in the location of scattered fruit trees may come from aerial photography, and from remote sensing devices which are being developed to discriminate vegetation types (Sykes, 1975). This may also apply to scattered remnants of primitive cultivars in remote and often inaccessable mountain regions where they are known to persist but their actual locations are unknown.

F

As has been pointed out previously, the priorities so far nominated are biased towards the economic importance of crops, and tend to exclude or give lesser prominence to species which have considerable importance in limited areas, or which are not regarded as of primary economic or nutritional significance, yet play a significant role in the nutrition or economy of large populations. Genetic resources of such species have very real significance, especially since some of them have so far not been subject to selection and breeding. Many vegetable crops, especially in the sub-tropics and tropics, are in this category, as are the wild relatives of several temperate-zone vegetables with mediterranean ancestors. Some of these species require and deserve urgent attention. The position is similar with many of the fruit species of South East Asia, where in many instances the genetic diversity extends from wild to cultivated status. Many of the fruits make important dietary and economic contributions, some fruit species are also useful timber trees, and some are attractive ornamentals. As S. Sastrapradja (1975) points out, agricultural scientists as a rule are interested only in the improved cultivars, leaving primitive material to botanists, who in turn feel that species with economic connotations are the responsibility of agriculturists. This dilemma is probably widespread and needs resolving. The number of species which at the recent Symposium of South East Asian Plant Genetic Resources were described as 'eroded' or 'seriously threatened' was large indeed. It is to be hoped that the co-operation between countries with related problems, which is emerging from this symposium, will bring forth concerted plans and, with support from IBPGR, concerted action.

It will be appreciated that a determination of priorities is not unequivocal, and that the real needs are more diverse than would wholly fit into a set of principles. There seems to be a need for a degree of flexibility which would give encouragement and modest support to enterprise from a variety of sources in all countries, and especially in those where genetic resources are located. An interest in genetic diversity is widespread throughout the applied botanical sciences – economic botany, evolution, ecology, agronomy, horticulture, forestry, nature conservation – and people may be willing to co-ordinate their own interests with fairly flexible objectives of a general plan. Once expertise is established in the centres of diversity – and this is growing rapidly – it may attract, assist and guide the participation of colleagues in universities and institutes, in their country and abroad. Strict priorities would need to be relaxed which might be an advantage, and the support, as has been shown by some of the most successful collecting efforts in the past, could be quite modest. However, there should be general acceptance of basic rules which should apply to all collectors, whether supported by public funds or not, that collected material and information should be shared with the country of origin if required, and that a sample should be deposited in a gene bank affiliated with the international conservation network. This is further elaborated in the next section.

Conservation

Exploration and conservation are the king-pins of the current problems of genetic resources. Exploration is to salvage threatened resources in the field, conservation to preserve new as well as existing collections. Even if no further material were to be added, the effective conservation of material now in possession of institutions all over the world is an important issue which requires serious attention. If in exploration the need is for urgent action in the field, on as broad a front as possible, *the need in conservation is for effective organisation*. In exploration the emphasis is on crops and areas, in conservation on facilities and their operation and co-ordination.

Conservation is safest and cheapest if life processes are reduced to the minimum level. This is the case in seeds preserved under conditions appropriate to each species. Live plants are subject to genetic change and to losses through parasites, climatic extremes or human error, but in some plants seeds are either not produced or cannot be stored for extended periods; hence live collections are inevitable. Wild plants are best preserved *in situ* within their indigenous communities. But representatives of particularly useful and/or endangered species can be successfully maintained in botanic gardens or experimental stations. In this section the present state and current problems of each of these groups are reviewed.

Conservation of seeds. The great majority of seed-reproduced economic species can be safely stored over long periods – decades, and probably centuries – without undue genetic change or loss of viability (Roberts, 1975). The advantages of long-term storage *versus* frequent reproduction are the avoidance of genetic erosion and loss referred to in the previous paragraph, and the economy of maintenance. The Working Group of FAO Panel of Experts (FAO, 1974) has specified storage conditions for long-term storage of 'conventional' seeds – i.e. those which can be stored at low temperatures and low moisture content – at two levels, 'preferred' and 'acceptable'. The majority of storage laboratories, including some of the largest, are in the 'acceptable' class, but some of these, and new storages now projected, are concerned to reach the 'preferred' standard, which is at -18°C or less, in air-tight containers, at a seed moisture content of $5 \pm 1\%$. The Panel has also specified operating procedures, including entry procedures, accession size, routine germination tests, regeneration, and documentation. None of these would be found burdensome by a well-run storage laboratory.

The Panel outlined the organisational pattern which is required for operating the system. It is to consist of 'base collections' which have the facilities outlined above, and the function of providing safe long-term seed conservation. Associated with them are 'active collections', whose functions include the multiplication and distribution of seed, regeneration of samples when required as a consequence of loss of viability or near-exhaustion of seed stocks, evaluation, documentation, and medium-term seed storage. The latter is required for the storage of the centre's own collection, and of seed stocks for distribution to other users. Such storages can be smaller and of a somewhat lower standard compared with base collections. The great majority of existing collections are 'active collections', actively engaged in some or all activities in genetic resources work, from exploration to evaluation and utilisation. Many institutions throughout the world are engaged in this kind of activity in relation to one or more crop species.

'Base collections' of the kind described are much smaller in number, and although many institutions maintain collections, relatively few have conditions which make it possible to maintain their collections without the attendant risks and losses already mentioned. This strongly emphasises the need for action to ensure that all assembled germ plasm which is worth preserving is *maintained under safe conditions of storage*. Safe storage can be defined as being conducted under conditions and procedures specified by the Panel of Experts, and with a *duplicate collection* kept under similar conditions in another storage, preferably in another country. Duplicate collections of base collections are regarded as *essential for the long-term safety* and reliability of valuable germ plasm collections.

A survey was conducted recently by FAO's Crop Ecology and Genetic Resources Unit (AGPE) of institutions likely to be equipped and willing to operate as base collections. They were asked (1) whether they were willing to participate in the proposed international network, (2) what were the capacity and physical conditions of the storage, (3) what proportion could be made available for 'international storage', i.e. for collections from other institutions. Of the 50 (out of 58 approached) institutions which replied, 42, or 84%, expressed a willingness to provide space for international storage. At least 30 institutions are willing to enter their entire collections, another 16 part of their collections. This high degree of willingness to participate is proof of the widespread concern of institutions best able to appreciate the need for determined action.

On the basis of size and quality of available storage space, 15 institutions were classified as *Main Centres*, and 16 others, with smaller and/or slightly inferior conditions, as *Associated Centres*. Twenty-one (21) of the total of 31 centres have an interest in a particular crop or group of crops, and the remainder, including some of the largest, are willing to store a variety of crops. However, some of the former might be prepared to accept a wider range of species, at least for duplicate storage.

It has been calculated on the basis of the returns received that at least 500,000 samples now stored under sub-standard conditions could be accommodated at base-collection standards if the required agreements can be brought about between FAO and the designated Main and Associated Centres. These *agreements should be drawn up and, hopefully, concluded without delay*, with a priority second to none. Agreement in principle having been reached at an earlier stage, it should now be possible to put it into effect.

At this stage much will be learned about the operational opportunities and difficulties of an international co-operative seed conservation network. But it must be realised that at the start it will be strikingly incomplete. Even were it possible to store the world's germ plasm in existing storages – which is far from being the case – the regional distribution would leave wide and dangerous gaps. There are vast areas without any storages of base-collection standard, including South and South-East Asia and Central America; but others, especially in Africa, have all too few storages. Clearly it is neither possible nor necessary to have substantial base collections in every institution, or even in every country. But regional quarantine restrictions, let alone technical needs and convenience, make *regional distribution of base collections an absolute necessity*. It is therefore essential that some of the worst gaps be filled without delay. As the FAO Working Group report (FAO, 1974) indicates, neither the capital nor the operating costs are excessive in relation to the value and in many cases irreplaceability of the material.

Mention must be made of research into the storage of seeds at very low temperatures (in liquid nitrogen) which would further reduce life processes and hence virtually eliminate genetic damage (Sakai & Noshiro, 1975). The results are encouraging and the difficulties, especially in the cooling and thawing processes, less than anticipated.

The preservation of the so-called '*recalcitrant seeds*', i.e. those which cannot be stored at low moisture contents, presents individual problems for species or groups of species. Some of these have been solved, but research is called for to improve and extend existing information. An interesting discovery that some seeds can be successfully preserved in a fully imbibed state (Villiers, 1975) is being further explored. *Research on recalcitrant seeds* is of special relevance in tropical species, especially in the many fruit species of South-East Asia.

Living plant collections. Species which cannot be reproduced from seed have already been discussed in a previous section. Seeds of other species cannot be kept for longer periods, and these include many temperate and tropical fruit species. Neither can pollen as yet be used in long-term conservation. Unrooted or rooted woody cuttings held at about 0°C have been stored for limited periods (up to 2 years) but longer term storage possibilities should be explored. These would include the most suitable type of material, the storage conditions and the regenerative procedure after storage (Howard, 1975). Germ plasm of species requiring vegetative forms of propagation therefore is being preserved in living collections maintained in experiment stations, research institutions, botanic gardens, and by commercial enterprises such as nurseries.

The maintenance of living collections presents difficulties attending to their complex and changing environment and the need for space and continued attention. The biggest single biological difficulty comes from the likelihood of virus attack. But the organisational and economic problems of space (especially for trees and large shrubs) and maintenance are considerable, with the further consequence that numbers and sizes of samples are likely to be much reduced by comparison with what is regarded as desirable in seed-reproduced crops. Against this it must be recognised, first, that vegetatively reproduced crops have uniform vegetative progenies, so that sample size is less relevant than in seed-reproduced crops; that multiple grafts can reduce space requirements; and that most of them are highly heterozygous, so that seeds they produce – or can be induced to produce by various means – reproduce highly diverse progenies. Nevertheless it is highly desirable that *research on ways to reduce the cost and effort* of maintenance be pursued and supported.

In the first instance attention should be drawn to various forms of maintaining germ plasm as smaller units than entire plants or seeds. A number of approaches have recently been reviewed, including meristem tissue and cell culture (see Frankel and Hawkes, 1975: chapters 25-27 by Morel, d'Amato and Henshaw). It appears that meristem culture has given considerable promise in the preservation of some species, but that the technical aspects of tissue culture conservation – which would open a wider field of conservation than is possible with meristem culture – is still not in a stage when it can be widely adopted, very largely because of the genetic instability of tissue culture.

Of the greatest importance, and perhaps not only for species which cannot be propagated from seed, are the recent developments in the storage of tissue culture at very low temperatures (-196°C). A number of authors (Anon., 1974; Nag and Street, 1973) found that tissue culture of a number of species, including *Daucus carota, Acer pseudoplatanus*, and *Atropa belladonna*, were stored from 100 days to 2 years without undue loss in cell viability. In one experiment, for example, the optimal cell viability was 65%. The essential components of the system were the cooling rate, the storage temperature, and the thawing rate. Both optimal cooling and thawing rates tend to be relatively high and the temperature of liquid nitrogen is far superior to higher temperatures of, for example, -20°C, -40°C or -78°C. A cryo-protectant was an essential part of the system and its nature has been explored by several authors. DMSO (dimethylsulphoxide) and glycerol seem to be the best protectants.

Morphogenetic potential in meristem cultures is unimpaired by the freezing preservation technique and accordingly normal plants were reproduced as is done from unfrozen tissue culture, producing flowers and seeds in the normal way.

No doubt these techniques will be further pursued and more widely explored; it must however be realised that the number of species which can be regenerated from tissue culture is still fairly limited. Here extensive research could be directly useful in increasing the efficiency of genetic conservation.

In conclusion, the problems of maintaining live collections of germ plasm are formidable, and every effort should be made to reduce the burden involved. It must be recognised, however, that in several countries live collections – of tuber, root or tree crops – are being maintained, especially in some tropical countries where land and labour are still available. Such efforts should be encouraged and supported. Indeed, there is an urgent need to establish collections of germ plasm of great value which is in great danger of impending extinction, as is the case with the many *temperate fruit species* with their gene centres in Iran, Turkey and Pakistan. Comprehensive national or regional germ plasm collections are a most urgent need and, in view of the value to the rest of the world, should be internationally supported. The case is as strong in South-East Asia (see the following section).

Conservation of wild species. Since an overview of endangered species and wildlife conservation is being prepared by IUCN, the present paper confines itself to matters directly related to the conservation of genetic resources actually or potentially useful to man. Three categories can be recognised.

A. Species of direct economic significance, including range, forest, drug or ornamental plants.

B. Wild species related to economic plants which are or may become useful as genetic resources for plant breeding.

C. Species of no known immediate economic use, though of ecological, aesthetic, social, scientific or, potentially, of economic relevance.

It is now generally recognised that the genetic diversity of wild species is most effectively and economically preserved within the communities in which they occur. A community in balance with a stable environment – the stability being subject to the general vagaries of natural environments – is the ideal model of long-term conservation. Here the general principles of nature conservation apply, as specified by IUCN, and recently by a task force organised by UNESCO and UNEP for the establishment of *biosphere reserves* (MAB,

1974) within the programme Man and the Biosphere (MAB) (see also chapter 8 in the present volume). The network of biosphere reserves is to include representative ecosystems of the world's biomes. The sites will be carefully selected for their representativeness and suitability, and the size and organisation of reserves will safeguard the integrity of an inner core area but provide a substantial buffer zone for approved human use, which of course would include the use as genetic reservoirs. Biosphere reserves will therefore have considerable importance for the long-term conservation of species within the categories specified above. The proposed inventories at inception, and thereafter at regular intervals, should be *indexed for species of actual or potential economic relevance*, and this information should be included in the genetic resources information system (see below).

The global distribution, international character and standing, size and organisational structure make biosphere reserves ideal reservoirs for genetic resources. Yet one must recognise that their number will be relatively small, and that their siting will not be able to take account of specific needs such as the preservation of particular species or communities of economic concern. Other forms of nature reserves, such as national parks and forestry reserves, offer additional opportunities as long as they are adequately safeguarded. This issue goes beyond the scope of this chapter.

Here it should be pointed out that the requirements for the preservation of genetic resources are not necessarily identical with those of long-term nature conservation. The distinction arises from the *time scale of concern* (Frankel, 1974) which is open ended for wildlife conservation, but limited to decades, or at most centuries, for categories A and B since human requirements are transitory and unpredictable over longer periods. This has significant consequences for the organisation and size of such reserves. First, legal safeguards are less essential than for long-term conservation, and, second, the ecological safeguards of size and organisation can also be more relaxed. On the other hand there is a greater demand for ecological diversity so as to include the largest possible range of genetic diversity. It follows that for the purpose of preserving genetic resources of wild species in categories A and B, the *standards* of security, size, organisation and management *can be somewhat lower* than is acceptable for long-term nature reserves, and that emphasis should be placed on the number and diversity of sites. This has two practical consequences. First, reserves dedicated to a great diversity of purposes could assume importance for the conservation of genetic resources; and, second, the limited time scale of concern would justify the designation of 'genetic reserves' for the protection of particular species or communities, even if the protected area is well below accepted standards for conservation.

In this regard there are similarities between the protection of endangered species in 'nature reserves ... set up to conserve just one species', which, in spite of shortcomings – the diminution or even destruction of other species present, and the threat to the protected species from visitors – are regarded as 'by and large successful' (Hunt, 1974). This, of course, is based on short-term observations. The long-term fate of such protective measures can scarcely be in doubt. But, as has been suggested, such considerations are of lesser relevance for the protection of species of economic significance.

When a species, or an ecologically significant or taxonomically distinct section of a species, is either needed for research or endangered in its natural habitat, steps akin to the conservation of domesticates (see above) may be called for, viz., conservation of seed, live plants, or both. Seed conservation of wild plants is now in progress at the Royal Botanic Gardens, Kew (Thompson, 1973), and probably in other botanic gardens. Many individual scientists have substantial collections of wild relatives of domesticates, often personally collected in their centres of diversity. Results of evolutionary, ecological or genetic research add greatly to the value of such collections. Steps should be taken to have duplicates deposited in base collections and recorded in the documentation system.

Live specimens of wild plants in the main have their only natural repository in botanic gardens, apart from collections assembled for research or breeding. Here, botanic gardens have an important role in genetic conservation which as yet is not generally recognised. However, a symposium held at Kew Gardens in September, 1975 explored this role in its various aspects, and has made recommendations for co-operative action by botanic gardens.

Finally, consideration must be given to species of prospective value to man. Such species are difficult to define. They stretch from plants which are now gathered as major vegetable food or as condiments in many parts of the world, in the forests of Southern Asia or the wasteland and scrub in mediterranean countries, indeed on the very outskirts of Rome, to potential raw materials for chemical and medico-chemical industries. Indications that species are worthy of attention come either from past usage, from taxonomic or other associations with species now used, or from new requirements by industry. The history of crop production fails to suggest that new major crops are likely to be discovered (as against new plants deliberately engineered by man). But there is reason for assuming that species may be taken into cultivation for specific ecological niches, or for requirements arising in nutritional, medical, chemical or other industrial research. Such leads should be taken up as they arise, but it hardly seems called for to collect and preserve a range of wild species on the basis of vague prospects. It would seem more purposeful to regard the preservation of potentially useful species as part justification for the conservation of ecosystems.

F*

Evaluation

Evaluation is an essential preliminary to utilisation. It may include no more than a site description of the place of origin and a few morphological or phenological descriptions, or it may extend to multidisciplinary studies including physiological, genetic, biochemical, plant pathological or other characteristics. All kinds of examination, at whatever level, have, and indeed should have, the common motivation of being related to *utilisation*, whether in some area of research, or in plant introduction, or in plant breeding. To give a few examples – large collections of wild wheat and *Aegilops* species have been analyzed for their protein characteristics in order to discover the ancestor that contributed the B-genome of the common wheat, *Triticum aestivum* (Johnson, 1975). Large collections of legume species from Africa and South America have been examined, under controlled environment conditions and in the field, for their suitability for different regions of Australia. An extensive search was made for wheats rich in protein and lysin; and the search for resistance to an enormous range of parasites is never ending. Indeed, with industrial and nutritional requirements becoming more specialised and sophisticated, and with the rapid progress in the basic sciences, it would be futile to conduct routine examinations of large collections, as has been suggested, apart from general and rather obvious characterisations. All others must be project-conditioned and project-specific to have any real meaning and, indeed, to attract intelligent operators. If this view needs defending, the very transience of present-day industrial objectives, let alone scientific information and techniques, argues against examinations which are not relevant to present or foreseeable objectives. The argument can be usefully inverted: evaluation, as the only rational lead to utilisation, must be scientifically and technologically at the frontier of knowledge; it is no longer mere routine testing. It demands imagination and good science as it merges into utilisation – the imaginative use of the best available information, materials and methods.

But if, in the writer's view, there is neither need nor scope for generalised evaluation, there is a real need for pooling resources, methods and information. As is evident from what has been said in the last paragraph, much evaluation is now carried out in laboratories, i.e. is not environment-specific. Laboratory methods are applied not only on chemical, biochemical or technological characteristics, but in entomology, plant pathology, genetics, physiology, and others. Such work requires expertise and equipment of a high order – and it is expensive. *Agreement on labour sharing and co-operation, on methods, and on the sharing of information* would benefit all nations. This could give a new dimension to the usefulness of genetic resources. In this area the proposed crop committees (see p. 129) could have a useful fact-finding and advisory role.

Documentation

A systematic descriptive documentation of collections is the key to their utilisation. It is no overstatement that the relatively limited use which has been made of large existing collections is mainly due to the deficiencies of existing documentation which may restrict the usefulness of a collection even to the institution owning it, and much more so to other potential users. The difficulty arises from the vast amount of information even on one single large collection which renders analysis very difficult. Moreover, there are no agreed standards and procedures which would facilitate the communication of information between collections, and between collections and users.

Developments which have taken place over the last two years have shown the method of overcoming most of the problems of documentation and information. Based on research carried out by information specialists over a number of years, a project was established jointly by FAO, CGIAR and the University of Colorado, under the title Genetic Resources Communication, Information and Documentation System (GR/CIDS). The system is based on the application of the EXIR(TAXIR) computer system which was specially developed for genetic resources requirements. In addition to developing further the programme itself, the FAO/University of Colorado group has established extensive working relations with a number of centres holding collections of maize, wheat, rice, peanuts, potatoes, sorghum, beans, cowpeas and cassava. The institutions include international research institutes, national centres, and members of organisations like Eucarpia. Crop data are required from these collaborators, and visits and workshops help to develop all practical aspects of the system so as to meet as far as is possible all user requirements; the research group is thoroughly user oriented.

The system has been designed to be computer hardware independent, i.e. it can be used, with minor modifications, on most of the available large computers. Current research explores the possibility of using minicomputers which could be operated independently, or connected to a large installation, for example by a microwave link.

Procedures have been worked out – and are constantly being further improved – to facilitate the introduction of GR/CIDS to new users. Careful orientation and education in all phases of data gathering and data use are provided on the spot by members of the team, and follow-up contact and help is given as needed. Relevant developments or improvements are passed on to users.

The reception of CIDS is highly encouraging. The system has been given to institutions in Colombia and Brazil, and others in Peru, Italy, USSR, UK and USA are negotiating. Clearly the wider the spread of an information system, the greater will be the benefit to the world as a whole.

Education and training

The growing interest and support for activities relating to plant genetic resources have raised the prospect of a rapidly growing demand for trained staff during the next few years. Two types of training courses have become established and are making useful contributions, viz., short courses, given at genetic resources centres and research institutes, and courses at university degree level.

1. Short courses (1-3 months) generate interest and participation in genetic resources activities in a region, as did the successful training course held at Bogor for participants from South-East Asia in February-March, 1975. The International Rice Research Institute provides training courses on plant exploration and conservation and related subjects. Training courses specifically directed towards urgent priority projects – in the immediate future the exploration and salvage of threatened primitive cultivars – could materially help to provide the necessary staff. Qualified people with local experience would have the advantage of familiarity with the environment, but may lack familiarity with practical techniques and the necessary theoretical background which such courses could supply. Unlike a university course, such *ad hoc* training should be highly specific – collecting cereals, root crops, fruit trees, etc. – and should include subjects directly relevant to the task. Such courses would be most effective if held at international or other institutes directly concerned with genetic resources in a particular crop.

2. A university postgraduate (M.Sc.) International Course in the Conservation and Utilisation of Plant Genetic Resources was pioneered in 1969-70 by Professor J.G. Hawkes, a member of the FAO Panel, in the Botany Department of the University of Birmingham. This course responded to the needs he, and the Panel, foresaw for people trained in the various phases of genetic conservation and in the principles underlying them. Sixty-three (63) students have so far passed through the course, the largest number, 15, in the current year 1975-76. Most of them have remained active in genetic resources work, about half of them in developing countries. Indeed, the small number of Birmingham M.Sc.s is having a marked impact in several important centres of genetic diversity. The reputation of the course is now well established as a training centre in a subject of rapidly growing importance. The rising demand is about to burst the seams of the Department and additional facilities and staff have now been granted by the University and by IBPGR to meet the foreseeable needs for the next few years.

Birmingham has remained the only university offering a special course and degree option on genetic resources. There has been a good deal of discussion about prospective staff requirements and the training facilities these would necessitate. Hence it is appropriate to consider this area in its broader perspective.

What is involved in the term 'genetic resources'? It was coined at the FAO-IBP Technical Conference of 1967, to include the areas covered in this overview – exploration and collecting, conservation, evaluation, documentation, and the training required for all of these. *Utilisation of genetic resources was the aim and purpose of it all*, where possible with emphasis on current needs, without neglect for potential and unpredictable needs for the future. While utilisation must dominate certain phases – especially, as we have seen, evaluation and documentation – in itself it was not conceived as an integral part of genetic resources work. Indeed, in practice the opposite is the case: much of the work on collections is integrated with utilisation. 'Utilisation' is a field of vast dimensions, including many fields of agricultural and biological sciences, whereas 'genetic resources' is, and should be, a limited field, created largely by the temporal need for emphasis rather than being a separate discipline in its own right. This point needs emphasising for two reasons. First, were it to be regarded as a long-term discipline, the emphasis on urgency of action would be reduced; second, genetic resources activities in the narrower and proper sense offer limited career prospects in the long-term should the field become overcrowded, as is not unusual in new or fashionable disciplines.

The Birmingham course has served, and continues to serve, a most useful purpose, and its expansion is appropriate. Nor would it come amiss if one or two similar courses were established elsewhere, especially in the tropics. Here one may bear in mind that the Birmingham course has been criticised for placing insufficient emphasis on the utilisation of genetic resources, and with this one may concur, though for somewhat different reasons from those adduced. If, as has been reasoned above, the genetic resources field, as interpreted here, is limited to what is regarded its proper area of relevance, the extension of training to related fields may be in the best interests of the student. Perhaps, rather than greatly expand training for genetic resources activities as such, it would seem appropriate to *introduce the basic scientific and technical information on genetic resources into agricultural and biological courses* in general, with practical specialised courses at genetic resources centres, base collections and documentation centres for those wishing to enter a career in such institutions.

In the years to come, pre-occupation with genetic resources is likely to shift from the current pre-occupation with the salvage, assembly and conservation of resources to their utilisation and development in ways which are beginning to emerge. To be sure, conservation will remain an essential pre-occupation, and is likely to extend to plants not in use at present, including wild species. But new approaches are likely to require workers with a knowledge of crop species, of their evolutionary pathways and variation patterns, and also of new ways of modifying and restructuring their genetic controls and physiological adaptations. In short, there may arise a need, especially in the larger genetic resources centres, of workers capable of participating in biological research which is likely to have profound effects on genetic resources of the future. The point of these remarks is that, in addition to the training and recruitment of workers in the more traditional – and for the greater part pragmatic – areas relevant to genetic resources, one may consider the possibility of attracting a small number of people capable of original thought and work in advanced and relevant areas of genetic research. This may apply in particular to international institutes and other institutions which assume major responsibilities in the future.

To be sure, there is a great deal to do at current levels of work: but it would be advisable to guard against genetic resources work becoming routine once the pioneering stage is past, with the result that it might fail to attract people with initiative and imagination.

Genetic resources networks

We have become accustomed to speak of a global network for genetic resources activities, and IBPGR was given as its basic function to promote such a network. In the light of the preceding sections of this overview, the objectives of the network as a whole should be as follows:

To assemble and make available for this and future generations a significant representation of the germplasm of actual or potential use to man. This involves the collecting of relevant cultivated or wild material in the field; the multiplication and distribution of material for present-day use; the long-term conservation of seeds (where possible) or of live plant material, or the *in situ* conservation of valuable source material; the gathering of information of value to users and its distribution; and, at all steps in all activities, the maintenance of agreed documentation systems as the only effective link between all operations and all participants.

To speak of a network for such diverse and wide-ranging activities, involving hundreds of institutions all over the world with widely differing interests and objectives is, of course, a figure of speech. It signifies the desirability of international co-operation in an area of common interest for the world as a whole. The object of the network is to strengthen links, promote agreed standards and procedures, ascertain and fill existing gaps in coverage, and stimulate the spread of material and information. The aim should be to achieve these ends with the minimum of bureaucratic formality and the maximum scope for institutional and individual initiative and co-operation.

A network is a co-operative association formed for a specific purpose. It will be the more successful *the closer the level of organisation is to the operational level*. If this kind of network functions, the task of the 'global' network is minimised. In the genetic resources field the operations defined in previous sections are distinct but interacting. Networks could therefore be limited to a specific activity such as exploration or conservation, or they could include several or all operations; they could have regional associations covering several crops, or they could be restricted to one crop or a group of related crops with or without geographical restrictions. In fact the pattern can, and should be flexible so as to achieve a practical objective which may be the sharing of facilities, of expertise, of material, of information or of a combination of any of these. Since networks are likely to play a critical role in the structure of activities and the allocation of funds, some comments are called for.

1. *Regional networks*, in the regions of genetic diversity in Asia, Latin America and Africa (see p. 127). The suggestion came from TAC (the Technical Advisory Committee of CGIAR) and at its request was elaborated by the Beltsville group of experts in 1972. It envisaged a group of associated national institutions, with one of them, equipped with facilities for storage, documentation, etc., assuming a co-ordinating and advisory role. Even at that stage doubts were expressed as to its feasibility and these have since been strengthened. A more practical form was proposed for South-East Asia at the recent symposium at Bogor. The genetic resources activities in member countries are to be co-ordinated by a committee which is to recommend the sharing of responsibilities, facilities, information, material and expertise, and IBPGR has been asked to assist in the formation of the network. The provision of an executive officer to the committee is under consideration. This appears to be a functional type of network in an area where there is considerable scope and urgency for exploration, where conservation is expensive (many tree crops), and where there are institutions in the different countries ready to play their part. A much needed long-term seed storage would be shared, as would be the documentation system. This type of network would extend over the whole range of activities and could be readily linked with others – with regional, crop specific (in this case through IRRI and ICRISAT), conservation, or documentation networks. The regional network itself would concern itself with any crops of the region agreed upon by the committee.

Regional activities are also undertaken by some national institutions. The Germplasm Laboratory at Bari, Italy, is performing regional functions in the central and western mediterranean area. A similar role could be performed by other institutions in regions where their expertise could play a useful role. In the mediterranean region, for example, there is scope for a project to collect vegetable species and their ancestors.

2. *Crop specific networks*, based on crop-specific international institutes or other institutions pre-eminent in a particular crop or group of crops. While the functions of such networks could be similar to those of regional networks – especially where the institute concerned is located in the main centre of diversity – their sphere of influence could reach well beyond the regions of genetic diversity. IRRI, the International Rice Research Institute in the Philippines, has assumed such a role in the course of the last few years, through co-operation throughout the rice-growing area in Asia and in other parts of the world. The effectiveness of such networks will largely depend on the people concerned and on their involvement in making a genetic resources network a success. It would be too much to expect that the pattern set by IRRI and one or two other institutes will be equally successful everywhere. To assume global responsibility for the genetic resources of a crop may therefore be neither generally possible nor desirable unless the nature of the responsibility is closely defined, for example with regard to the designation of exploration targets, the co-ordination of documentation or the organising of training courses. Long-term conservation of seeds need not necessarily be a function of such networks since other institutions may be available to act as base collections.

It must be prominently borne in mind that the expertise of national institutions, as well as the materials in their collections, are likely to exceed those of international institutes. The proposed crop co-ordinating committees (see p. 129) could have an important role in planning the activities of such networks and in attracting participation.

3. *Conservation networks* do not necessarily have regional or crop-specific connotations. Basically a few storage laboratories could preserve, and even duplicate, the world's seed collections on a long-term basis. That this would be neither functional nor safe – quite apart from political considerations – was discussed above (p. 133). Yet there is scarcely a need for facilities of base collection standard in every kind of network, although medium-term storage facilities, which can be small and inexpensive, should be widely distributed. However, there is a need for *collaboration between base collections* on standards and procedures, on labour sharing in conservation, on duplicate collections, and on documentation. There is therefore a clear need for a co-ordinating body in which the International Seed· Testing Association (ISTA) may play a part.

The conservation of live material could best be visualised in a regional context, although there is scope, as has been shown in tuber crops, for more widely based associations.

4. *Information networks* have already been discussed. These can, and no doubt will, assume dimensions and directions which are functionally appropriate. The flexibility of CIDS facilitates its

application in any appropriate kind of context.

5. *The global network*. The term 'global network' can be, 'and has been interpreted in the past, as a loose association of networks of the kind suggested in the preceding paragraphs, with a degree of planning, co-ordination, and as far as possible technical and financial assistance on the part of an international agency which could only be FAO. With the establishment of IBPGR, in close association with FAO, a new situation was created. IBPGR assumed 'responsibility ... for recommending policies and developing programmes in close collaboration with and with the help and advice of FAO', for objectives which include the whole range of genetic resources activities covered in this paper, not only at planning and co-ordinating levels but, subject to approval by CGIAR and through FAO and presumably the CGIAR-supported international institutes, at action levels. This in itself represents a tremendous advance over the previous state of affairs when there was, at best, good science, ideas and programmes, but resources were lacking for any but the smallest practical enterprises, and major collecting activities, let alone the initiation of an effective documentation system – advocated by the Panel for many years – had not even a remote chance of execution. The participation of UNEP has added further to the resources of the new management.

This organisation, now in its second year, is faced with a number of problems. As a deliberative, but not executive body, it relies on its secretariat for tactical support, i.e. for the action arising from its decisions and recommendations. At the present stage this task is very large indeed, seeing that none of the component parts, i.e. the various kinds of networks, as yet exists. At the same time the urgency of the situation in gene centres where genetic resources – *the original and principal objectives of the enterprise* – are melting away, calls for rapid, indeed drastic action with any means available. The Board has approached its tasks on a broad front and, although some priorities have emerged, the logistics of the programme appear to require an executive far in excess of that which is available or foreseeable. One may ask whether the range of activities at this stage might be limited to those essential for tackling the most urgent issues, and whether the method devised by FAO and the Board in developing GR/CIDS on a contract basis with a university could be applied in other major priority projects, thus freeing Board and secretariat from detailed planning and executive functions.

This may be an example of the process of devolution of planning and authority which no doubt will become necessary. Perhaps this could also come from greater reliance on expert participation over a broader range of topics than has so far been thought necessary. The crop co-ordinating committees are a good start; a parallel development of 'problem oriented' expert participation is equally needed. In this process Eucarpia in Europe, and SABRAO, the corresponding organisation in Asia and Oceania, may have a part to play. If the world's genetic resources are to be salvaged and 'activated', the surest way of achieving this end will be to secure active and direct involvement of the scientific community.

Summary and conclusions

1. The problem of the conservation of genetic resources is to explore and collect the vanishing genetic heritage, to evaluate, conserve and document the material for the benefit of present and future generations.

2. Notable advances have been made in the *organisational superstructure* and in political and public awareness, but relatively little in terms of material collected or of conservation becoming comprehensive.

3. The Consultative Group on International Agricultural Research (CGIAR) established the International Board for Plant Genetic Resources (IPBGR) to promote, in close association with FAO, genetic resources activities on a global scale, with access to financial support through CGIAR, and with further support from UNEP. International agricultural research institutes supported by CGIAR are to assume co-ordinating responsibilities for a number of major crops.

4. Little or no progress has been made in *exploration and collecting* of genetic resources, but techniques have been clarified, and priorities for exploration targets have been established. Emphasis is on major crops and on present-day needs for plant improvement. However, care must be taken that mission-oriented priorities do not infringe upon the salvage of threatened material of potential value in the future – even the near future – and that minor crops of national or regional significance are not left out. There is a need for greater flexibility which could be achieved by encouraging broad participation on the part of institutions and individuals in all parts of the world.

5. The conditions of *conservation of seeds* of existing and new collections require urgent attention to safeguard their long-term survival and integrity. The FAO Panel of Experts on Plant Exploration and Introduction has provided standards, procedures and an organisational structure for the conservation and distribution of seeds, and FAO staff has conducted an extensive survey of the size and technical standards of storage space offered by institutions for international storage. Agreement on an international scale should be concluded as a matter of urgency. 'Base collection' facilities are needed in areas where none exist, in

South-East Asia, Central America and parts of Africa.

6. Encouragement should be given to the *conservation of living collections* of species which cannot be preserved as seeds. Research is needed into methods for conserving tree crops to reduce costs.

7. *Wild species* are best preserved within their natural communities. Inventories of nature reserves, such as the Biosphere Reserves organised within the MAB programme, should be indexed for species of actual or potential economic significance, and endangered species should be preserved in botanic gardens or research institutes. Collections assembled for research should be duplicated in base collections and included in the documentation system.

8. *Evaluation* should be problem-oriented, i.e. directly related to utilisation. There is wide scope for labour sharing and co-operation on methods and the sharing of information.

9. Much progress has been made in advancing a system for *documentation and information* (GR/CIDS) in a project jointly established by FAO, CGIAR and the University of Colorado. Much experience has been gained with the EXIR system, and many institutions are negotiating its introduction.

10. Specialised short-duration courses (1-3 months) on particular topics and a small number of university courses, such as that pioneered at Birmingham University, are likely to meet the short-term needs for *education and training* at the level of likely genetic resources activities in the next decade. Further needs might best be met by inclusion of basic information in normal university courses, complemented by practical courses in genetic resources centres. There seems to be no justification for building up genetic resources into a discipline of its own.

11. A global network can be workable only if its component parts are close to the operational level. The proposed *regional networks* in centres of genetic diversity have for their primary aim the exploration and conservation of genetic resources within the region, with co-operation in evaluation and documentation and the sharing of basic facilities. Co-ordination of activities, materials and facilities is to be through a regional committee. *Crop-specific networks*, based on international or national institutes, can play a most useful role as demonstrated by IRRI. A *conservation network* may, but need not, have regional or crop-specific connotations. There is a need for agreements on standards and procedures, on labour sharing in conservation, and on duplicate collections. *Documentation networks* will emerge as essential components of any form of network or association which may emerge.

12. The global network to be promoted by IBPGR and FAO can be visualised as stimulating and co-ordinating component parts and attempting to fill gaps. In its formative stage it faces logistic problems which are likely to delay urgent priority actions. Devolution wherever possible, by direct participation of appropriate institutions and by greater involvement of the scientific community, could help to relieve pressure on Board and secretariat and accelerate the execution of programmes.

APPENDIX

Priorities for Exploration and Collection designated by two or more meetings of the FAO Panel of Experts and the Beltsville group:

Wheat, rice, sorghums, millets, barley
Phaseolus, soya, *Arachis, Pisum, Vigna*
Potato, cassava, sweet potato, yam
Banana, temperate, subtropical and tropical fruits
Sugarcane
Cotton, coffee, cacao, rubber
Forage species
Cucurbits

REFERENCES

Anon. (1974). Abstracts 94-96 in 3rd International Congress of Plant Tissue and Cell Culture, Leicester, 1974.

FAO (1969, 1970, 1973). Third, fourth and fifth session of the FAO panel of experts on plant exploration and introduction. Rome, FAO.

FAO (1974). Proposed standards and procedures for seed storage installations used for long-term conservation of base collections. Rome, FAO.

Frankel, O.H. (ed.) (1972). *Survey of Crop Genetic Resources in Their Centres of Diversity*. Rome, FAO/IBP. pp. 164.

Frankel, O.H. (ed.) (1972). *Survey of Crop Genetic Resources in Their Centres of Origin*. Rome, FAO/IBP. pp. 154.

Frankel, O.H. (1974). Our evolutionary responsibility. *Genetics*, **78**: 53-65.

Frankel, O.H. and Bennett, E. (eds.) (1970). *Genetic Resources in Plants — Their Exploration and Conservation*. Oxford, IBP Handbook No. 11. Blackwell, pp. 554.

Frankel, O.H. and Hawkes, J.G. (eds.) (1975). *Crop Genetic Resources for Today and Tomorrow*. IBP Synthesis Vol. 2. Cambridge, Cambridge University Press, pp. 492.

Harlan, J.R. (1975). Our vanishing genetic resources. *Science*, **188**: 618-21.

Harlan, H.V. and Martini, M.L. (1936). *Problems and Results in Barley Breeding*. USDA Yearbook of Agriculture, 1936: 306-46.

Hawkes, J.G. (1975). Vegetatively propagated crops. *In* Frankel, O.H. and

Hawkes, J.G. (eds.). *Crop Genetic Resources for Today and Tomorrow*. Cambridge, Cambridge University Press, 117-21.

Howard, B.H. (1975). Possible long-term cold storage of woody plant material. *In* Frankel, O.H. and Hawkes, J.G. (eds.). *Crop Genetic Resources for Today and Tomorrow*. Cambridge, Cambridge University Press, 359-67.

Hunt, P.F. (1974). Ecosystem reserves. *In Succulents in Peril*. Supplement to IOS Bull., **3**: 11-12.

Johnson, B.L. (1975). Identification of the apparent B-genome donor of wheat. *Can. J. Genet. Cytol.*, **17**: 21-9.

MAB (1974). MAB Task Force on: Criteria and guidelines for the choice and establishment of biosphere reserves. *MAB*, no. 22, UNESCO.

Marshall, D.R. and Brown, A.H.D. (1975). Optimum sampling strategies in genetic conservation. *In* Frankel, O.H. and Hawkes, J.G. (eds.). *Crop Genetic Resources for Today and Tomorrow*. Cambridge, Cambridge University Press, 53-80.

Nag, K.K. and Street, H.E. (1973). Carrot embryogenesis from frozen cultured cells. *Nature*, **245**: 270-2.

Roberts, E.H. (1975). Problems of long-term storage of seed and pollen for genetic resources conservation. *In* Frankel, O.H. and Hawkes, J.G. (eds.). *Crop Genetic Resources for Today and Tomorrow*. Cambridge, Cambridge University Press, 269-96.

Sakai, A. and Noshiro, M. (1975). Some factors contributing to the survival of crop seeds cooled to the temperature of liquid nitrogen. *In* Frankel, O.H. and Hawkes, J.G. (eds.). *Crop Genetic Resources for Today and Tomorrow*. Cambridge, Cambridge University Press, 317-26.

Sastrapradja, S. (1975). Tropical fruit germplasm in South East Asia. *In* Williams, J.T. and Lamoureux, C.H. (eds.) *Plant Genetic Resources in South East Asia*. Bogor, 33-46.

Sykes, J.T. (1975). Tree crops. *In* Frankel, O.H. and Hawkes, J.G. (eds.). *Crop Genetic Resources for Today and Tomorrow*. Cambridge, Cambridge University Press, 123-7.

Thompson, P.A. (1973). Techniques for the storage of seed of species and ecotypes. *In* Hawkes, J.G. and Lange, W. (eds.). *European and Regional Gene Banks*. Wageningen, Eucarpia, 65-6.

Villiers, T.A. (1975). Genetic maintenance of seeds in imbibed storage. *In* Frankel, O.H. and Hawkes, J.G. (eds.). *Crop Genetic Resources for Today and Tomorrow*. Cambridge, Cambridge University Press, 297-315.

11. Preserving Britain's historic farm animals

J.L. Henson

Ever since man first began to domesticate wild animals he has been breeding selectively for those characteristics which happened to suit his particular needs. To start with he merely killed or castrated any male animals which did not conform to his requirements. Later he brought in males which had the characteristics he wanted and culled out females which were below average.

In time this process gave rise to a great variety of breeds of domestic stock, all stemming from a common wild ancestry, but each developed quite differently in different areas. Usually the breed took the name of its district which led to a great local pride in the breed, which was then consciously fixed as a type, often with its own 'trade mark'. Where possible the trade mark chosen was a dominant characteristic transmitted to all its progeny regardless of the breed with which it was crossed.

Examples of this are the white face of Hereford cattle, the black, polled appearance of the Aberdeen Angus, the white tail of the Old Gloucester cattle, and the black face of the Suffolk sheep. Each breed developed useful commercial characteristics of production and climatic adaptation which may or may not be of use to modern agriculture, but which should not be forgotten.

During the course of our history, food tastes and farming systems have changed, so that many breeds which once played an important part in our economy have fallen out of favour. Some have in fact been lost, while others are on the point of extinction. Once a breed has gone it is lost for ever, and for some years scientists and enthusiasts have been trying to create a national awareness of the valuable genetic material which is being and will be lost unless a serious attempt is made to preserve our numerically small breeds.

It was not until European Conservation Year, in 1970, that attention was drawn to the activities of a working party set up by the Zoological Society of London and the Royal Agricultural Society, to advise on the preservation of our rare breeds. A 'Gene Bank' of rare breeds, previously established at Whipsnade Zoo, and consisting of seven breeds of sheep and three breeds of cattle, was moved to the National Agricultural Centre, Kenilworth, Warwickshire and the Cotswold Farm Park, Guiting Power, Cheltenham, where they are successfully breeding and are on view to the public. An organisation has now been formed for the purpose of co-ordinating this work, and its title – The Rare Breeds Survival Trust – was inspired by Sir Peter Scott.

Some of the historic breeds which still survive today have come down to us since early domestication in Stone Age times, almost unaltered by man's breeding techniques. Some, like the little brown Soay sheep, have survived on remote islands on which they were isolated by advancing civilisation. Others, like the wild White Park cattle, have survived in private parks thanks to their sporting attraction for hunting kings in the past, and their beauty and elegance today.

Some breeds have continued in commercial use down through the ages by bending to meet the current needs of the day. Longhorn cattle were the first breed to be taken in hand by the great livestock improvers of the nineteenth century, who developed draught animals into beef cattle. There are now only 200 cows left of the breed in Britain, but only the best have survived and the current demand for a large, lean carcass has brought this and the South Devon, another once minor breed, back into demand.

The Cotswold sheep, descended from the Roman longwool, brought here during the Roman occupation, was a large animal, bred almost entirely for its huge fleece of long, lustrous wool. It was the wool from these sheep which brought great wealth to the Cotswolds in the sixteenth and seventeenth centuries, when wool was the most important product of this country. At that time they roamed the hills in their thousands, but there are now less than 200 ewes left. They were forced out of use by the Australian wool trade and later by man-made fibres. Their great size counted against them with the demand for a small joint – but who is to say that their genes for great wool, staple strength, and their size of carcass, as meat prices continue to increase, will not be of use in the future?

Some breeds have made a vital contribution to agriculture during our history, but have outlived their usefulness and been replaced by modern innovations. The Old Gloucester cattle (without which there would be no Double Gloucester cheese) and the Portland sheep (which gave the gene for out of season lambing to its descendant, the Dorset Horn) are examples. The Suffolk sheep is one of our most important providers of fat lamb sires and its main progenitor, the Norfolk Horn, became extinct in the pure form only last year. Although two small flocks of 'bred back Norfolks' remain at the National Agricultural Centre and the Cotswold Farm Park, for the pure Norfolk Horn it is too late. I believe that it is very presumptuous of anyone to say that because a breed appears to have no commercial use to them today, it will never be of any use in the future, and should be allowed to become extinct.

For many breeds it is already too late, particularly in the pig world where commercial pressures have perhaps been greatest. In the last few years we have lost breeds like the Lincoln curly coat, the Oxford Sandy and Black, and the Dorset Gold Tip. Let us hope that, in this age of commercial hybrids, there are enough enthusiasts left to continue breeding the Berkshire, the Middle White, the ginger Tamworth, and the Gloucester Old Spot, so that commercial pig breeders of the future will have pure lines to return to, instead of having to import stock from abroad with its associated risks of disease.

Luckily, in the poultry world breeds have been kept alive by private enthusiasts, keen to compete at shows. Most, like the Old English game, descended from the fighting cocks, have their own breed society. Those which have not, like the heavily crested Houdan and the Yokohama, with its magnificent flowing tail, are looked after by the Rare Poultry Breeds Society. To keep a breeding flock of poultry in the back yard is a relatively inexpensive hobby, but hard pressed commercial farmers of today cannot be expected to keep breeds of cattle or heavy horses, which once worked their land, purely out of sentiment.

What then is to be done to preserve the breeds we have left? Already a census of rare breeds has been taken by Reading University, assisted by the Ministry of Agriculture, and this is in the process of being brought up to date by the Field Officer of the Rare Breeds Survival Trust. Survival Centres, such as those at the Cotswold Farm Park in Gloucestershire and the Drusillas Cattle Collection near Alfriston in Sussex, as well as preserving specific breeds, do a vital public relations job, acting as 'shop windows' for rare breed survival.

Here the public can see examples of most of the breeds which are in danger of extinction, displayed in a farm setting, and while learning something of their own history as well as that of the animals, they can be encouraged to help by joining the Rare Breeds Survival Trust. Such centres cannot hope to preserve all our breeds on their own, and the Council of the Trust consider it vital that breeds should be preserved in their own local environment for which they have become adapted, since otherwise their character is sure to change.

Council members who are experts in the field of genetics, fertility, and animal husbandry, will be available to advise individual breeder members. The Trust, through its monthly magazine *The Ark*, is able to act as a clearing house for ideas as well as livestock. On 27 September 1975, the Trust staged the first Show and Sale ever to be held, devoted entirely to rare breeds, at the Royal Show Ground, Stoneleigh, Warwickshire. As and when it collects sufficient money from private members and national companies and institutions, it will be able to ease some of the economic pressure off breeders, who can then concentrate on pure line breeding, rather than being forced to outcross with more currently popular breeds in order to compete commercially.

The little Orkney sheep are now only kept by the crofters on the sea shore of North Ronaldsay Island, where they live almost entirely on seaweed. Although examples of these can be seen at Survival Centres, the main bulk of the breed should be preserved, unchanged, in the native environment to which it has become adapted. Obviously it is extremely dangerous to have the whole of one breed on one small island; foot and mouth disease could wipe out the breed overnight, or an oil slick, which would be easy to imagine, with all the drilling for oil in the North Sea, could contaminate the seaweed and remove their diet. The Rare Breeds Survival Trust decided that the situation was so acute that 'fire brigade' action was required. They therefore purchased the island of Linga Holm off Stronsay in the Orkneys as a sanctuary for an alternative breeding group of Orkney sheep from North Ronaldsay. The island is 142 acres of grazing, and there is ample kelp, the seaweed on which they live. One hundred and eighty sheep were moved on to the island in August 1974 and this spring over two hundred lambs have been born on the island. Who is to say that in the hungry, overcrowded world of tomorrow a breed able to survive on a wild and windswept shore, living on seaweed, will be of no value?

The Trust also decided that it was important to have rare breed bulls available through artificial insemination. Many members of the Trust only have one or two cows of a rare breed and therefore cannot afford to keep a bull especially for them. In the past this meant using services from readily available breeds such as Herefords and Friesians, and these cows have, therefore, been playing no part in the continuation of their own breed. It is obviously dangerous to have only one bull of a breed at A.I. as this would encourage inbreeding. It is, therefore, the Trust's aim to have a minimum of three unrelated bulls of each breed available in the next year or two. Semen has already been taken from two of my Old Gloucester bulls and work is underway on bulls of the White Park, Shetland, and Longhorn breeds.

The conservation of rare breeds has very sound scientific justification, although in this enlightened age conservation should not need commercial justification. Let us hope, therefore, that sufficient national support will be engendered to ensure that this living part of our heritage will not be lost for ever, and that the example of the Trust will be followed in other countries throughout the world so that diverse genetic material in the world's domestic animals will be saved for posterity.

SUMMARY OF DISCUSSION IN PART III

The first part of this discussion was concerned with population numbers and Brothwell felt that we should be thinking about reduced population numbers if these were considered right for Britain. Bennett's view, however, was that there was no ideal population number for a country and that even in the most highly populated countries amenity values could be preserved. Her view was the optimistic one that no control of population was necessary since this would find its own level, both in developed and in developing countries.

A discussion on the relative importance of the advanced versus the primitive cultivars was developed by Hutchinson who pointed out that for cotton most of the spectacular breeding advances were made by the use of advanced ones. In contrast, the primitive cotton cultivars had little relevance. He also pointed out the difficulties he had encountered in the conservation of genetic stocks through genetic erosion. A particularly valuable point was made which is worthy of quotation in full:

'We need to maintain very carefully a balance between the maintenance of the variability now being generated in the advanced cultivars as against the variability that remains to us from past times. I think one thing that is worth a little emphasis is that new variability is being generated in these vast commercial agricultural populations that are growing now and we need to watch that also. I think that modern plant breeding legislation really trimmed up and refined to meet the needs of legally minded people who have to enforce it is very inimical to the emergence of the kind of variability that can arise in modern advanced populations and this I think is so important that it should be discussed in the main discussion because a group of the authority of this group here might find some way of expressing this opinion that it is complete nonsense to say that you may not put out as a new variety anything that is not absolutely pure and absolutely definable. We are selling our birth-right for the plant breeders' rights legislation and this, I fear, is going to be very much to our detriment.'

Sencer (Turkey) asked about evaluation, since Frankel had previously stated that this was a waste of time if not linked to plant breeding objectives. In reply, it was stated that in the past there had been an over-emphasis on evaluation, merely for evaluation's sake, whilst anything that was not evaluated had been regarded as of no use. Evaluation is a continuing process, starting at the moment of collection when field data should be continually added from screening and other work. As Frankel summed up: 'What really matters in evaluation is the project-oriented part, since that is what the plant breeder is really looking for. As an old plant breeder I feel that all the rest are trimmings.' So, attributes which have a real meaning to breeders should be described, but those which have not are likely to be useless.

Much interest was taken in Henson's paper on rare breeds and many questions were asked. Concern was expressed on the dangers of inter-breeding in those rare breeds where an insufficient gene pool was maintained, and the speaker himself was well aware of this danger, instancing the difficulties he had had when he took over the Norfolk Horn Sheep from Whipsnade. By skilful outcrossing and backcrossing the breed has been re-created, though some vital genes may of course have been lost in the process.

Waddington offered congratulations to Henson on the creation of the Rare Breeds Survival Trust, saying that he had been prevented from doing something similar just after the war for economic and other reasons. Henson also pointed out that the rare breeds had survived largely because the old landed gentry found them aesthetically pleasing in their parks, but, unfortunately for pigs, these animals were not considered objects of beauty and hence the old breeds have largely disappeared. In certain instances they can be imported from abroad, where many British breeds, which have disappeared from Britain altogether, still exist.

Frankel expressed surprise that more had not been done with the preservation of frozen semen and even frozen ova, since he felt that the number of individual cows kept of some breeds was dangerously small. However, Henson stated that in fact a semen genetic variation bank is being laid down by the Milk Marketing Board, both of rare breeds and of commercial breed strains. The same kind of project is also under way with sheep.

Waddington expressed a slightly different view by considering that at least some animals ought to be allowed to roam about the surface of the earth rather than be kept, as it were, in a semen bank. In fact, the cost of keeping a few sample animals around would not be much more than that involved in the storage of semen. At least some breeders would then be able to look at them from time to time to see if they possessed the characters that were being sought. Henson heartily agreed, saying that he hoped he would always live surrounded by his rare breeds, and those of us who have enjoyed his Cotswold Farm Park would certainly echo this view.

At the end of this discussion it was felt that all participants saw the urgent need for conservation of genetic resources, both of crop plants and farm animals, and it was hoped for the latter group that the movement to preserve old breeds would spread throughout the world. Conservation of related wild and weed species of crops was also agreed on as a worthy objective, and Frankel's paper contained an excellent account of the present position for crop genetic resources over the complete field.

PART IV
FORESTRY CONSERVATION AND DEVELOPMENT

12. Development and conservation of forest resources

K.F.S. King

Most of the inhabitants of the developing countries are hungry and under-nourished. Many are affected by one disease or another. The brains of a high proportion of the children in these countries are permanently damaged because of a low intake of essential nutrients in early childhood. Many are blind for want of vitamin A. A considerable number of those who manage to live to a ripe old age never attain what, in the developed world, would be considered a normal state of health. In short, the chances are that most people born in a developing economy can never fully enjoy what are considered by most to be basic necessities. They are doomed, at best, to a half-life.

All of this is already known to the people of the developed world. Indeed the people of the developing countries themselves are fast becoming aware of their condition. These aspects of their plight are mentioned, therefore, not to provide new knowledge, nor to elicit sympathy, but to lay the foundation for a thesis: all development and all conservation must have as its ultimate objective the enhancement of human life. The strategy of development may be controversial, but not the objective.

If this goal of the enhancement of human life is to be achieved, there must be facilities for the eradication of disease and the attainment of acceptable standards of health. More and better houses must be constructed, suitable training and educational institutions established, agricultural production increased and employment opportunities provided. Today, in the developing countries, levels of unemployment as high as 20% are considered acceptable by some. Yet, in the developed countries, a 5% rate is thought to be a tragedy.

Much has been said in recent years about the necessity for more aid, for an increased transfer of resources from the rich countries to the poor, for more relevant technical assistance, and for better terms of trade between the developed and the developing countries. These factors can, indeed, play an important rôle in the attack on under-development. However, true development can only be achieved by the involvement of the people of the developing countries in the solution of their problems. The mere transfer of knowledge, of technology, of capital, in itself, is not enough. The developing countries must depend upon themselves and must utilize their own resources.

The forests are one such resource. It has been estimated (FAO, 1964) that there are 3,779 million hectares of forests in the world. 1,464 million hectares have been classified as unproductive, and 75 million hectares as protection forests. Therefore, productive forests cover 2,240 million hectares. The developing regions account for about 55% of the world's entire forest area, but in 1973 the value of exports of forest products from tropical developing countries came to only about 15% of the world's total trade in forest products. Finland and the Republic of the Congo have land areas and forest estates of approximately the same size. Yet, in 1973 the value of forest products exported from Finland was sixty times greater than that of the Congo. Latin America has more than five hectares of forest land per person, compared with a world average of about one hectare per person. Yet the region imports more timber products, in terms of value, than it exports. For many reasons, some biological, some economic, some administrative, and some political, large areas of a potential developmental resource are either neglected or receive scant attention.

Nevertheless, it has been demonstrated that in a number of developing countries the forestry and forest industries sector possesses a number of economic and technical characteristics which enable it to act as an important base for economic growth. And this for several reasons. (FAO, 1962, 1969).

As has been mentioned, one of the main social problems in many developing countries is increasing unemployment. This is mainly caused by the drift of population from the country to the town, since the rate of job creation through urban industrialisation is not high enough to absorb these migrants. Any undertaking which provides significant employment opportunities in such areas can therefore play an important part in rural stabilisation and in general economic development.

Some forest industries, particularly the less capital-intensive types such as sawmilling, are somewhat flexible in their locational requirements. Most, however, like the pulp industry for example, are more or less tied to the forested areas. The economics of location thus favour the establishment of forest industries near the source of the raw material. By creating significant employment opportunities in such areas, forestry and forest industries can therefore provide an excellent means of alleviating the problems of unemployment.

Another characteristic is the ability of forests to yield a great number of products which vary considerably both in their properties and in the uses to which they can be put. This diversity is caused partly by the floristic composition of the forests, partly by the multiplicity of products obtainable from a single tree, and partly by the fact that the composition of wood is such that it is capable of providing the raw material for a group of related but widely divergent industries. Forest products therefore range from simple commodities such as fuelwood and sawlogs to complex products such as pulp and paper, from by-products like resins, latex and essential oils to particle board and plywood.

This catholicity of end use is one of the chief reasons for the importance of the forestry and forest industries sector in the developmental process. The products which the forests yield and the processes employed to convert these products into other articles are such that there appears to be some type of forest industry suitable for virtually every stage of economic development.

As a result, varying intensities of capital and labour are demanded, different skills are required, and there is therefore the possibility of growth by stages. In addition, this group of industries possesses a feature which makes it eminently suitable for the attack on economic under-development. Forest industries not only slip easily into the existing economic structures of developing countries, they also provide the basis for succeeding stages of economic development. Much of the demand for wood products comes from other industries, and the inputs of many wood-using industries are products of other industries. Through these forward and backward linkages, the expansion of forestry and forest industries can therefore act as a stimulating force for many other economic activities.

Finally, forestry and forest industries earn and save foreign exchange. Two attributes are valuable in this context. First, the income elasticities of demand for forest products in the developed countries are, in general, high. Second, there appears to be a growing dependence on tropical forests, as it seems that further expansion of high-quality hardwood consumption will be based on tropical hardwoods.

I have spent some time on the relevance of forests and forest industries to development, because I wished to emphasize that this resource, the forest, can play an important rôle, in its productive capacity, in alleviating the poverty and the misery of the people who live in the developing world. But the forests perform other functions which may be as important to man's existence.

Forests reduce the incidence of soil erosion not only beneath the trees, but also in areas adjacent and far removed from them. They thus contribute to the prevention of the siltation of rivers and reservoirs, and they protect farmlands from denudation. They regulate and purify water supplies by retarding run-off during the wet seasons and releasing water during the dry seasons when it is most needed. In this way they minimise the incidence of droughts and floods. In this connection, it is more than a coincidence that in Bangladesh, in Ethiopia, in the Sahel Zone, and in Somalia, indeed in almost all the areas in which there have recently been severe shortages of food supplies, the forest vegetation has been razed to the ground.

In addition, the forests protect crops from the harmful effects of winds, thus increasing agricultural crop yields, especially in those areas on their leeward sides. Moreover, forests provide food and shelter for wild-life, and recreational facilities for the community. Further, the forest ecosystem absorbs heat and noise, and acts as a climatic buffer in many regions of the world.

It is sometimes argued that the utilisation of the tropical forests for productive purposes, for development, would militate against the forests' capacity to provide those services which are also essential for man's well-being. Some go further than this. They allege that the exploitation of these forests for the production of wood, would lead to the complete removal of the forests with all the ills attendant upon such a catastrophe. Indeed, one eminent British ecologist, an undoubted expert on the ecology of tropical forests, has asserted that within twenty to thirty years the tropical rain forests will have disappeared (Richards, 1973).

Let us consider this last point. The latest figures available in the Food and Agriculture Organisation of the United Nations indicate that in the *temperate* regions the situation is as follows. In Europe, the annual increment of the forests is estimated to be 330 million cubic metres, and the average annual removals are 323 million cubic metres. In North America, annual increment is over 500 million cubic metres, but removals are under 400 million cubic metres. In the USSR, the annual increment is 874 million cubic metres but removals are a mere 358 million cubic metres.

In the temperate zone, therefore, the amount of wood removed from the forests each year is somewhat lower than the forests' increment, that is, than its growth during the same period.

Complete data are not available for the tropical regions, but the information which we possess for individual countries indicates that, in general, removals are very much below increment. Indeed, the ratio of removals to increment is considerably smaller than that for the temperate countries.

It is not intended to paint too rosy a picture. These global figures which have been presented refer to the forests as a whole. For individual species, however, the situation is likely to be somewhat different, because exploitation is often selective and the removals of certain species may well be much higher than their replacement or increment. Nevertheless, even in the Philippines and in Indonesia, for which we have some information, and about which there are frequent tales of a disappearing forest, the annual increment, taken as a whole, appears to be higher than average annual removals.

Are the exploitation of the forests for productive purposes, and the retention of the forests' capacity to provide those services which have been earlier described, compatible? It *is* possible in managing forests to provide both the goods that are needed for economic development and to maintain their protective and recreational services. Indeed, this synthesis of conservation and utilisation has always been the *raison d'être* of the forester.

Over the years foresters have evolved a range of silvicultural and management systems. These vary from the clear-felling system in which there is a total removal of the forest crop to the group of selection systems in which only a very few trees might be removed. Between these two extremes there is a number of systems, the essential difference among which is the intensity of the removals. Allied with these systems are management systems designed, in many cases, to sustain the yields from the forests, and to ensure their continuity.

Under proper management, when the clear-felling system is employed, the crop removed is quickly replaced by 'artificial' plantations, in order that the soil might not be exposed for too long periods. The other systems are so designed that soil exposure is reduced to a minimum. Indeed, as a general rule, in the humid tropics, soil exposure through forestry activity is not a serious problem, for growing conditions are such that the trees removed are almost always replaced by some sort of naturally regenerated vegetation. This even in the frequent cases in which there is severe damage to the residual forest during felling operations.

It is not being suggested that these management practices and silvicultural systems are employed to a great extent in tropical forestry. What is being emphasised is that the knowledge exists to ensure that the forest cover remains, or if it is removed or disturbed is quickly replaced. The problems of tropical forestry, in so far as the practising forest manager or silviculturist is concerned, is not how to maintain soil cover (this he knows), but how to increase productivity, how to regenerate particular species, and how to obtain the best economic returns from his forests.

The forest manager and silviculturist are primarily concerned with exploiting those species which are marketable. They often, therefore, deliberately eliminate species which are unmarketable and which they identify as weeds. Their aim is to obtain a stand of trees, a forest, in which there are only species which are known to be saleable. These are relatively few in the tropical forests. Consequently, they deflect and arrest successions, change the floristic composition of the forest over time as well as over space, and so alter the original environment. Thus, it is possible, even when employing 'natural regeneration' systems, for the forester to be responsible for the elimination of tree species which have a restricted distribution. Indeed, where clear-felling systems and artificial regeneration are practised, most or all of those species which occur naturally are removed. Conversely, under systems of artificial regeneration, exotic species are often introduced into a completely new environment.

The forester does not *preserve* the forests. He does not respect their virginity, for its own sake. He *uses* the forests. If it is considered desirable, he ensures that cover is maintained, either (on the one hand) by some or most of all of the original species, or (on the other) by exotic species. If it is considered desirable, he ensures that the yield from the forests is sustained. He *conserves* the forest.

Two consequences might flow from this. First, some species might eventually disappear. The International Union for the Conservation of Nature and Natural Resources (IUCN) has suggested that twelve species of trees which are large when mature, and twenty-nine which are small, mainly hardwoods of the tropics, are threatened with extinction. The International Union of Forest Research Organisations has indicated that a larger number of forest species is endangered, but not so seriously as to be classified as being threatened with extinction.

However, although the number of species threatened with extinction does not appear to be great, there is a danger that certain ecotypes may disappear, or lose their integrity.

The second consequence of forest exploitation and forest management might be, not the elimination of tropical rain forests as Richards (1973) has suggested, but their transformation. It is likely that in the course of the next century the species composition of these forests will be altered and their physiognomy changed. Already there is evidence of this in many parts of West Africa, for example, and in northern South America. The important point, however, is that there have been no noticeably adverse effects on soil, climate and on water-relations in these areas.

Nevertheless, if we are to preserve our heritage, and if we are to have available a background of information and a pool of biological resources for experimentation, research, and observation, so that we might profit in the future, efforts should be made both to preserve those species and ecotypes which are endangered and to maintain representative areas of plant formations and ecosystems throughout the world.

In some countries, e.g. Kenya, Nigeria, Tanzania and Uganda, reserves have been or are being established with the specific objective of preserving threatened forest species. In others, the best seed stands have been set aside, both for seed collection purposes and for *in situ* conservation of threatened species (Bouvarel, 1975). This is an interesting development for it combines the possibilities of both short and long term benefits.

Conventional arboreta and tree collections for the *ex situ* conservation of forest tree species exist in many countries, but usually on a small scale. However, these are not to be preferred to *in situ* natural reserves and seed stands. In arboreta and tree collections only a few species of a genetic unit are normally represented, and there is also a great probability of hybridisation.

The preservation of forest formations and ecosystems presents a greater problem. It is true that in most countries of the tropics forest reserves have already been established and, within these reserves, areas have been set aside in which no interference is permitted. Yet, because of the necessity of establishing relatively large blocks for the adequate protection of the forest formations and ecosystems and because of the further necessity of establishing a protective 'surround' for the inner core of protected forests, there is a danger that in the future there would be a demand for these blocks of land to be utilised either for conventional forestry or for agriculture.

We cannot devise a formula which will ensure that these forest reserves are maintained. The general practice is to promulgate laws which state that the reserves may be put into use only after a substantial majority of the legislature has voted to de-reserve. Such laws exist in most of the developing countries with sizable forest estates. But laws have been known to be ignored and to be changed.

I have argued that forest exploitation *in itself* (even over-exploitation, in the sense of a greater volume of wood being removed than is being replaced in a given period) is not harmful to the environment, if ecological conditions are stable. However, in areas in which one or more factors of the environment might be critical, over-exploitation of the forests can have, and does have, the most disastrous effects. It is important, therefore, that the most careful and thorough investigations be conducted in areas which appear to be marginal for plant production, and in which the ecological conditions seem to be brittle, before any form of land-use is permitted.

The destruction of tropical forests is caused mainly by shifting agriculture, by the clearing of the forests for the establishment of perennial agricultural crops such as cocoa, coffee, oil palm and rubber, and by the burning of the forests by herdsmen.

Shifting cultivation is the most important factor. The system is practised in Africa, South America, Oceania and South-East Asia. It provides sustenance for 250 million, or 7% of the world's inhabitants. It destroys large areas of forests. It has been estimated that one-third of the total land area used for agriculture in South-East Asia is still under shifting cultivation, and that in Africa, south of the Sahara, the area of closed tropical high forest has shrunk by at least 100 million hectares from its original extent mainly because of this system. In the Far East as a whole, it is thought that there are about 24.5 million shifting cultivators who annually fell forests up to approximately 8.5 million hectares, and that the total area under shifting cultivation is 103 million hectares.

The Food and Agriculture Organisation of the United Nations recognises that it is necessary to reconcile the conflicting demands of the farmer and the forester for forest land, particularly with regard to shifting agriculture. It is attempting to systematise a practice which originated in Burma in the nineteenth century, but which has since spread to very many countries in all the tropical regions of the world. This system of utilising the labour of shifting cultivators and farmers to establish forest plantations is coming to be known as *agri-silviculture* (King, 1968).

Basically, forest trees are planted by the farmer after the forest has been exploited. At the time of the establishment of the forest plantation, the farmer inter-crops the forest trees with various kinds of agricultural crops. Generally, he stays on the land until the forest canopy is closed. He then moves on to another area to be planted with forest tree crops. In this system, therefore, the exploited forest is replaced, the farmer is given land for the provision of food crops, and a valuable economic resource is provided for future utilisation. When the forest plantations established by the farmer are ready for felling, the process is repeated.

The establishment of timber plantations, by this and other conventional means, has, over the last twenty years or so, spread rapidly in the developing countries. FAO has estimated that at the end of 1974, the area under man-made forests, as the jargon describes them, was 90 million hectares.

Reforestation and afforestation projects are executed mainly for the production of industrial timber. They, therefore, to some extent possess many economic advantages over mixed tropical forests: they can be tailor-made to suit the requirements of industry; they are generally homogeneous and compact, and can therefore be harvested more economically than can the natural forests; their locations can be chosen, not only with biological considerations in mind, but also with transportation costs, labour availability and other requirements of industry in view.

In addition to these mundane and industrial uses, however, they are employed for other reasons which may perhaps be more acceptable to conservationists. They protect soils which would otherwise be exposed; they are established for sand-dune fixation and soil-stabilisation; and, as we have seen, they are useful in the preservation of forest genetic resources.

Many conservationists object to their very presence, however (Budowski, 1976). They allege that there is the danger of long-term deterioration of the soil, particularly when coniferous species are planted in the humid tropics. We do not know much about this, but a series of studies is to be conducted in various countries, by FAO, on the effects of plantations on various aspects of soil fertility. Conservationists stress that the monocultures thus established may be easily destroyed by pests and diseases. This is of course a possibility. They claim that the wild-life under plantations is not as varied as that in the natural forests, and that the removal of natural forests would lead to their extinction. There is no general evidence of this. Recent research in some *Pinus radiata* forests shows that the wild-life in them does not differ substantially from that of nearby natural vegetation. In Venezuela, a very great increase in wild-life has been observed in *Pinus caribaea* plantations, including predators. This plantation is on sandy soils (Budowski, 1976).

It should be emphasised that these claims have no validity when *afforestation* is being considered. That is, when plantations are being established on open savannas or on land already bare. Indeed, *afforestation* clearly improves the biological quality of the environment.

The most important objection of the conservationists concerns *reforestation*: the establishment of plantations where there were forests, usually natural forests. They argue that the conversion of the diversified and highly complex ecosystem of the natural forests to a forest of relatively simple structure and little or no floristic diversity is fraught with danger.

Obviously, the ecosystem is changed whenever the forest is used, is disturbed. It is often difficult, however, to judge whether the results of interference, in this case the clearing of the forests, are harmful or beneficial. In an intensive study in New Hampshire, it was found that clear cutting reduced the flow of amonia-nitrogen to higher plants, increased the flow of amonia-nitrogen to nitrifying organisms, decreased the output of water as vapour, increased the output of water as a liquid, increased the rate of losses of nitrate-nitrogen and other ions from the ecosystem, increased the movement of hydrogen ions to cation exchange sites in the soil, increased the movement of stored energy to respiration, increased fertility and eutrophication of stream water, and so forth.

It must be repeated that the establishment of plantations will permit the retention of the remaining natural forests for a longer period than would otherwise have been the case. It must also be urged that plantations should not be established unless there are adequate species trials to ascertain the suitability of the species to be planted to the climatic and edaphic conditions of the plantation area.

Man's progress throughout the ages has been achieved by harnessing and controlling the forces of nature. In particular, he has enabled himself to advance, in great part because of his 'domestication' and improvement of the flora and fauna which he found in his environment. The forester's predilection with plantation forestry and with the homogenisation of the natural forests is in the tradition of his *successful* forebears.

It is sometimes argued that our knowledge of the wet tropics is so insignificant that we should do little or nothing until we know more. There is some wisdom in caution, and certain ecological ground rules and guide-lines should be established.

Land capability classification and land-use planning should generally precede the utilisation of new lands in the humid tropics. In particular, a policy of caution should be followed when one or other of the environmental factors necessary for the sustained utilisation of the land under the form of land-use intended is known or is discovered to be inadequate. Nevertheless, it must be recognised that a great number of the bio-climatic obstacles to land-use can be overcome by

G*

modern technology.

I end as I began. Development and conservation are for people, and are about people. Many of the proposals made for conserving the world's natural forests would lead to the perpetuation of under-development in the tropical world. It should not be forgotten that man is an important and often essential factor in the ecological mix. In fact, I venture to suggest that he is the most important factor.

REFERENCES

Bouvarel, P. (1975). Analysis of the Global Programme proposed by the FAO Panel of Experts on Forest Gene Resources. *Paper presented to the Second Meeting of the International Board for Plant Genetic Resources.* Rome, May, 1975.

Budowski, G. (1976). Forest plantations and nature conservation. *Paper submitted to the Committee on Tropical Forestry.* Rome, FAO.

FAO (1962). The role of forest industries in the attack on economic underdevelopment. *The state of Food and Agriculture, 1962.* Rome.

FAO (1964). *World Forest Inventory, 1963.* Rome.

FAO (1969). Modernizing institutions to promote forestry development. *The State of Food and Agriculture, 1969.* Rome.

King, K.F.S. (1968). *Agri-silviculture.* University of Ibadan.

Richards, P.W. (1973). The tropical rain forest. *Scient. Am.,* **229**: 58-67.

13. Depletion and conservation of forest genetic resources

R.H. Kemp and J. Burley

Depletion of the natural forest resources of the world is now so apparent that it has led to widespread concern for their conservation. The destruction of forests and their replacement by permanent agriculture, or some other continuing form of land use, was most rapid in the more industrialised and more heavily populated countries; however, even for some non-industrialised countries, with relatively low population density, such as most of Africa a quarter of a century ago, it has been estimated that the area of closed forest had already at that time been reduced to a third of its original extent, largely as a result of shifting cultivation (Schantz, 1948). During the ensuing twenty-five years the rapid rise in human populations, and the increasing demands made by the industrialised nations on the world's diminishing resources of forest, have increased the rate of removal.

At the same time progress has been made towards the creation of artificial forests, through the selection of relatively few, fast-growing species, chosen for the qualities of their form and timber, and through the development of techniques for their intensive cultivation. Such artificial forests, usually of a single species, are needed to provide the increased volume of wood that the world demands from decreasing areas of forest land. This process has proceeded furthest in the more advanced industrial countries, many of them situated in the north temperate zone where there are very few indigenous tree species, and has usually involved the introduction of exotic species or provenances from other countries. Even in the tropics, where there are several thousand woody species, the number likely to be used in creating artificial forests is very low – perhaps only 10-20 in a single country – and of these some or all are likely to be exotic species. As in agriculture, great improvements in forest productivity may be achieved through selection of the most suitable species, provenances and families for propagation and breeding.

The creation of intensive timber plantations in this way is not advisable, nor even possible, on all forest lands. Much of the remaining natural forest exists only because it grows on soils too poor to sustain intensive agriculture and therefore not apt for the development of large human populations. The most efficient use of such areas may be made by management of the natural forest to increase its productivity, perhaps by planting desirable species within the forest, without disturbing the natural vegetation to the extent that would cause a serious loss in the site capability through soil exposure, leaching or erosion. At the same time the creation of intensive plantations on previously deforested, depleted or degraded sites may reduce the demands on the remaining areas of forest, and also on other land better suited for agricultural use. Nevertheless, as a result of the pressures to increase productivity, and the many problems encountered in the management of multi-specific high forest ecosystems, it has often been found easier to improve production by replacing such forests with high-yielding plantation monocultures. Conservation, therefore, which was previously one of the main objectives of forest management in many countries, has been set apart from the main activities of forest production, and restricted to the reservation of relatively small areas of forest as Strict Natural Reserves (SNR) or Virgin Jungle Reserves. These usually are accorded very low economic value in national development plans and this, together with their smaller size, makes them less secure reservoirs of genetic diversity than the earlier more extensive reserves of managed natural forest.

Depletion of genetic resources

An inventory of the present genetic resources of forest trees throughout the world would still reveal great richness and diversity, with relatively few species in danger of extinction (perhaps 40 or 50 out of tens of thousands). However, we are now in a period of very rapid change. The most rapid and extensive destruction of forest now occurs in more remote areas such as Brazil, Indonesia and Papua New Guinea. The rate of destruction of natural tropical forest in Malaysia has been calculated to be 0.03 hectares/minute (Wavell, 1975) and in the Amazon Basin of Brazil, for example, a single private company has been felling and burning forest at the rate of 12,000 hectares/year during the past five years, to make way for plantations. Carnheiro (1971) estimated that about 3 million hectares of forest are destroyed in Brazil annually. There can be little doubt that local populations and even whole species of forest trees may rapidly disappear as this process continues.

Does this matter? For most industrial purposes the wood of a great many species may be equally acceptable and, if a sufficient volume of consistent quality can be assured, as may be achieved from well managed artificial forests, industry can adapt within certain limits to use the wood of any one of these species. However, compared to agriculture the development of forest resources, as opposed to their simple exploitation, is still at a very early stage. The majority even of the few species already in cultivation are only one generation or less from the original wild populations. Technology in the use of timber and other products derived from trees is advancing rapidly, and may demand different qualities in trees in the future. The great majority of tropical species are still unexplored and may be only known botanically, perhaps from relatively few specimens.

The danger is twofold. Of the species already known to be of value for use in highly productive artificial forests very few have been explored adequately, if at all, to determine the genetic variation between different provenances, and their relative value in different environments. The economic importance of provenance differences has been amply demonstrated for many tree species; also generally accepted are the need for a broad genetic base to a long-term breeding programme, and the value of diverse populations as safeguards against epidemic diseases or pests. One danger, therefore, is that valuable provenances of such important species may be extinguished before they can be evaluated or utilised. Examples of species so endangered in some areas of their natural range are *Eucalyptus deglupta*, *Pinus caribaea* and *P. kesiya*, all of great importance to tropical forestry.

It is often the populations at the extremes of the natural range which are most in danger, yet these could prove to be among the most important for degraded and deforested sites too poor for sustained agricultural production. The more efficient use of such sites for wood production from forest plantations could be an important factor in reducing the demands on, and the rate of destruction of the remaining areas of natural forest.

The second danger is to the many thousands of species of unproved and often unexplored value, the great majority of which occur in tropical regions, where the rate of forest destruction is now most rapid. Although the number of tree species at present known to be in danger of extinction is small, the loss of many ecotypes is certain and whole species will be increasingly threatened over the next two or three decades. At the same time the market demands are changing rapidly with advancing technology, and may place very different values on structural and chemical characteristics of trees in the future. We therefore cannot afford to dispense readily with any species whatever its current economic importance.

International concern

The growing awareness of these dangers received its first major expression at the FAO/IBP Technical Conference on the Exploration, Utilisation and Conservation of Plant Genetic Resources (Rome,

September 1967) and through the IBP Handbook No. 11, 'Genetic Resources in Plants – their Exploration and Conservation' (Frankel and Bennett, 1970) which resulted from that conference. The other result of importance to forestry was the constitution of the FAO Panel of Experts on Forest Gene Resources, which has since met and reported three times (FAO, 1969, 1972, 1974a), and has helped greatly to co-ordinate national and international action in this field.

In general terms the action needed is evident. For the species of known value it is to explore, collect, evaluate and conserve their genetic resources. For the majority of species of unknown or uncertain value it is to ensure their conservation by setting aside areas of natural forest as representative samples of the main forest ecosystems. The major constraints on such action are not only financial but, perhaps even more important, relate to the lack of information on what needs to be conserved, on where it should be done and above all on how to do it (see the UNEP/FAO report on methodology of forest genetic resource conservation, FAO, 1975).

Although the general principles of conservation of genetic resources in forest trees may be the same as those applicable to crop plants there are important differences, mainly arising from the different scales of time and space involved. Trees are large as individuals and require large areas of land to accommodate an adequate population. They are long lived and usually require many years to reach sexual maturity. Moreover, because of the extensive area of his crop, and the relatively low financial yield per unit area and per unit of time, the forester has much less scope than the agriculturist to manipulate the environment to suit his crop. The selection of ecotypes well suited to the local environment, including the infrequent occurrence of periodic hazards such as drought and disease, is therefore vitally important and the conservation of a broad range of ecotypes is essential. The development of a methodology appropriate to the conservation of forest genetic resources will therefore require extensive and prolonged research.

The dangers of losing genetic diversity are greatest in the tropics, and particularly in the high forest ecosystems, where, paradoxically, there is the greatest diversity of species, where forest destruction is most rapid and where the resources of expertise and finance available for conservation are very limited. By contrast, in Britain, for example, where the initial genetic diversity in terms of tree species was very low, and where the activities of commercial forestry have in some ways increased diversity through the introduction of exotic species, there is now a strong tendency to restrict the intensification of wood production from coniferous monocultures, in favour of the conservation of less productive natural woodlands, mainly for their recreational or amenity value. Such conservation is clearly desirable but is only possible through our dependence on imported timber for 90% of our total annual requirements. To some extent therefore the conservation of unproductive British woodland may contribute to the loss of genetic resources elsewhere in the world, particularly in the tropics. At the same time the developed countries' demands for agricultural products also contribute to forest destruction in less developed countries, as evidenced by the conversion of large areas of virgin forest in the Amazon basin in Brazil to rangelands, to provide beef for export to North America and Europe. It is therefore appropriate that developed countries should take the lead in providing technical and financial support for the conservation of forest genetic resources in developing countries.

Conservation of selected species

The longevity of forest trees is a great advantage to their genetic conservation since the same population can be retained for a very long period essentially unchanged. In many cases the life of the tree greatly exceeds the storage life of its seed or pollen. With appropriate planning and control, therefore, local ecotypes can readily be conserved without the danger of annual depletion of the gene pool that may occur in crop plants. Nevertheless some ecotypes are more immediately valuable for forest production than others and, since we are dealing with wild populations which often possess great variability even within the local population, there are strong economic advantages in improving populations by elimination of less desirable individuals. As improved populations become widely established in artificial forest, often far outside their area of origin, then even if some of the original populations are retained for genetic conservation they may risk losing their genetic integrity through contamination from the introduced stands. (e.g. Libby *et al.*, 1975). However, with suitable care representative samples of many ecotypes may be retained through successive generations, following, for example, the Finnish model of "standard stands" (Hagman, 1971).

For species threatened with extinction the International Union for the Conservation of Nature and Natural Resources (IUCN) has issued data sheets, published in the series of Red Data Books, revised periodically. In addition to the tree species listed there as facing extinction many more are known to be in danger in a part of their range, entailing the imminent loss of valuable ecotypes. For these a similar series of data sheets is being prepared under the auspices of the International Union of Forest Research Organisations – Subject Group S2.02.2 Conservation of Gene Resources (Roche, 1974).

The long term objective of conservation is the rational use of the available resources and it is necessary therefore not only to conserve, but also to investigate and evaluate genetic diversity. Within species this is done by provenance trials in the field and by biosystematic studies in the natural forest, plantation, arboretum, herbarium, glasshouse, laboratory and so forth. For practical purposes replicated and truly comparable field provenance trials are essential. The occurrence of large genotype × environment interaction effects is of great importance when populations are introduced to areas outside their normal range, often to different countries or even continents (Burley and Kemp, 1972). There are numerous examples of tree species which are of the greatest economic importance in the creation of artificial forests in exotic situations but of very low economic importance in their area of origin (e.g. *Pinus radiata* D. Don). In such cases the evaluation and even the conservation of the genetic resources may have to be undertaken by countries other than the country of origin. International co-operation in seed collection and provenance trials of a number of species, particularly some North American conifers, has been successfully promoted by IUFRO and has undoubtedly contributed to the conservation of ecotypic variation through its evaluation, and through the establishment of small exotic populations on many sites in different countries. Until the mid-1960s, however, such activity was confined almost entirely to a few species of temperate zones.

In tropical zones, where the potential gains from exploration and conservation are probably much greater, bearing in mind the great diversity of species and ecotypes and the fast rates of growth, very few countries have the resources of staff or funds to undertake exploration and conservation on a wide scale, and certainly not beyond their own borders. Nevertheless the most promising species for afforestation in many tropical situations are exotics, and are often of less interest to their country of origin. Many *Eucalyptus* species might be cited as examples from large forest plantations in Africa, Asia, South America and elsewhere, although in their native Australia they may not be cultivated at all. In this case, since Australia has well developed forestry services and advanced research facilities, the Forest Research Institute in Canberra conducts systematic collections of eucalypt seed for seed origin research and samples are distributed free to many countries. This work is part of the programme co-ordinated by the FAO Panel referred to earlier and is partly supported by a financial contribution from FAO. Although collection has concentrated mainly on species of commercial importance, the conservation status of all species can be kept in view and action can be taken in respect of any species seen to be threatened by extensive land clearance. The means exist to conserve at least some wild populations *in situ*, and, most importantly, the entire natural range of most important eucalpyts lies within the single country.

For most tropical species the situation is quite different, since their natural range extends through several countries, none of which may have either the means or the incentive to explore and conserve their genetic resources. In these circumstances the initiative, organisation and finance for the work must come from outside. Since many tropical countries wishing to introduce exotic species are developing countries, and a large number may be interested in the same species, exploration and seed collection have increasingly been undertaken as a form of technical assistance, by research institutes or organisations based outside the region of collection, even though this involves complex problems of planning and organisation (Kemp *et al.*, 1976). However, a major advantage of centralised planning of exploration and collection is that it can be continued into the organisation of the provenance trials on an international scale, with more effective exchange of information, and perhaps beyond this into programmes of selection and breeding (Burley and Kemp, 1973). An example of this is the Central American Pine Provenance Research Project, conducted by the Commonwealth Forestry Institute, Oxford University (Kemp, 1973a, 1973b, 1973c, 1973d). Over 40 countries are co-operating in this research and seed has already been distributed for more than 300 trials. Centralised analysis and interpretation of the results of such trials facilitates estimation of the importance of genotype × environment interaction effects and the exchange of information between countries.

In the course of exploration on this and similar projects, such as that of the FAO/Danish Forest Tree Seed Centre working in Southeast Asia (Keiding, 1972; FAO, 1974a) the urgent need for conservation of the genetic resources of some important species, such as *P. caribaea*, has been revealed. For a variety of reasons, such as the fragmented nature of the distribution, difficulties of access and above all difficulties in effective control, the conservation of endangered ecotypes of tropical species *in situ* very often cannot be assured (e.g. Kemp, 1975). For this reason it is necessary to attempt conservation *ex situ* also. Similar considerations undoubtedly apply to many other valuable species which are still awaiting adequate exploration.

Conservation ex situ. A primary task of the FAO Panel of Experts on Forest Gene Resources has been the preparation and periodic review of a list of species urgently in need of exploration, evaluation and conservation. The list is arranged geographically and divided into three priority classes, according to the intrinsic importance of the species and its current status in exploration and conservation. Since the list is largely composed of species of known value for use in fast growing plantations the majority of them are pioneer species for which techniques of cultivation are already known and which do not present serious problems of seed collection or seed handling. This combination of attributes is significant in the context of *ex situ* conservation. Although the inclusion of a species in a major planting programme is itself some guarantee of conservation, it is only partial, based on a sample from a part of the natural range, and is subject to subsequent genetic selection according to economic criteria. For this reason the creation of plantations intended specifically for conservation of genetic resources must be considered (Bouvarel, 1970).

As outlined by Guldager (1975) the objectives of *ex situ* conservation of forest genetic resources may be to retain as far as possible the same genotype frequencies, or in some cases the same gene frequencies, as the original population (static conservation) or to allow changes in gene frequencies according to the forces of natural selection in the new exotic habitat (evolutionary conservation) or by deliberate selection (selective conservation). There are great practical problems involved in maintaining genetic integrity, related principally to the efficiency of sampling of the original populations, differential survival and growth of the sampled genotypes *ex situ*, the size of the breeding population so established and the type of mating that occurs within it. There are many problems also of establishment, treatment and management of such conservation stands, particularly if they are to be maintained as international gene pools providing seed and clonal material for seed orchards and clonal banks. For proper control of such a scheme a much better understanding of forestry population genetics will be required in future and for this, as well as for the practical problems of establishing and managing *ex situ* conservation stands, extensive fundamental and applied research is needed, under a continuous and co-ordinated programme in several countries.

When undertaking conservation *ex situ* the recording and dissemination of information regarding the origin, genetic history (Jones and Burley, 1973), and distribution of material is essential, and this should also embrace material in provenance trials and other small collections as well as the major conservation stands. The problems involved have been discussed by Finlay and Konzak (1970) and in the forestry context specifically by Burley *et al.* (1974), who stressed the value of computer based programmes for data storage and retrieval. The development of an efficient system for gathering, storing and retrieving information will itself require research (Roche, 1975a).

Seed and pollen storage. As emphasised by Frankel and Bennett (1970) the possibilities for using seed storage to conserve genetic resources should be explored and used to the full, and certainly much more fully than has so far been planned. Seed storage facilities are relatively simple and inexpensive compared with the complexities of managing *ex situ* conservation stands in the field. Methods of seed and pollen storage for the conservation of plant genetic resources have been described in some detail by Harrington (1970) and Wang (1975). It is fortunate that many of the species likely to be used in artificial forests for wood production have seed with some degree of natural dormancy, or at least the ability to survive for long periods under conditions of low humidity and low temperature. Although most studies have been done on temperate species, seed of many tropical species, including most of the important *Eucalyptus* and *Pinus* spp., can be successfully stored for several years in this way, and research on very long term storage is in progress. The storage of tissue in culture may perhaps also be of value in the future although it does not appear to be practical with present knowledge (Wang, 1975).

The possibility of genetic changes in seed or pollen, particularly in long term storage, whether as a result of differential survival between genotypes in a seed lot, or because of mutation effects, must be considered and investigated (Allard, 1970; Frankel and Bennett, 1970; Harrington, 1972). Wang (1975), however, considered that with appropriate methods of seed collection, handling and storage, present evidence suggests that genetic changes such as have been observed in aged agricultural seeds are not common in tree seeds. The major limitation on the use of seed storage in forest genetic resource conservation at present is very short seed viability in some species, particularly among those from tropical high forests.

Conservation of forest ecosystems

As pointed out by Frankel and Bennett (1970) the ideal model of long term conservation is "a community in balance with a stable environment – the stability being subject to the general vagaries of natural environments ...' In forestry terms this implies the setting aside of selected areas of forest for the purpose of genetic conservation *in situ*. In the last few years, with the growing public appreciation of the need for nature conservation, and the setting up of organisations in some countries specifically charged with this task, the possibilities for genetic conservation *in situ* have certainly improved. Internationally co-ordinated action such as the International Biological Programme (particularly on the Conservation of Terrestrial Communities – IBP (CT)), the UNESCO Programme on Man and the Biosphere (Project 8 – Conservation of natural areas and of the genetic material they contain) and the IUCN/WWF conservation programme has helped to define priority areas and to initiate conservation measures. Again it is in the developing countries, and especially in the tropics with their great resource of genetic diversity, that more effective action is now most urgently needed.

Whereas in many industrialised and developed countries the conflicting demands on land may be greater, the machinery for the resolution of such conflicts, given public awareness of the need for nature conservation, tends increasingly to work in favour of the permanent conservation of some areas of natural forest. In many developing countries the social and economic priorities demand the maximum use of limited resources of land and forest, to meet the immediate basic needs of rapidly growing populations. Moreover the complexity of tropical high forest ecosystems, within which 100-200 tree species may occur in a single hectare, while the number of breeding individuals of a single species may be only one or two per hectare, may demand the setting aside of very large areas of forest. Since genetic resource conservation of such wild populations is concerned with genetic differences which can not be directly identified but only surmised, it must be concerned with population samples, possibly along environmental gradients such as latitude or altitude, and the areas involved must therefore be either extensive or scattered, and in the latter case very difficult to manage (Frankel and Bennett, 1970).

Nevertheless the very complexity of the systems, and the large number of species involved, mean that conservation *in situ* is the only practical possibility for conserving the genetic resources of most tropical tree species. The majority of these species are known only taxonomically and virtually nothing may be known of their ecology or genetics, but there is evidence of the interdependence of the flora and fauna and the practical impossibility of attempting the conservation of many species independently of their ecosystem (Roche, 1975b). The problems of seed storage also have been little studied in many tropical areas and the seed of some species, particularly those of ever-wet tropical high forests, may lose all viability within a few weeks, or even days of seed fall. Several tropical countries are setting aside areas of forest as Strict Natural Reserves (e.g. Nigeria, Uganda) or Virgin Jungle Reserves (Malaysia) but progress is slow in comparison with the rate of clearance of the remaining areas of forest.

While the social, political and economic difficulties that delay or prevent the creation of such reserves are often decisive in themselves there are also technical problems arising from lack of knowledge of the dynamics of tropical ecosystems and of the breeding systems of the principal species involved. A fundamental question which must be asked is how large an area of forest is required for genetic resource conservation. The answer can only be given in terms of the necessary minimum number of individuals required of each species and this is not yet known. Estimates vary from as low as 200 (Dyson, 1974) to 10,000 (Toda, 1965) but no precise estimate is possible until the breeding systems of the species concerned are understood. For many trees, even those of major commercial importance, no information is yet available concerning the reproductive system (self-pollination, cross-pollination, apomixis or some combination of all of these) or genetic system, governing the manner and extent of population differentiation and gene flow between populations (e.g. Stern and Roche, 1974).

At a recent international symposium (Burley and Styles, 1976) more than twenty papers reflected the need for and growing interest in research into breeding systems and other aspects of forest genetic conservation in the tropics. The knowledge of population structure and effective population size is fundamental to effective action on conservation *ex situ* also and is therefore of high priority for research.

International co-operation

Priorities. For a great part of the world's population, including most of the tropical countries where the threat to forest genetic resources is greatest, the over-riding priority is increased production of food. This requirement dominates not only national efforts and expenditure but also international aid programmes. Nevertheless the most recent report of the FAO Panel (FAO, 1974a) lists more than 300 tree species in need of exploration, evaluation and conservation. The principal concern of the FAO Panel of Experts on Forest Gene Resources has been to determine priorities and to ensure that the facilities and resources available are used to maximum effect. Despite severe financial constraints this has resulted in intensified exploration and the collection of seed and other scientific material from many provenances of some valuable species during the last 6 years. At its third session, in May 1974, the Panel agreed on a global programme for the improved use of forest genetic resources, with particular emphasis on their conservation (FAO, 1974b). The programme is designed to co-ordinate financial and technical inputs from many sources, including international organisations, bilateral aid programmes and national government organisations. The initial plan covers a 5-year period but it is intended as the start to a much longer-term project that should continue for several decades.

The global programme. In developed countries the exploration and conservation of their genetic resources is normally within the competence of the national governments and organisations, although the benefits may be made available to other countries and even other regions. The global programme is therefore concerned primarily with action on behalf of developing countries.

Exploration and seed collection form the largest item in the proposed global programme, largely financed, as hitherto, by bilateral aid funds. Collection of additional quantities of seed of selected provenances is planned, for genetic conservation *ex situ*, in conservation plantations. Initially this work will concentrate on four species of importance in tropical forestry, and the plantations will be established on several sites in a number of tropical countries. Funds are proposed under the global programme to meet some of the direct costs of planting and tending, during an initial period of five years, on the understanding that reproductive material will later be made available internationally. Seed collections for *ex situ* conservation of the species concerned are already in progress under bilaterial aid programmes, such as the CFI programme, financed by the UK Ministry of Overseas Development. The conservation plantations are planned on at least two sites in each of eight selected countries in Africa, Asia and South America.

Conservation *in situ*, by creation of SNRs or their equivalent, depends essentially on action to be taken by the country concerned, since it involves legislation, land acquisition, protection and public education. However, external aid is often needed in research and the training of staff. Financial provision has been made in the global programme for expert consultancies, training fellowships and travel in connection with pilot studies in tropical areas. This section of the programme is entirely dependent on new funding requested from bodies such as the United Nations Environment Programme (UNEP), FAO and IUCN. So far UNEP has commissioned a study on the methodology of conservation of forest genetic resources, published by FAO (1975) and this includes recommendations for further action.

The role of the United Kingdom. The United Kingdom, because of its dependence on imported timber, has a special interest in, and also perhaps a special responsibility for, the conservation of forest genetic resources in developing countries. The financial contributions of the UK to international agencies, as well as its bilateral aid (for example through the programmes of the CFI, Oxford and the Institute of Terrestrial Ecology, Edinburgh) are already large, and British scientists have played a prominent part in promoting international co-operation and action through FAO and IUFRO. However, the proposed global programme, even if finance is obtained for its full implementation, will only go part of the way towards meeting the urgent needs for research and training. It is in these fields particularly that much more use could be made of existing resources in universities and research institutes in the UK.

Some research problems, even for tropical species, might be solved by studies in the laboratory alone, if suitable facilities were made available and the material supplied in the right condition. This applies to many seed studies, particularly seed storage problems. Other examples might be found in forestry population genetics, involving chemotaxonomic methods (studies of iso-enzymes, volatile oils, etc). Some such studies are already in progress in connection with the CFI programme but much more could be done if more facilities and more expert staff were applied to the problems.

Overseas students in the UK for training at post-graduate or post-doctoral level could contribute more to solving problems of immediate and practical importance in the course of their research, if relevant subjects were identified and material made available. Such research might then more readily be continued in their own countries, given the necessary facilities and equipment.

Some aspects of research, such as the study of breeding systems, floral biology and seed dispersal, cannot so easily be divorced from the forest environment. However the manner in which universities in Britain can contribute to such research, and at the same time assist in training staff overseas, is illustrated by the collaborative project between the Universities of Aberdeen and Malaya, on the reproductive biology of some rainforest trees (Soepadmo and Ashton, 1974).

As emphasised by Roche (1975c) much more attention should be given to teaching the methodology of conservation of forest genetic resources at both university and technical levels. The University of Birmingham has taken the lead internationally in post-graduate education by offering on M.Sc. course in the Conservation and Utilisation of Plant Genetic Resources. In addition to the need to increase the training capability at this level it may be necessary to mount short training courses at different levels in countries overseas.

In all of these activities, in both research and training, the links between the United Kingdom and the other nations of the Commonwealth provide a basis for international action where it is most urgently needed, in tropical countries.

REFERENCES

Allard, R.W. (1970). Problems of maintenance. *In* Frankel, O.H. and Bennett, E. (eds.). *Genetic Resources in Plants – Their Exploration and Conservation*. Oxford, Blackwell, 491-4.

Bouvarel, P. (1970). The conservation of gene resources of forest trees. *In* Frankel, O.H. and Bennett, E. (eds.). *Genetic Resources in Plants – Their Exploration and Conservation*. Oxford, Blackwell, 523-9.

Burley, J. and Kemp, R.H. (1972). International tropical provenance trials and genotype-environment interactions. Proc. IUFRO Genetics-SABRAO joint symposium, Tokyo.

Burley, J. and Kemp, R.H. (1973). Centralised planning and international co-operation in the introduction and improvement of tropical tree species. *Commonw. For. Rev.*, **52**: 335-43.

Burley, J. *et al.* (1974). Information collection, storage and retrieval in forestry. Paper 10th Commonw. For. Conf., pp. 39.

Burley, J. and Styles, B.T. (1976). *Tropical Trees. Variation, Breeding and Conservation*, London, Academic Press, 243.

Carnheiro, N. (1971). World wood review – Brazil. *World Wood*, **12**.

Dyson, W.G. (1974). A note on the conservation of tree species *in situ*. *In* Report of the 3rd Panel of Experts on Forest Gene Resources, Rome, FAO.

FAO (1969). Report of the first session of the FAO Panel of Experts on Forest Gene Resources. Rome, FAO.

FAO (1972). Report of the second session of the FAO Panel of Experts on Forest Gene Resources. Rome, FAO.

FAO (1974a). Report of the third session of the FAO Panel of Experts on Forest Gene Resources. Rome, FAO.

FAO (1974b). Proposals for a Global Programme for improved use of forest genetic resources. FO: MISC/74/15. Rome, FAO.

FAO (1975). *Report on the Pilot Study on the Methodology of Conservation of Forest Genetic Resources*. Rome, FAO. pp. 117.

Finlay, K.W. and Konzak, C.F. (1970). Information storage and retrieval. *In*

Frankel, O.H. and Bennett, E. (eds.). *Genetic Resources in Plants – Their Exploration and Conservation.* Oxford, Blackwell, 461-5.

Frankel, O.H. and Bennett, E. (eds.). (1970). *Genetic Resources in Plants – Their Exploration and Conservation.* Oxford, Blackwell, 554.

Guldager, P. (1975). *Ex situ* conservation stands in the tropics. *In* FAO, *Report on a Pilot Study on the Methodology of Conservation of Forest Genetic Resources,* Rome, FAO, 85-92.

Hagman, M. (1971). The Finnish standard stands for forestry. Proc. 13th Meeting Committ. For. Tree Breed. in Canada. Ottawa, Can. Forest Service.

Harrington, J.F. (1970). Seed and pollen storage. *In* Frankel, O.H. and Bennett, E. (eds.). *Genetic Resources in Plants – Their Exploration and Conservation.* Oxford, Blackwell, 501-21.

Harrington, J.F. (1972). Seed storage and longevity. *In* Kozlowski, T.T. (ed). *Seed Biology, vol. 3.* London, Academic Press, 145-240.

Jones, N. and Burley, J. (1973). Seed certification, provenance nomenclature and genetic history in forestry. *Silvae Genet.,* **22**: 53-8.

Keiding, H. (1972). Collection of pine seed in Southeast Asia with emphasis on provenance sampling. *In* Burley, J. and Nikles, D.G. (eds.). *Selection and Breeding to Improve Some Tropical Conifers.* Oxford, Commonw. For. Inst., 17-28.

Kemp, R.H. (1973a). International provenance research on Central American pines. *Commonw. For. Rev.,* **52**: 55-66.

Kemp, R.H. (1973b). Status of the C.F.I. international provenance trial of *Pinus caribaea* Morelet, September, 1973. *In* Burley, J. and Nikles, D.G. (eds.). *Tropical Provenance Research and International Co-operation.* Oxford, Commonw. For. Inst., 10-17.

Kemp, R.H. (1973c). Status of the CFI international provenance trial of *Pinus oocarpa,* Schiede, September, 1973. *In* Burley, J. and Nikles, D.G. (eds.). *Tropical Provenance and Progeny Research and International Co-operation.* Oxford, Commonw. For. Inst., 76-82.

Kemp, R.H. (1973d). Status of the proposed C.F.I. international provenance trial of *Pinus pseudostrobus* Lindl., September, 1973. *In* Burley, J. and Nikles, D.G. (eds.). *Tropical Provenance and Progeny Research and International Co-operation.* Oxford, Commonw. For. Inst., 106-9.

Kemp, R.H. (1975). Central American pines – a case study. *In* FAO. *Report on a Pilot Study on the Methodology of Conservation of Forest Genetic Resources.* Rome, FAO, 57-64.

Kemp, R.H. *et al.* (1976). Current activities and problems in the exploration and conversation of tropical forest gene resources. *In* Burley, J. and Styles, B.T. (eds.). *Tropical Trees. Variation, Breeding and Conservation.* London, Academic Press, 223-33.

Libby, W.J. *et al.* (1975). California conifers – a case study. *In* FAO, *Report on a Pilot Study on the Methodology of Conservation of Forest Genetic Resources.* Rome, FAO.

Roche, L. (1974). Gene resource conservation – IUFRO working party S2.02.2. *In* FAO, *Forest Genetic Resources Information* no. 3. Forestry Occ. Paper, 1974/1. Rome, FAO.

Roche, L. (1975a). Guidelines for the methodology of conservation of forest genetic resources. *In* FAO, *Report on a Pilot Study on the Methodology of Conservation of Forest Genetic Resources.* Rome, FAO, 107-13.

Roche, L. (1975b). Tropical hardwoods – a case study. *In* FAO, *Report on a Pilot Study on the Methodology of Conservation of Forest Genetic Resources.* Rome, FAO, 65-78.

Roche, L. (1975c). Priorities for research and action. *In* FAO, *Report on a Pilot Study on the Methodology of Conservation of Forest Genetic Resources.* Rome, FAO, 115-7.

Schantz, H.L. (1948). An estimate of the shrinkage of Africa's tropical forests. *Unasylva*, **2**: 66-7.

Soepadmo, E. and Ashton, P.S. (1974). The reproductive biology of some rain-forest trees: second annual report for 1974. University of Aberdeen (mimeographed).

Stern, K. and Roche, L. (1974). *Genetics of Forest Ecosystems.* Berlin, Springer-Verlag. pp. 330.

Toda, R. (1965). Preservation of gene pool in forest tree populations. *Proc. IUFRO Special Meeting (Section 22), Zagreb.*

Wang, B.S.P. (1975). Tree seed and pollen storage for genetic conservation: possibilities and limitations. *In* FAO, *Report on a Pilot Study on the Methodology of Conservation of Forest Genetic Resources.* Rome, FAO, 93-103.

Wavell, S. (1975). Jungle warfare. Guardian Newspaper, May 21st 1975. London, Guardian Newspapers.

SUMMARY OF DISCUSSION IN PART IV

Although the contributions by King and by Kemp and Burley were given in separate sessions, it seems better that the chapters and the relevant discussions for each should be placed together.

The discussion was started by Dimbleby who, referring to King's statement that we knew little of tropical forests, asked how then was it possible to say that tropical rain forest had little effect on the soil? He further stated that it would be a valuable contribution to our knowledge of tropical forests if parts could be set aside as controlled samples in order to give us some reference to the original conditions when the remainder was changed by exploitation. King agreed and said that this was already being done in various parts of the world, even though he feared that such control areas might disappear through human population pressure. King further stated that there had in fact been no observed reduction in soil production capacity in tropical forests nor in the water relationships of these areas. It was only when the shifting agriculturalist over-farmed the soils by taking out the accumulated nutrient provided by the forest that the soils became degraded. This was not due to the forests as such, however.

Bennett referred to another of King's points in which forest areas were taken for conservation before destruction had taken place but pointed out that there were countries such as India and other semi-arid areas of the world where the forest cover had been ruthlessly cut down already. King agreed that great care needed to be taken with marginal zones, since droughts and floods have taken place, according to climate, when forest cover has been removed. A positive step to be taken for such areas is to adopt a policy of reforestation so as to recover some of the original ecological conditions. A negative step is to 'put in quarantine' such marginal areas and prevent forest exploitation altogether in them.

Since forests are long-term yielding systems, Bennett asked whether in any of these marginal forest zones actions and planning of the right kind were being carried out by the governments concerned. King assured her that this was so, and that extensive reforestation projects were under way south of the Sahara and north of the green belt in West Africa. Governments were concerned but often had no financial resources. There was also the problem of protecting trees from nomadic herdsmen, which must really be solved by education. He emphasised, however, that the political will existed to plant and protect forests in that region.

A very real problem mentioned by Hutchinson was that, if the pressure was to be taken off the forests, the productivity of the existing agricultural lands needed to be improved. He cited an instance in the former Belgian Congo where, under shifting agriculture, in order to grow two years' crops the land had to be rested for 30 years. It would obviously have taken very much longer to regenerate forest, and in these very poor conditions of soil, swidden agriculture would surely have been impossible. Such problems also occur in other parts of Africa, in India and in parts of South America. However, he was certain that one should take courage from the tremendous recuperative powers of nature, and he provided examples of this from the contrasting environments of north Yorkshire on the one hand and Medellín in Colombia on the other. The lessons to be learned from these examples were that we should improve the productivity of agricultural lands and, at the same time, make use of the extraordinary capacity of forest lands to regenerate if they are given half a chance to do so.

David Harris contrasted clearly the stable and shifting kinds of tropical agricultural systems. The stable system is in the minority now, he thought, and was found in areas of low population or with deliberate population restriction. The shifting or pioneer mode is the more destructive and is seen now over large parts of the tropical forest areas of the world, especially in South America, where the object is to dispose of the forests as a preliminary to the introduction of cattle.

Referring to Kemp and Burley's paper, Bennett asked whether forest trees which live so long were extremely heterozygous and if this fact would limit the numbers required to represent a given level of genetic diversity. In reply, Burley said that studies on pioneer species such as tropical pines bore this out, so far as isoenzyme studies had shown, though even this heterozygosity differs between populations. On the other hand, in climax forest species, the distribution pattern of individuals and the mating system is different. Individuals are more isolated and he suspected that there was a greater degree of self-pollination, leading to greater homozygosity. However, the data are scanty, and the evidence which does exist varies according to species and areas. Thus, in Nigeria two species of *Terminalia* and *Triplochiton* have completely different distribution patterns, one in clumps and one in more or less continuous forest, indicating that the mating systems and the mechanisms of gene flow might be quite different.

The problem of tree germplasm conservation by tissue culture was also raised, and Burley replied that it had not yet been tried for trees as far as he was aware. The problem that had not yet been solved was to find ways of regenerating plants from cell or suspension cultures, although it would obviously be of the very greatest importance.

Methods of early flowering induction as a way of speeding up breeding was discussed and, although it was said to be of little interest in the tropical pine plantation work, it was not thought of in any case as a particularly promising economic activity. Early induction of flowering was possible in some species but practical applications had not yet been developed.

PART V
AN ASSESSMENT OF THE GREEN REVOLUTION IN INDIA

14. Success in the Indian Punjab

Manohar Singh Gill

The increase in the production of food grains in the Punjab in the last decade has been dramatic. Data are given in Table 14.1.

Table 14.1 Production of cereals in the Indian Punjab, 1960-61 to 1972-73

Thousand metric tonnes

Year	Rice	Wheat	Total cereals
1960-61	229	1742	2453
1965-66	292	1916	3000
1971-72	920	5618	7623
1972-73	955	5368	7399

Source: Punjab statistical abstract, 1973

Though the acreage under wheat has gone up from 1.4m.* hectares in 1960-1 to 2.4m. in 1972-3 and that under rice from 0.23m. to 0.48m. over the same period, the increased production is not only the result of expanded sowing. The increase in productivity has been impressive by any standards as Table 14.2 shows.

Table 14.2 Yields of rice and wheat in kgs per hectare

Year	Rice	Wheat
1950-51	956	1042
1965-66	1000	1236
1972-73	2007	2233

Sources: Punjab statistical abstract 73, and *Bihar and Punjab: A Study in Economic Disparity,* Economic and Scientific Research Foundation, N. Delhi, 1973.

* m. = million throughout this paper.

H

The term 'green revolution', so much in disrepute with scholars these days, is not, therefore, altogether a misnomer at least in the case of the Indian Punjab. As a result of the partition of 1947, and the reorganisation of 1966, the Indian Punjab is a small triangle with its base on the Indo-Pakistan border and its head in Chandigarh, the new Corbusier-designed capital. It has an area of only 50,000 sq.kms. and a population of 13.5 millions. The net sown area is a little over 4 million hectares. In terms of size, this Punjab is dwarfed by the Pakistan Punjab with its area of 204,000 sq.kms., its population of 38 millions and its net sown area of 9.7 million hectares. Because of the successive changes in its boundary, the Indian Punjab is now essentially an area of Sikh agriculture. The partition saw the departure of the Muslims, and the reorganisation of 1966 and the creation of the state of Haryana took away most of the Hindu peasantry of the areas close to Delhi. It is the agricultural breakthrough achieved in this small corner in North-Western India, and the reasons thereof, that we shall attempt to examine in this paper.

The term 'green revolution', however apt it may be, does tend to convey an impression of a sudden improvement, achieved almost entirely on account of a single factor – the import of the 'miracle' dwarf wheat seeds from Mexico. It also tends to convey in some way the notion that the Mexican dwarf wheats were the first improved varieties of wheat to be seen by the Punjab peasant. Neither impression is correct. To consider the second one first, Dr. Clive Dewey (1974) in examining the agriculture of the Punjab over the 1870-1940 period has recorded the remarkable work done by Albert and Gabrielle Howard at the Imperial research station of Pusa, and by David Milne at Lyallpur, in the production of improved wheats in the first two decades of the present century. By the first world war over a million acres were planted with the Pusa wheats. These were followed by wheats bred in the Punjab, type 11 in 1913, 8A in 1919 and thereafter by two new hybrids. Dr. Dewey records that by the end of the second world war more than 2.8m. hectares were under improved varieties. These new varieties played as important a part in the increase in production in the old pre-partition Punjab, as did the increase in irrigation which rose from 2.8m. hectares to 6.9, from the early 1890s to the early 1940s.

Dr. Randhawa (1974), the Vice Chancellor of the Agricultural University in Ludhiana, has carried the story on. He writes: 'In the 'thirties commendable wheat-breeding work was done by Dr. Ram Dhan Singh at the Agricultural College and Research Institute, Lyallpur. Two of his varieties C518 and C591 made a great impact on wheat production. However, the genetic potential of these tall wheat varieties was limited and their yields under ideal conditions of cultivation rarely went beyond thirty quintals per hectare. The averages were much lower. After the establishment of the Punjab Agricultural University, an excellent variety of tall wheat, C306, was released in 1965. It has a very good grain quality with a yield potential about 30 percent higher than C518 and C591. It proved to be the highest yielding tall wheat variety not only in Punjab but also in Haryana, U.P., Rajasthan and Bihar. However the real breakthrough came with the import of dwarf wheat varieties from Mexico, followed by rapid local selections therefrom, and the speedy expansion of their cultivation with matching and needed agronomic improvements suggested by the PAU scientists.' 150 strains of the dwarf wheats were received in India in 1963 from Dr. Borlaug. The PAU scientists quickly selected two promising strains and to save time used the device of multiplying them in the high valleys of Lahaul-Spiti in the May-September period of 1964. PV18, the first of the new selections, gave an average yield of 4690 kgs per hectare against 3291 kgs per hectare from C306, the best local variety at the time. Soon another two varieties, Kalyan-sona and Sonalika, were put out. It is apparent that though the long hoped for breakthrough came with the Borlaug dwarf varieties, the Punjab had a long tradition of breeding and cultivating new and better varieties of wheat. But the Punjab green revolution is not the simple story of the release of the new wheats in 1966-7. The results achieved in 1966-72 are a complex amalgam of many separate factors going back to the partition of 1947. That the Borlaug seeds fell on 'fertile ground' in the Punjab, and achieved their greatest success in the sub-continent, is due to the building up of an infrastructure which prepared the way for their coming.

The consequences of partition

Looking at the prosperity of the Punjab today, few realise that its current wealth is largely self-created, by the most sustained hard work that any people have had to do. The impoverished East Punjab came off poorly in the partition (Randhawa, 1954). The West inherited 55% of the population, 62% of the area, 70% of the canal irrigation built by the British, and 70% of the income of the old province. The exchange of people was almost even, 4.3 millions coming to the East against 4.2 going away. But while the Hindus and Sikhs had abandoned 2.7m hectares of land in Pakistan, of which 1.7m. were irrigated, 0.9m. perennially, there were only 1.9m. to offer to them, of which 0.53m. hectares were irrigated, barely 0.16m. perennially. The famed canal colonies around which had been built the prosperity of the old Punjab were gone. After four decades the Sikh peasants had come back to the villages from which they had gone out to seek the new wealth. Ian Stephens records that 40% of this entire people, almost all agriculturists, had become refugees in 1947. Such was the situation which faced the Indian Punjabis in 1947. The new province was in deficit in foodgrains by 35,000 tonnes.

The refugees were not allowed to solidify into a parasitic and helpless accretion in the camps. In the very first winter they were given temporary allotments of land, loans for seed and cattle and encouraged to sow the winter crop. A separate Rehabilitation Section manned by the ablest civilians was set up and for the next three years they worked hard to sort out the claims and draw up schemes of resettlement. The concept of a standard acre based on an area of land capable of producing 350 to 400 kg. of wheat was evolved to compute the claims. More important, in view of the shortage of land, a system of graded cuts from 25% on the smallest claim, to 95% on the biggest one was worked out and applied rigidly in spite of resistance from the lobby of big farmers. The East Punjab had always been an area of small holdings and small self cultivating peasant proprietors. This is why men had gone out from this crowded area to seek their fortunes in the new canal colonies, and even abroad, from China to California. The influx of refugees and the policy of graded cuts helped further to level the holdings situation downwards.

In most ways the East Punjab had suffered grievously from the partition. But in one sense it had gained. The refugee farmers who trekked across the border were no ordinary men and women. To quote Calvert (1936), on the effect of the canal colonies upon this virile and responsive human material: 'Upon the human element their effect is no less remarkable; the opportunities for hard work under more responsive conditions than those which prevailed in their home districts have moulded the character of the colonists and developed a sense of pride in their economic well-being that should strengthen the opposition to any tendency towards a lowering of the standard of living.' The refugee farmers held true to Calvert's judgement of their character. They had known a better economic standard, and they were not easily going to abandon it, no matter how adverse the circumstances. If they now had fewer acres they simply had to get more out of them. Many sold the jewellery of their women to buy the first tractors. They were the first to try tubewells seriously; they were the first to risk sending their girls, often alone, on cycles or buses, to schools in the cities. One could go on enumerating the innovations of the refugee on the Punjab scene, but it is sufficient to say that the refugee grasped at every means that would restore his standard of living. By April 1950 these men had been settled on their new allotments in the Punjab villages on a permanent basis, and could begin to invest in improvements of the land.

Land reform and re-allocation

Immediately after partition the Punjab Government passed a series of Land Reforms Acts. Occupancy tenants were given full rights, and a ceiling of thirty standard acres placed on holdings. Randhawa records that 647,740 occupancy tenants were given proprietory rights over

0.75m. hectares. The Ceiling Laws, howsoever imperfectly implemented they might have been, had one effect from the point of view of the State's agricultural production. The biggest holdings were either acquired by Government, sold out or broken up to avoid seizure. Absentee landlords disappeared completely. Men either cultivated the land or sold out and moved away. And so the area cultivated by owners increased from 51% in 1947, to 81% in 1969-70. Today, tenancy cultivation has dropped even further. In 1973 the ceiling was further reduced to 18 standard acres per family. The Punjab never had the great zamindaris of U.P. and Bihar. The few big estates which were in the West were left in Pakistan. The cumulative effect of the post-independence land legislation has been to break up the Punjab agricultural lands into a large number of medium sized self-cultivated holdings, as Table 14.3 shows.

Table 14.3 Holding size by number and by area occupied

Size (hectares)	Number (percentage)	Area occupied (percentage)
up to 1	23.4	2.5
1 to 4	39.1	23.4
4 to 8	23.9	33.2
8 to 20	12.0	32.5
20 and above	1.6	8.4
Total	100.0	100.0

Source: National sample survey No. 144. Seventeenth round September 1961 — July 1962.

This preponderance of self-cultivating middle rank peasants provided the ideal conditions for the introduction of the new technology based on the new seeds plus water and fertiliser, for an owner cultivator would have both the incentive and the capability to invest in the new inputs.

Indian agriculture has always suffered from fragmentation, even of tiny holdings. These are wasteful of the peasant's energy, and a bar to investment in irrigation and other land improvements. Hubert Calvert, Registrar of Co-operative Societies Punjab 1915-25, first introduced the idea of voluntary consolidation of holdings by co-operative societies, and by 1947 almost half a million hectares had been consolidated. The Punjab Government made consolidation compulsory from 1948. A new department was set up, and Sardar Partap Singh Kairon, the most dynamic Chief Minister the State has known, made it his prime concern during 1956-64, his years in office. He took it upon himself to convince his fellow jats of the benefits, and to prevent the injustices that were likely to arise due to the scale and speed of the operation. Touring furiously and keeping a sensitive ear to the ground, Kairon was able not only to maintain the speed and momentum of the programme, but also to ensure that by and large the peasantry got a just deal. By the time he resigned in 1964 the programme had been accepted and two thirds of the work completed. By 1969 his successors were able to announce the completion of the re-allocation of the entire 3.7m. hectares of agricultural land in the States of Punjab and Haryana. These two are the only States in either India or Pakistan to have completed this work. The effect of consolidation on the Punjab was immediate and dramatic. In 1950 the State had hardly any tubewells. In 1972-3 she could boast of 180,480 of them, providing more than half of her greatly expanded irrigation. In contrast, the West Punjab (Pakistan), which by 1972 had consolidated less than 50% of her cultivated area, had sunk only 75,000 tubewells by that year.

The consolidation of land was almost complete by the time the Borlaug seeds arrived in 1966, and was one of the main reasons for their success. Farmers cultivating widely scattered plots could hardly have invested in the water and fertilisers that the new wheats demanded. With their holdings effectively consolidated, they immediately began to look for ways of making improvements, above all by the sinking of wells and tubewells.

Water

Water has always been the key input and the ultimate determining factor in Indian agriculture. Lyallpur and Montgomery grew with the life-giving waters of the great canals. But the East Punjab had lost almost all the canals. Less than 30% of the irrigated area of the old Punjab had fallen to her share. The new Punjab could not replace the lost lands, but it was determined to replace the lost canals. The Bhakra-Nangal project on the Sutlej river became the symbol and hope of its future. By 1960-1, 54% of the net sown area was irrigated, largely due to the new canals. By 1972-3 the percentage had risen to 72%, the result since 1966 of the massive tapping of ground water with tubewells.

Today, canals account for less than 50% of the irrigation in the Punjab. The increase of canal irrigation was the result of a major investment, consciously made and efficiently used. Over the 1951-67 period the Punjab spent Rs 108 per hectare on irrigation against an all India average of Rs 41. The building of the Bhakra complex added tremendously to the electricity potential of the State — at the time of partition there was only a small hydel plant at Jogindernagar in the Kangra valley. Government encouraged the use of electric power for tubewells and for lighting in the villages. Today something like half the tubewells are run on electric power, and more will be connected when power is available. Of the 12,000 villages in the State nearly 7,000 have electricity for home use. The percentage of the consumption of electric power for agriculture has risen from 15% in 1960-1 to 35% in 1969-70. Such has been the rise in power consumption that in East Punjab in 1974-5 against a demand of 800MW there was only 476MW available. Agricultural use has been a major factor in the creation of this shortage. The increase of water and power in the fifties and early sixties undoubtedly helped to prepare the ground for the seeds that were to come in the late sixties. Without abundant water the Mexican wheats would have been of little use to the Punjab farmer. In fact the wise ones among them − even those farming canal irrigated land − do not move to Mexican wheats until they have their own tubewell to supplement the erratic canal supply.

Education and the agricultural university

Education was expanded considerably, the literacy rate going up from 15% in 1951 to 29% in 1961. Among women literacy stood at 17% in 1961. The opening of schools and colleges − the money for which was invariably contributed by the villages themselves − helped to widen the mental horizons. The establishment of an Agricultural University in Ludhiana made a tremendous impact on the thinking of the peasants. From the very beginning the University maintained a close link with those it was meant to serve. Farmers had free and easy access, and so when the seeds came the Ludhiana University was very quickly able not only to promote the new seeds but also to inculcate the new package of practices. The success story of the district of Ludhiana in Indian agriculture is in no small measure due to the presence of the Agricultural University.

Credit and the co-operatives

The Borlaug seeds and the package of practices that was advocated with them had no hope of success unless they were backed up with a package of services. The farmer had to acquire fertiliser and additional water. To buy these he must have money. In many ways the problem of Indian agriculture is the problem of credit. The co-operatives grafted onto the agriculture of India by the British at the turn of the century were meant to pull the peasant out of the clutches of the moneylender. Involved too much in the purity of the doctrine, and therefore insisting on credit created largely by the thrift of the farmer himself, they succeeded in doing nothing of the kind. In 1950-1 they provided only 3% of the peasants' credit needs (RCSC, 1954). In the Punjab they perhaps provided about 8%. The Government of India, committed to using co-operatives as the main instrument of serving the farmer, changed the policy radically. Becoming shareholders in the co-operative banks, they proceeded to channel massive funds into agriculture. Credit had always been given against security, and had never been tied to identifiable productive purposes. Clearly security requirements had to be dropped if the large majority of farmers were to benefit. The credits must also be tied to production. And so the Reserve Bank of India evolved the crop loan system. Under this system short term credits of less than a year's duration were to be given by the co-operative banks through the village credit societies for the specific purpose of growing a crop, and were to be recovered when it was harvested. To ensure productive use a part of the loan was to be given in the shape of fertiliser; to enable every farmer, big or small, to benefit it was to be given without mortgage security. For investments in wells, pump sets, etc. separate medium and long term loans were to be given. These co-operative loans were to form the backbone of the credit and input services that were so necessary to the new wheats.

Some idea of the expansion of co-operative credit can be had from the fact that in 1974 the Indian co-operatives were estimated by the Reserve Bank of India (personal communication) to provide 35% of the total crop production credit needs, and 56% of the investment funds needed by the farmers. Studies in Ludhiana show that the co-operatives provide something like 60-65% of the farmers' loan needs; along with the nationalised Banks they account for nearly 80%. The predominance of institutional credit in the Punjab is also borne out by the fact that over the years 1966-72 the State is estimated to have absorbed nearly 10% of the total credit given in India.

In the Punjab the crop loan system was accepted and vigorously introduced from the winter of 1966, just in time to serve the new agricultural strategy. From the start emphasis was laid on loaning in the shape of fertiliser to ensure productive use. From 1967-8 to 1973-4 a total of Rs 3215m. of short term crop loans have been given in the Punjab; of these as much as 64% was in the form of fertiliser. The long term loans increased from only Rs 3.1m. in 1960-1 to Rs 163m. in 1972-3. In this way the institutional agencies in the Punjab provide most of the farmers' credit, and the moneylender is no longer an important social phenomenon. Institutional credit has not achieved such a prominent position anywhere else in the sub-continent, and even in West Punjab (Pakistan) barely Rs 150m. were so given in 1971-2.

The relation between production under the new agricultural programme and the supply of credit from the co-operative is shown in Table 14.4.

There has sometimes been the impression that co-operative loans are cornered by the few to the detriment of the many. If this had been true, the large scale expansion of production in the Punjab would not have taken place. The distribution of co-operative loans (in Rs m.) in the Punjab in 1971-2 was as shown in Table 14.5.

Two points emerge from this analysis. Firstly the size of the Punjab loaning programme. This works out at Rs 103 per hectare of cropped area of short-term production credit alone, against an All-India

Table 14.4 Agricultural production and co-operative credit in the Punjab

Year	Production (m. tonnes)		Co-operative services (m. rupees)		
	Rice	Wheat	Short term loans	Long term loans	Fertiliser distributed
1960-61	0.24	1.72	117.6	3.1	20.7
1965-66	0.29	1.92	275.5	16.4	104.7
1968-69	0.47	4.50	619.6	132.9	354.6
1970-71	0.69	5.15	572.6	195.6	426.5
1972-73	0.96	5.36	620.2	162.6	490.0

Source: Registrar of Co-operative Societies, Punjab

Table 14.5 The distribution of co-operative loans in the Punjab, 1971-72 (Rs m.)

Total loans	Loans to farmers with holdings			Loans to tenants and agricultural labour
	up to 2 hectares	2 to 4 hectares	above 4 hectares	
612.6	141.9	168.3	221.1	81.3

Source: Reserve Bank of India, *Review of the Co-operative Movement in India, 1970-72*, p. 83

average of Rs 35 (Ministry of Co-operatives, 1974). Secondly the spread of the Punjab loans particularly over the tenants and small farmers.

Marketing

Up to 1966 the administrative organisation was that while the co-operative department promoted co-operative societies, the job of agricultural production was that of the agricultural department. Each worked in its own separate compartment and jealously guarded its domain. Thus the agricultural department procured and distributed fertilisers, pesticides, etc., and the co-operatives distributed credit in their own way without relating it in any way to the agricultural programmes of the State. Any failures could be easily blamed on one's rivals. The re-organisation of the Punjab in 1966 and the creation of Haryana provided an opportunity for a much needed administrative reform. In November 1966 a Development Commissioner was appointed with total responsibility for rural development. For the first time the co-operative and agricultural departments came under one master, and the two had to work in 'double harness'. It was made

H*

clear that the Director of Agriculture was to provide the package of practices to the peasant; the Registrar of Co-operative Societies was to be responsible for the package of services, the loans, the fertiliser, the pump sets, the seed, the pesticides, etc. The Agricultural Department was divested of its trading in these commodities, a job hardly suited to a Government Department.

In parallel with this, the marketing structure was greatly developed. Markets, regulated, controlled and organised by Government, were expanded rapidly from 1967 on, to cater for the rising production. Links were built from the main highways so that today nearly all villages are accessible by metalled roads. The trading functions formerly undertaken by the Agricultural Department were transferred to the Markfed, the State co-operative marketing federation, on a commercial basis. The Markfed raises credit from the commercial banks thus relieving the hard-pressed State budget of this burden. Within a few years it built more than 300,000 tons of storage in the countryside to stock and distribute the needed inputs. It maintains 4,000 or more village depots – almost one to every three villages – for this purpose. The federation buys and stocks the fertilisers, the pump sets, etc. and ensures their availability at the right place and the right time. The distribution by the co-operative marketing federation also ensures productive use. The system is simple. The farmer is sanctioned loans by the co-operative banks through his village society. Against these the Markfed supplies him fertiliser or pump sets or other inputs through the same village society. The banking and the marketing structures have their common base in the village society. The Punjab Markfed with an annual turnover of something like Rs 2000m. has become one of India's great co-operative success stories. It distributes almost Rs 500m. worth of fertiliser a year; it has in the years since 1967 distributed something like 30,000 diesel pumping sets; it has an aerial spraying unit with helicopters, harvest combines and an extensive set-up for the processing of agricultural commodities like oilseeds, cotton, etc.

The marketing co-operatives were also involved in the procurement, storage and despatch of foodgrains to other provinces. The wheat procurement of approximately 3 million tons every year is entrusted by Government to the Markfed, the Food Corporation of India and the State Food Corporation, in almost equal measure. The Markfed's extensive modern storage facilities are invaluable for this purpose. But at the level of the markets the local co-operative marketing society is used as the sole buying agent for Government. The Punjab Government for many years has given up buying through grain dealers, and has in fact abolished their functioning in the food grain trade. This year (1975-6) the entire wheat surplus is to be bought by the three agencies through the local marketing co-operatives. This was successfully done in 1971-2 but then given up for a short period to fall in line with national policy.

Thus the Punjab co-operatives underpin the entire process, from the growing of the crop to its marketing. Each crop season is jointly planned by the Director of Agriculture and the Registrar of Co-operative Societies under the control of the Development Commissioner. It had been said that given the Borlaug seeds the first State to make the organisational effort would reap the benefit. The Punjab administrators more than anyone else realised the truth of this statement. In the last analysis the green revolution was to be a revolution in the organisation of the application of inputs to the new seeds. The Punjab State, by divesting the Agricultural Department of its inappropriate trading functions and making it concentrate on its prime job of extension, and by successfully organising the Co-operative Department for the effective and commercial distribution of all the inputs from credit to fertiliser, succeeded in making the best use of the new seeds. The rapidity with which the area under high yielding varieties was expanded bears witness to this fact. The area under the new wheats rose from 681 thousand hectares to 1589 in 1970-1, constituting in that year 69% of the total area under wheat. Today, almost the entire area has shifted to the new seeds. Compare this with the Pakistan Punjab where during 1970-1 only 53.4% of the total wheat area was under the Mexican varieties (PDRP, 1972).

Since 1971 the Indian Punjab has begun to increase the sowings of rice. The new rice varieties grown under tubewell irrigation have had considerable success in the State, and the Punjab is beginning to emerge as a major rice growing area also. That she is having considerable success in this is visible from the jump in rice production since that year. In the last few years the Punjab has been exporting 700 to 800 thousand tons of rice also, and has become the major supplier to the central buffer stock.

Conclusion

The Punjab, then, was not only able rapidly to expand the area under the new varieties, but more important, was able adequately to service it with the inputs of fertiliser, water and credit. She was able to make these facilities available to almost all her farmers. This is why she has been able to do better than all the other wheat growing States of India. No doubt the fixing of a minimum procurement price of Rs 76 per quintal in 1966 – which has been slowly raised to Rs 105 now – helped to make the whole proposition attractive. But it is nobody's case that the Punjab or any peasant can be persuaded to produce more without considerations of personal gain. In any case the same attraction was available to all the wheat growing States, and yet not all of them responded in equal measure. The answer lies in the whole complex amalgam of the farmers' attitudes and the State's organisational capabilities. If one is out to make comparisons perhaps

Table 14.6 Increases in area, yield and production of wheat and rice in the Indian and Pakistan Punjabs

	Area (m. hectares)			Yield (kg./hectare)			Production (m. tonnes)		
	1960 -61	1970 -71	% increase	1960 -61	1970 -71	% increase	1960 -61	1970 -71	% increase
Wheat									
Indian Punjab	1.40	2.30	64	1244	2238	80	1.72	5.15	199
Pakistan Punjab	3.38	4.39	30	886	1138	28	2.90	4.87	68
Rice (paddy)									
Indian Punjab	0.23	0.39	69	1009	1765	75	0.23	0.69	200
Pakistan Punjab	*	0.73		905	1344	48	0.50	0.97	94

*not available

Source: 1. Punjab Statistical Abstract 1973, Punjab Government, Chandigarh (India).
2. Punjab Development Review and Prospects 1972, Punjab Government, Lahore (Pakistan).

the most fruitful area of study lies in a comparison of the two Punjabs. Beginning from a common geographical and cultural heritage, with the Pakistan Punjab enjoying an advantage in the division of the land and irrigation assets in 1947, they have shown widely divergent performances in the green revolution as Table 14.6 shows.

The new seeds were available to both alike. The two countries enjoyed the same opportunities and faced the same problems in the procurement of fertiliser. The wide disparity in achievement emphasises the importance of those other factors of social structure that have in fact been so significant for the success of agricultural development. The agricultural growth rate of the Indian Punjab has been 6.6% over the period 1952-3 to 1969-70 and that of India 3.1% over the same period (Commerce, 1972). According to Nulty (1972) that of the Pakistan Punjab over the 1959-60 to 1969-70 years has barely been 2%. One can make many guesses of the reasons for the decline of the canal colonies and the rise of the poorer eastern half. The maldistribution of land in the West Punjab, the predominance of tenancies, the lack of an institutional credit structure able to serve the majority of the medium and small farmers, the failure to complete the consolidation of land holdings, and the inadequacy of those two main carriers of all progress – literacy and the road system – may be suggested as among the more important factors concerned.

Such then, in brief, is the story of the Punjab's recent agricultural success. In terms of India's food supply, the Punjab has made a massive contribution. In 1965-6 actual market arrivals were 0.78m. tonnes of wheat and 0.31m. tonnes of paddy. In 1971-2 they were 3.12m. tonnes and 1.30m. tonnes respectively (Kahlon, Sharma and Deb, 1974). This increase has made it possible for the State procurement organisation to purchase 2.5-3.0m. tonnes of wheat every year in recent years. In the summer of 1973 out of the total of 4.5m. tonnes of wheat procured in the country, the Punjab alone accounted for 2.7m. tonnes. In the 1972-3 season, of the national rice procurement of 1.19m. tonnes the Punjab's share was 0.76m. tonnes. (NCDC, 1972-3). It would be no exaggeration to call this small State the bread basket of India. No doubt the new seeds have been the key to this achievement, but much work had been done to prepare receptive ground for them. When they did arrive they were backed up with an impressive organisation effort.

Many problems remain to be tackled. It has not been possible to maintain the purity of the seeds nor to multiply the new varieties quickly and adequately. Seed production programmes continue to lag, both in the Punjab and in the rest of India, and are partly responsible for the fall in production in the last one or two years. The expansion of credit has brought the expected problem of rising overdues. The shortage of electricity has hit irrigation. The oil crisis has caused a problem both of fertiliser and of diesel oil for the pump sets. There is a long and hard road ahead, but the people of the

Punjab have travelled a hard road with spirit and determination, and the achievements of the past give good ground for hope for the future.

For references and acknowledgements see the end of Chapter 16.

15. Progress and problems in Tamil Nadu

J.C. Harriss

From being a deficit state in the production of rice during the 1950s, Tamil Nadu (in the south eastern corner of India, with Madras its capital) began to produce a surplus by the late 1960s. In the early 1970s Government publications began to mention a 'rice revolution'. Statistics showed, for example, a 25% increase over the previous year in total rice production in 1970-1, and a 19% increase in yield per hectare. The total rice production of 5.3m. tonnes in 1971-2 compares with an average figure of 3.7m. tonnes for the period 1965-9, an increase of 44%. So it was that the State government could claim: 'Tamil Nadu ranks 7th among the major rice producing States in the country in respect of area under rice but holds the third position in rice production because of its high productivity rate ... Thus it is a legitimate claim that if wheat revolution is going on in Punjab, rice revolution is going on in Tamil Nadu' (TNEA, 1973).

Such claims, though made with justice, are tempered when it is pointed out that the yields obtained on research stations with high yielding varieties (HYVs) of paddy* have been in excess of 6000 kgs/hectare, and that average yields/hectare in Japan in 1971 were 5250 kgs, whereas Tamil Nadu claimed an average of only 1973 kgs in 1971-2. Disparities between performance on experimental stations and on farmers' fields are expected and are perhaps inevitable, and they are certainly no greater with rice than with other crops. What is more important is the evidence for wide differences in performance within and between major rice growing regions, which indicate the limitations of the progress that has been made thus far in Tamil Nadu.

---

*The term HYVs has come to connote short strawed, fertiliser-responsive varieties of cereals bred in international plant breeding institutions. The wheats were bred at CYMMYT in Mexico, and the rices at IRRI in the Philippines. Paddy is the name for rice in its raw state. When milled the yield of rice from paddy is about 50% by volume or 66% by weight.

Contributors to increased rice production

The introduction of new HYVs of paddy is one of several factors which have to be considered together in examining the reasons for the spurt in production at the beginning of the 1970s. The aims of the Fourth Five Year Plan for Tamil Nadu were that 37% of the additional targeted production of foodgrains would be derived from HYVs, 25% from expansion of minor irrigation and 21% from increased use of chemical fertilisers. It is not certain that the different components of the 'package' have contributed to increased production in quite the proportions suggested by these planning targets, and there are those who argue that there has been a 'fertiliser revolution' or a 'pumpset revolution' rather than an 'HYV revolution'. In any case a basic factor is that whereas expansion of rice production was hampered in the late 60s by poor rainfall, especially in 1968-9, the early 70s were years of good monsoons. This favourable trend was reversed however in 1973-4, and even more disastrously so in 1974-5 when rainfall fell further below average than at any time since the years of the Great Famine of 1876-8. Reports suggest that production of foodgrains will be down to 5m. tonnes from 7.5m. tonnes in 1973-4, a sad indication of the extent to which cultivation is subject to rainfall variability.

Precipitation is highly variable over most of the State, so that a decisive factor in the expansion of paddy production, even though it has obviously not guaranteed it, has been the considerable increase in 'minor irrigation', principally from wells with electric pumpsets. Rural electrification has proceeded very far in Tamil Nadu. At the end of 1971-2 91% of villages in the State had received electricity supplies, as against 38% and 34% respectively in the neighbouring States of Karnataka and Andhra Pradesh, themselves well above the national average of 21% (TNEA, 1973), and the State has about 55% of all the electric pumpsets in India. Numbers of electric pumpsets increased fivefold between 1961 and 1972. Increased use of groundwater for irrigation has been especially important in Chingleput and in South and North Arcot Districts, which together with Thanjavur are now the surplus producing districts of the State (TNEA, 1973). Thanjavur is a delta area which is uniquely favoured in terms of irrigation facilities, enjoying the use of water from the Kaveri-Mettur Scheme and producing 25% of the paddy output of Tamil Nadu from about 12% of the gross cultivated area. Chingleput and North and South Arcot Districts, which are based mainly on tank and well irrigation, together produced 36% of the State total in the early 70s from about 25% of the cultivated area. More than 40% of the irrigated area of these districts was cropped twice, a much higher percentage than in all except one other district. Thus it is that Mencher (1974) has suggested that '... the massive increase in well irrigation in Chingleput and in South and North Arcot Districts, and irrigation facilities that allow for a second crop in Thanjavur' has been very largely responsible for the 'rice revolution' of Tamil Nadu.

The extent of the contribution of chemical fertilisers to the increase in production is indicated by the increase in consumption. Offtake in 1971-2 was more than double the average offtake of the period 1965-9. The contribution of the new HYVs is more difficult to estimate. The area under new varieties is difficult to determine, for it is well known that the system used for reporting results in over-estimation of acreages in official statistics. Official estimates for the area under HYVs in 1972-3 in the 6 taluks of North Arcot District studied by a joint Cambridge University-Madras University research project, ranged between 39% and 48% of the paddy acreage, whereas the data from the project, based on a random sample survey of cultivators, showed only 13% for the same year. In 1973-4 some official estimates claimed that 60% of the gross paddy acreage of the State was under HYVs, but this seemed very unlikely in view of the fact that 75% of the gross paddy area is in the main wet season when adoption rates, according to many research studies and for reasons which are discussed below, are very low. (For discussion of official estimates and comparison with the results of the research project, see Chinnappa, in press.)

The record of Tamil Nadu is then one of progress, though with some important limitations, and one in which the contribution of new varieties *per se* is not at all clear. The limitations of the existing HYV technology and the constraints on the improvement of paddy production in Tamil Nadu are discussed here in the light of field experience gained especially in North Arcot.

The complexity of rice farming

In comparison with other crops rice is unique in its water relations. On the one hand it tolerates flooding as no other crop can, and on the other it seems that the primary reliance of the plant for nourishment is on the 'medium' rather than the 'substrate'. To quote Grist (1959) 'the supply and control of water ... is more important than the type of soil'. Furthermore, the difference between the water regime of rice and other crops makes for acute problems when attempts are made to diversify the agricultural economy of rice growing areas.

Field preparation requires the flooding of the field and the creation of a deep 'ooze' by several ploughings or by repeated tillage with hand tools, and the quality of the 'ooze' that is achieved influences the outcome of the crop. After sowing or transplanting in a well soaked field with little standing water the field has to be kept wet, with the level of the water in the field being increased steadily as the plant grows and flowers, after which it has to be drained off until at harvest time the field is dry. It is also important that the water in the fields should not stagnate but be kept gently flowing and periodic drainings are necessary for weeding and fertilisation. There are different local systems of water control, and HYVs have requirements of their own, but in all regimes there is a very delicate balance between too much and too little water at all stages of cultivation.

So rice farming requires especially careful management at the field level and that in turn introduces problems which often have to be handled by the whole community of a village or small locality. Without wishing to invoke Wittfogel's (1957) theories concerning 'hydraulic societies' and 'oriental despotism', a number of detailed studies do show how closely social organisation and decision making in agriculture are linked to the requirements of irrigation. This is perhaps especially so in areas like Thanjavur where cultivators whose fields are supplied by gravity irrigation from canals have very little individual control over the vital matters of supply and drainage of water to and from their fields.

Field preparation, and especially transplanting, which in most Indian conditions seems essential for high yields, are labour intensive operations for which even small semi-subsistence farmers need to hire labour. It is in the major paddy farming districts that especially large numbers of landless labourers are found. Even so, short but very acute peaks of labour demand create temporary scarcities which further constrain the farmers' decisions. Delayed transplanting, due to labour difficulties, is a major cause of low yields.

It is generally accepted that environmental conditions in the major rice areas of India, amongst which those of Tamil Nadu are very important, are more uncertain than those of the major wheat areas (Barker and Mangahas, 1971). These basic uncertainties are compounded by the intricate and interlocking decisions that are involved in rice farming, especially when two or three crops are cultivated in one year.

Farm size and land tenure

A debate of long standing in Indian agricultural economics has been concerned with the relative efficiency of use of the factors of production by farmers in different holding size classes, and under different tenurial conditions. The literature includes much polemic and little science, but it is agreed that the soundest conclusion is that cultivation is generally more intensive and yields higher on small holdings rather than on large (Bell, Byres and Lipton, 1974), though it may be necessary to revise this conclusion because the factor market is currently so organised that large farmers have been more successful than small farmers in taking advantage of HYVs, in spite of the theoretical scale neutrality of the 'new technology'. It is generally agreed that the terms of many tenancy agreements, which are often based on sharecropping, are such as to limit the likelihood of adoption of intensive cultivation practices. On the whole, tenancy conditions are worst in the rice farming areas, while some of the most favoured areas agriculturally, like Thanjavur and the delta of the river Godaveri, also have relatively high proportions of large holdings and particularly exploitative agrarian structures dominated by absentee landlords. These institutional and social structural factors have had a profound effect upon the progress of rice farming, and upon the no less vital question of the distribution of benefits. Some observers hold that the kind of 'agrarian reform' which followed Partition on the plains of the Punjab is the major factor responsible for the success of agricultural development there. Certainly the structure of agrarian social relations in the rice areas has always to be taken into account.

New varieties, water and fertilisers

It has often been suggested that part of the potential of the new high yielding varieties lies in the fact that they are of shorter duration than earlier varieties, a characteristic which enhances the possibility of multiple cropping. In the delta of Thanjavur it is true that the new varieties are of relatively short duration as compared with local varieties. It is as well, however, to be wary about the use of the term 'traditional varieties' in Tamil Nadu where rice breeding has a long history, and one finds that most of the so-called 'traditional varieties' are in fact the product of earlier phases of research (compare M.S. Gill, concerning wheat breeding in the Punjab, in Chapter 14), and this has had some influence in increasing the double cropped area. However, shorter duration varieties have to be harvested in wet weather, and it has not been found easy to fit new cropping patterns into the rhythm of the seasons.

The argument on duration has to be reversed for a tank and well district like North Arcot. There the existing HYVs are of about the same duration as some of the most popular local varieties and of substantially longer duration than one of them, a variety called *kullan kar*. This one variety was grown on 21% of the annual gross paddy acreage in the area in North Arcot surveyed by the Cambridge-Madras project in 1973-4 (see Chinnappa, in press). It is a 90 day variety, in comparison with 120-130 days for IR 20, and 130-150 days for IR 8 – the two most important HYVs. It is thus much better suited to the water-scarce conditions of two of the three possible paddy seasons of the year than are the HYVs from IRRI. Farmers with wells with assured water supplies can undertake cultivation of the HYVs in these seasons, but even many who do own wells cannot be sure that the water will not give out before the end of the growing seasons, especially in circumstances of marked secular decline in the water table (Madduma Bandara, in press).

It makes sense for farmers to continue to cultivate the traditional variety even though its yield potential is much lower, because not only does it require less water, but it also does not require costly chemical inputs or indeed such careful management as the HYVs. Even the most profit-conscious farmers have to consider the advisability of cultivating *kullan kar* on at least a part of their farms in the two dry seasons, if they are to obtain production at all. Efforts have been made to introduce a variety bred in Tamil Nadu, known as 'Karuna' (or Co33, the product of a cross of IR 8 with ADT 27, an improved variety developed in Tamil Nadu in the early 1960s), which requires only 105 days in the field. But although it has been very successful in Thanjavur, where it was developed, it was not found so effective in North Arcot.

Constraints relating to water supply have also been important in the delta and canal irrigated areas. There it seems that one of the major obstacles to the successful introduction of HYVs lay in the need for co-ordinated decision making between individual cultivators in the large areas fed by gravity irrigation (Hopper and Freeman, 1969), though this difficulty has apparently been very largely overcome in Thanjavur.

To return to the tank and well irrigation areas: as we have seen, local varieties have a powerful ongoing advantage in the two dry seasons. However, since the paddy cultivated in these two seasons makes up only about 25% of the gross acreage, it would still be possible for HYVs to dominate if they could be cultivated successfully in the main wet season. Unfortunately, the existing HYVs are less well suited to wet season conditions than to dry in North Arcot, and by inference in all the other major paddy districts except perhaps Thanjavur. The Cambridge-Madras survey found only 4% of the paddy area under new varieties in 1972-3, and 8% in the wet season of 1973-4 (in comparison with 13% and 11%, and 26% and 16% respectively for the two dry seasons; Chinnappa, in press).

Those farmers who did take up HYVs in the wet season of 1973-4 in North Arcot were rarely rewarded with results commensurate with the level of expenditure required, and in fact yields in the first dry season were 22% higher than in the wet season. The reasons for the poor performance of the new varieties in the wet season are not fully understood but it seems that a combination of lower insolation and higher humidity – which in turn enhances the probability of pest attacks – is mainly responsible. It has been found elsewhere also, that the comparative advantage of the new varieties is least in the wet season, and that year to year variability is particularly marked during that season (Barker and Mangahas, 1971).

The combination of water supply and seasonal constraints seriously limits the potential of the existing HYVs, and their effects are further strengthened (in the short term at least) by soil conditions. It appears that IRRI varieties were developed on well-drained soils at the research station at Los Baños, and they do not grow as well on the heavy clay 'ooze' soils of North Arcot, which are the soils of the old paddy lands, as on the dryland soils recently put under paddy by the expansion of irrigation from groundwater sources, the limitations of which have been mentioned above.

Economic constraints

As if this combination of biological and environmental factors was not enough we find also that price differentials weigh heavily against the new varieties in the wet season in North Arcot, which is the period during which particularly fine varieties of rice can be cultivated. These varieties (most notably *Arcot kichili*) command such a high price in the market as to give farmers profits as high or higher than those that they can obtain with the HYVs (cf. also Barker and Mangahas, 1971). This is of course an additional twist to the well known consumer preference against the new varieties because of either their taste or their cooking qualities. Price differentials have, however, been eroded in the general steep and frightening rise in paddy prices that has followed upon shortages obtaining since early 1974.

It seems probable that so far as North Arcot is concerned the adoption of HYVs reached a peak in the main dry season and the wet season of 1973. Even at the beginning of this period, urea, the main chemical source of nitrogen, was in short supply and often only available at black market prices. By the end of the period it had become chronically short and in a matter of a fortnight at the end of 1973 black market prices doubled, while compound fertilisers also increasingly became available only on the black market. For North Arcot farmers there was little scope for substituting organic manures for chemical fertilisers, because their usage of organic materials was already intensive. Indeed the price of urban compost went up more than the price of chemical fertilisers at the end of 1973. At the same time recurring electricity shortages were reducing the availability of groundwater to those with wells. These factors, together with low rainfall, led to a reduction in the area under HYVs in the main dry season of 1974 in comparison with the coverage in 1973.

Conclusion: the prospect and the need

The main burden of this paper has been to point out that there are no simple plant breeding solutions to the problems of Indian agricultural development, especially in the case of rice farming, with its peculiarly intricate relations with the physical and human environments. The existing HYV technology has proved to be of only limited suitability in the conditions of North Arcot District, and though no sweeping generalisations should be drawn it is true that these conditions are fairly representative of the greater part of the paddy acreage of the State. Although rice production has been increased in Tamil Nadu in the 1970s the changes involved fall far short of what was expected, or indeed of what was claimed for the 'green revolution'. The reasons for this are both technological and socio-economic.

The HYVs that have been distributed most widely up to the present were bred at an international research station remote from South India to meet the specific requirements of high fertility conditions and assured water supply. The range of HYVs available from IRRI is far too narrow to meet the variety of other conditions in Tamil Nadu, and in particular the range in length of season. Moreover circumstances with regard to fertility level and water supply have changed with the change in cost and availability of fertiliser, and with power shortages and the fall in the water table.

It is true that great efforts are being made to develop varieties within Tamil Nadu adapted to the particular conditions of different regions, using the IRRI varieties crossed with local strains. But even within the State, plant breeding has tended to concentrate on the most favoured localities. As in the case of the variety called *karuna* mentioned above, what has tended to happen has been for varieties that have proved successful in one or two places to be distributed widely, into areas for which they are apparently not suited. This is certainly one way of proceeding, but discussions with plant breeders in South India served to convince Chambers (in press) that there is a great deal of scope for consideration of alternative priorities in plant breeding research, and that the scientists involved may have been basing their choices on too restricted a range of criteria. The conventional wisdom that 'technology is neutral' is misleading in so far as the decisions made by agricultural scientists about their priorities do have considerable social and economic effects. Chambers suggests that from amongst the very large number of alternative or complementary characteristics towards which breeding may be directed the selection of such objectives as preference for (*inter alia*) stable to unstable seed; varieties with high yields of calories under conditions of low fertility which have high slopes in the early stages of their nitrogen response curves; varieties with water stress tolerance; short duration varieties; and varieties which will fit into existing farming systems and existing or anticipated farm labour demand profiles, will tend to help farmers in less favoured environments, and the smaller, poorer farmers in general. The decision-making process is likely to benefit from a multi-disciplinary approach such as is being employed in the activities of the International Crop Research Institute for the Semi-Arid Tropics (ICRISAT) at Hyderabad.

It is not claimed, however, that choices about technology can be expected to be substitutes for social and economic reforms. It has been a major criticism of the 'green revolution' that its chief beneficiaries are those who were already in possession of a disproportionate share of the communities' resources. This is no more than is to be expected, for the wealthy and powerful are those who are best able to turn to advantage technological developments that are potentially available to all. Indeed, in attempting to promote technological change the expert and the adviser perforce seek out the members of the community who have the enterprise and the skill to exploit new potentialities. And in India, at least, 'experts' and 'entrepreneurs' usually come from the same social groups and have interests in common. It is to be expected then that any other forms of technological change brought about by plant breeding would be equally susceptible to appropriation by the rich and powerful, and it may well be that the 'distributive preferences' suggested above are not feasible alternatives given the existing power structure in South Asia. All that is claimed here is that there is a latent potential in plant breeding research. If growth through technological advance is to be associated with greater justice in the distribution of its products (and many economists now argue that economic growth in South Asia *requires* greater distributive justice), the revolution that is ultimately required is not technological but social.

For references and acknowledgements see the end of Chapter 16.

16. The Indian achievement

J.B. Hutchinson

In chapters 14 and 15 of this section on the green revolution in India, accounts are given of the outstanding success in increasing wheat production in the irrigated northwest of India, and of the considerable, though not so spectacular, success in increasing rice production in irrigated areas of Tamil Nadu. Wheat constitutes 25% and rice 40% of the production of food grains in India, so these successes have been of very great importance. Indeed, it is not too much to say that without them there could have been no chance at all of keeping control of India's food supply problems. Nevertheless, the successes with rice and wheat must be looked at in proper perspective. It is misleading to call them revolutionary. 'Revolution' carries the connotation of a sudden once-and-for-all change, that stands or falls by its completeness and success. It is in this sense that the 'green revolution' has been condemned as a failure. It has been neither complete nor universally successful. We shall not be clear on the achievements and limitations of recent agricultural change in India unless we define the situation in different terms. A process of change and development that has gone on at least from the time of Partition, and has its roots much further back in time, is not properly termed a 'revolution', and an achievement that has virtually been confined to two major crops, and to a part of the irrigable alluvial lands of India, should never have been reported in revolutionary terminology.

Review

To evaluate the significance of recent changes in India's agricultural productivity, it is necessary to give a brief account of the position in the vast areas of India that have not yet attracted the attention of those who write of the 'green revolution'. The irrigated lands of India amount to 30m. hectares out of a net sown area of about 140m. hectares (Swaminathan, 1973), and even on the irrigated areas the 'green revolution' technology has not been universally applied.

On the rain fed lands, little change has yet taken place. They are unresponsive to the new technology because of the hazards of the monsoon. Nevertheless, an analysis of the main factors in crop improvement suggests that there are real possibilities of improving their productivity. The crop races now in cultivation are adapted to production at a low fertility level. They grow slowly over as long a period as there is likely to be either rainfall or residual soil moisture, and thereby achieve a modest production. If they are fertilised during the rains, growth is fast and vigorous, and a crop cover is established that cannot be supported on the declining water supply as the monsoon ceases. Thus it is no use making good the lack of fertility while in fact production is limited by lack of water in the latter part of the growing season.

The hope of progress

The key problem is again water. Monsoon rains are not subject to human management, but it is possible to define for any area a period in the monsoon season when the rainfall is reasonably reliable. With the repertoire of crop genotypes now available to the plant breeder it is a straightforward breeding enterprise to breed varieties with a duration equal to the period of reliable rains, plus a limited extension into the dry season to allow for maturation and ripening off. This involves establishing a substantially shorter crop duration than at present, which at current fertility levels would result in lower yields. However, with the better relationship between monsoon water supply and crop duration, there would be a satisfactory return from the use of fertilisers. Thus, plant breeding would be devoted to the exploitation of the higher fertility levels now attainable, but whereas on irrigated lands the major change has been in plant height and straw stiffness, for the rain lands it will be in crop duration, in conformity with the dictates of the water regime. This is the principle on which the interaction between water supply, fertility level, and crop variety can be modified to advantage on the rain fed lands.

Though the monsoon is both unmanageable and unpredictable, there is much that can be done to improve the effectiveness of the rain after it falls. On the great black soil tract of mid India – 64m. hectares in extent – percolation is very limited after the first rains and runoff and erosion are serious. But the soils are retentive and, if the rainfall is well managed, winter crops can be grown on stored moisture. On the red soils – 72m. hectares in extent – soil moisture capacity is low and cropping on stored moisture very hazardous. But there is much to be done to improve percolation rate, moisture storage, and root range, thereby giving a degree of security to the crop in the face of capricious and unreliable monsoon rains. The organisation of control of runoff, reservoir storage where possible, and maximisation of percolation and soil storage on the great rain fed farm lands of India present a challenge to the soil scientist and agronomist, and offer the hope of great improvements in productivity.

The problem of energy costs

A very serious problem arises from the scarcity and high and rising price of fertilisers. The break-through with wheat in northern India and the steady rise in rice production are just as seriously in jeopardy from the rise in input costs as is the prospect of extending the improvement in productivity to the rain fed lands. India, like western Europe, needs to re-think agricultural policy radically to take account of changing fertiliser and energy costs. In the long term, it is the cost of fixed nitrogen that is the key to fertiliser policy. Potash is not limiting on most Indian soils. Phosphate deposits have been located in India, and will presumably be used increasingly to meet her own needs. But manufactured nitrogen fertilisers are, and must always be, expensive in energy terms, and India's indigenous sources of energy are limited.

The alternative of biological fixation has been only inadequately studied, but in fact a large proportion of the nitrogen used by higher plants is fixed by the lower organisms, either in root nodules or free living in soils and rice paddies. There is therefore an alternative to high energy cost fertiliser, and the urgent need is for research into the intensification and management of biological fixation.

Conclusion

Rice and wheat are the two most important crops in India, and in both, production has increased very greatly in the past 25 years. It is important to remember, however, that these increases have been gained almost entirely on irrigated lands. These increases in production to which the name 'green revolution' has been applied are not derived from the breeding of new varieties of these crops, but from a complex interaction between increased fertility due to fertilisers, better management of irrigation water, and improvement in the social and economic situation, as well as new varieties bred to be responsive to these improved circumstances. The close interdependence of these factors is made very clear by the comparison of the great success of wheat in the Punjab with the much more modest improvement of the rice crop in Tamil Nadu.

Even more important in assessing the significance of the 'green revolution' is the fact that it only applies, so far, to a limited sector of India's crop lands. Water management is an essential feature of the 'green revolution' technology, and only one fifth of India's crop lands are irrigated. Moreover, the new technology has not been universally adopted, even on the irrigable wheat growing areas. The breakthrough took place in the northwestern sector, between Delhi and the Pakistan border. Wheat is also grown on similar alluvial land, with ground water below, throughout Uttar Pradesh and Bihar, but the greater part of that vast tract is still an area of cereal deficit. It is not too much to say that it could make a massive contribution to India's food reserves in the same way, and by the same techniques, as the Punjab has done.

Thus even on the irrigated lands it is not a revolution that we are discussing, but a process of agricultural change that has been spectacular in some favoured areas, modest in some others, and without noticeable effect in vast tracts of India's countryside.

Looked at as a continuing process of change, the scope for further advance is more impressive than the progress already made. The enlargement and diversification of the rice breeding programme will, over time, produce the wide range of varieties necessary for the exploitation of fertility and of water supplies in the rice areas. The extension of crop improvement to the rain fed lands can be foreseen, in terms of better soil management and more efficient use of monsoon rains with the use of new crop varieties.

All these technological advances can be forecast, but the human factor remains in question. Gill has shown how closely the agricultural advance of the Punjab depended on the imagination, enterprise, and determination of the Punjab farmer, both local and immigrant, following Partition. These great human resources overcame the constraints of limited land, inadequate water, and an antiquated land use system. It has not yet been possible to mobilise human resources to this extent in the rest of the great alluvial area. Moreover, in the rice areas such as Tamil Nadu, the constraints of rice agriculture, the population pressure that goes with rice farming, and the associated complex and interdependent social system, have so far proved too resistant to change for the kind of enterprise that was successful with wheat in the Punjab to succeed with rice in Tamil Nadu.

What has gone on in the past decade has been a great achievement, but it must be evaluated as a part of the long term race between population and the food supply on which it depends, and not as an incident to be named and recorded in isolation. Looked at in this way, the prospects for the future are encouraging. Great increases in productivity have been achieved in a limited sector of Indian agriculture. Though the problems of the vast remaining areas are intractable, the means of their solution are beginning to emerge, and the magnitude of the increases in production that might be achieved in them is such as to give real hope for the future.

Acknowledgments

The opportunity to make this comparative study of the 'green revolution' in India arose from the circumstance that the three authors were associated with the Centre of South Asian Studies in Cambridge during 1975. M.S.G. was on study leave to write up the history of the co-operative movement in the Indian Punjab. J.C.H. was writing up his contribution to an interdisciplinary study of agrarian change in the rice growing areas of Tamil Nadu and Sri Lanka, and on this interdisciplinary study J.B.H. acts as an agricultural consultant. We take this opportunity to thank the Director and staff for making the facilities of the Centre available to us.

REFERENCES for chapters 14, 15 and 16

Barker, R. and Mangahas, Mahar (1971). Environmental and other factors influencing the performance of new High Yielding Varieties of wheat and rice in Asia. *In Policy, Planning and Management for Agricultural Development.* Oxford.

Bell, C., Byres, T.J. and Lipton, M. (1974). *In* Lehman, A.D. (ed.). *Agrarian Reform and Agrarian Reformism.* London, Faber and Faber.

Calvert, H. (1936). *The Wealth and Welfare of the Punjab.* Lahore, Civil and Military Gazette.

Chambers, R. (in press). *Challenges for Rural Research and Development.* Cambridge, Centre of South Asian Studies.

Chinappa, Nanjamma (in press). *Adoption of the New Technology for Paddy Cultivation in the Survey Area.* Cambridge, Centre of South Asian Studies.

Commerce (1972). Annual number.

Dewey, C. (1974, ms.). *The Agricultural Output of an Indian Province.* University of London, Institute of Commonwealth Studies.

Grist, D.H. (1959). *Rice,* 3rd edition. London, Longmans.

Hopper, W.D. and Freeman, W.H. (1969). From unsteady infancy to vigorous adolescence: rice development. *Economic and Political Weekly, Review of Agriculture,* March 1969.

Kahlon, A.S., Sharma, A.D. and Deb, P.C. (1974). *In* Hunter, G. and Bottrall, A.F. (eds.). *Serving the Small Farmer: Policy Choices in Indian Agriculture.* London, Croom Helm.

Madduma Bandara, C.M. (in press). *Hydrological Consequences of Agrarian Change.* Cambridge, Centre of South Asian Studies.

Mencher, J. (1974). Conflicts and contradictions in the Green Revolution: the case of Tamil Nadu. *Economic and Political Weekly,* Annual no.

Ministry of Co-operatives (1974). *Annual Report 1973-4.* New Delhi, Government of India.

National Co-operative Development Corporation (1973). *Annual Report, 1972-3.* New Delhi, Government of India.

Nulty, L. (1972). *The Green Revolution in West Pakistan.* New York, Praeger.

Punjab Development Review and Prospects (1972). Lahore, Government of Pakistan.

Randhawa, M.S. (1954). *Out of the Ashes*. Chandigarh, Punjab Public Relations Department.

Randhawa, M.S. (1974). *Green Revolution: a Case Study of the Punjab*. New Delhi, Vikas.

Rural Credit Survey Committee Report (1954). Reserve Bank of India.

Swaminathan, M.S. (1973). *Our Agricultural Future*. Sardar Patel Memorial Lectures. New Delhi, Indian International Centre.

Tamil Nadu Economic Appraisal (1973). Madras, Government of Tamil Nadu.

Wittfogel, K.A. (1957). *Oriental Despotism*. New Haven, Yale University Press.

SUMMARY OF DISCUSSION IN PART V

The reaction to the papers on the green revolution in India was one of considerable interest and appreciation. The first part of the discussion was concerned with mechanisation. Thorpe asked whether much future in mechanisation could be envisaged in either rice or wheat lands. Hutchinson was against the importation of machinery since it was so often brought in without the slightest idea of whether it would be of any value. However, though citing instances of the misuse of machinery in India, he agreed that there should be mechanisation in the shape of water pumps, combine harvesters, helicopters for distributing fertilisers, thrashing machines and the like. These needed to be brought in gradually, and with due regard for traditional methods.

Comments on fertilisers elicited the response from Hutchinson that India produces about half her fertilisers in factories situated in various industrialised parts of the country. Half is imported, but for that which is produced internally the energy base is almost all imported. Phosphates are also all brought in from outside but deposits have now been found which will reduce the amount imported in the future.

Gray raised an interesting point on the production of compost, following on from the work of Sir Albert Howard, saying that he had been associated with a project near Hyderabad in the arid regions and asking if Howard's ideas could be brought up to date. Organic fertilisers are used a very great deal in India according to Hutchinson, although he thought that Howard's imagination had rather got the better of him. The big problem, surely, was that, although organic fertilisers should be used as much as possible, there simply were not enough to go round.

Problems of irrigation were also discussed; here again there are difficulties with depletion of resources, and Harriss pointed out that the wells in Coimbatore are now so deep that three pump sets are needed to bring water to the surface. In regions with which Harriss was familiar there was always heavy dependence on well irrigation.

However, Hutchinson made the point that in northern India there had been a considerable rise in water level since canal irrigation had been installed. By and large, however, the lesson that an aquifer is a reservoir and cannot be expected to yield more than flows into it had still to be learned.

Waddington was concerned to hear that around Delhi the so-called green revolution was being applied by rich men, very often civil servants buying up farms, who ousted the small-holders and ran the farms efficiently, thus making large profits. Hutchinson believed that this was a local phenomenon but quoted the old text, 'to him that hath shall be given'. In the Punjab the peasants themselves have become prosperous and have been running their small plots, on the whole very efficiently. Only when peasants and government co-operate can this sort of policy become effective. Waddington, however, had some reservations, quoting the example of Europe where it was the great landowners who made the improvements. He did not feel too concerned about the civil servants from Delhi making the profits from big yields, since it still increased production.

Hutchinson was inclined to agree, but felt that the Punjab experiment was a good one since the Sikh peasant could live on a 4 hectare holding. If he could produce a good crop from that it must be valuable, since there was only a limited amount of land, and there would be nothing else for him to do in any case. So this seems to be the answer in lands with plenty of labour, to help the peasant to help himself, with proper government support and just enough mechanisation to aid him where needed but not enough to throw the peasant out of work. Crop varieties, fertilisers, irrigation all play a role, but the really important factor seems to be good financial support, social organisation and a tradition of hard work.

PART VI

ECODEVELOPMENT: THE WAY AHEAD

17. The balance between food production and conservation

M.W. Holdgate

There is a question implicit in the title of this chapter. If a balance needs to be struck between food production and conservation, does this mean that these two activities can or do compete and conflict? My aim is to explore how far this is so and, where the conflict is real, to examine how it can be resolved. For both food production and conservation are components of land management, and the pursuit of a balance between them is an element in the search, however idealistic it may be, for some 'optimum' land use policy.

Food production: the background

It was as a food gatherer, and later food producer, that man had his first substantial impact upon the ecological systems of the world. The uniqueness of man's impact has arisen not because he was at any time in his evolution separate from natural systems, but because of the rapid rise in his numbers and even more dramatic change in the nature of his interaction with the environment and other species. For within a few millennia he has passed through many stages: initially a rare gatherer of easily obtained foods, and then, not necessarily in strict sequence, a weapon-using hunter, fire raiser, axe-wielder, domesticator of plants and animals, generator of energy, maker of pesticides and fertilisers, scientific geneticist and biochemist, and conservationist. No other dominant organism in evolutionary history has affected the plant and animal communities of the world in so many different ways in so short a period.

Fig. 17.1 summarises the sequence of ecological impacts. Stage S_1 represents the unaltered system, changing ($S_{1.1} \ldots S_{1.n}$) in response to climatic and other natural factors and evolutionary developments. It retains full ecological diversity (D). Today such systems are rare, occurring chiefly at the poles, amid high mountains, on remote islands and in the deep seas – and even here modern man's impact on the

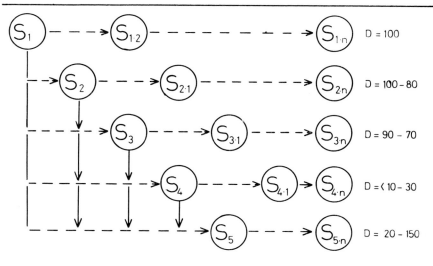

Figure 17.1. Diagrammatic representation of stages in environmental modification by human impact, with notional changes in diversity.

whole biosphere through pollution has some slight effect.

Stage S_2 and its sequential derivatives represent a system in which man is a hunter-gatherer, taking selected plants. Usually these have large energy stores in stem, root or fruit, digestible when raw or after simple cooking and lacking dangerous or unpalatable alkaloids and other substances. Many species are commonly taken, but the cropping rate is low and unlikely to modify the structure of the system. Similarly, many invertebrates, birds eggs, young birds and small mammals would be cropped. The coastal zones, with their abundant molluscs and many small fish which can be trapped in pools or behind corrals on a falling tide, offered special attractions to such cultures. As hunting techniques developed, the chance of taking bigger animals, yielding more food energy per unit effort arose. The kind of energy balance and population density such a system might support is given in the first line of Table 17.1, simplified from Odum (1967) and relating to rain forest in Zaire or Amazonas. One person/km^2 might gather 0.4 KCal/m^{2}yr. Probably you would do a lot better on a diverse shore. Ecological diversity and ecosystem structure is unlikely to be affected by such cultures until fire and forest clearance permitted overkills above the sustainable yield of a population (Martin, 1971). In prehistoric times such overkills seem especially to have affected large, long-lived herbivores with low reproductive capacity. Even with such impacts, it is unlikely that diversity was reduced much below 80-90% of the original.

The development of plant cultivation, and the closely-linked superimposition upon it or parallel development of domesticated herbivores were a third and fourth stage combined as S_3 in Fig. 17.1

Table 17.1 Energy input, cropping and human support levels from four systems (from Odum, 1967 and Institute of Ecology, 1971)

System	Energy input (Kcal/m^2 year) (Kcal/m^2 year)		Human food (Kcal/m^2 year) (Kcal/m^2 year)		Population supported	
	Solar	Fossil fuel	Plant	Animal	On land/ Km^2	In city
Rain forest	1.5 x 10^6	0	0.4		1	0
Uganda grazing	1.5 x 10^6	0	19.5	0.2	25	0
India: monsoon zone	1.5 x 10^6	0	245	27	230	50
United States: rable	1.5 x 10^6	135	1000	0	60	2000

and in the second line of Table 17.1. At such a stage, human population densities still tend to remain low, pastures are entirely composed of species native to the area and food yields are slight. But it is also at this stage that ecological structure is greatly altered and nutrient depletion can be severe. Likens *et al.* (1970) recorded in the Hubbard Brook catchment a net loss of 65-90 tonnes of nutrient salts/yr in run-off from cut forest as against 4.5-6 tonnes/yr from uncut woodland. The loss from the uncut system could be made good by rainfall and soil weathering in the year; it is evident that even if the loss from cut forest were to continue for two years only and then revert

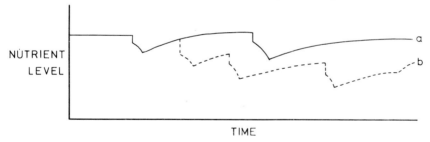

Figure 17.2. Schematic pattern of nutrient depletion and restoration under intermittent cultivation (a) in stable mode (b) under excessive cropping.

to the previous level, as scars were healed by herbaceous growth, it would take over twenty years for the nutrient levels in the system to be restored. In a tropical forest system some 90% of nutrients may well be locked up at any one time in the standing crop of trees; the destruction of the forest, especially by fire, disperses these materials into the air, or accelerates their removal in drainage, often leaving truncated soils of low fertility with little resistance to erosion in heavy and irregular rains.

Harris (Chapter 4 above) points out that shifting cultivation can be stable if human population densities are low and there is ample time for nutrient restoration between periods of intensive land use. Fig. 17.2 illustrates the principle. Such cultivation involves a considerable range of plants in a multi-layered system, amidst large tracts of wild country; domestic stock similarly co-exist with wild animals so that, while ecosystem structure is altered, species diversity is little impaired. Following the Hubbard Brook model, it is likely that the time interval between cultivations will need, as a minimum, to exceed the time under cultivation by a factor of ten, and preferably twenty; this means that only 5-10% of the total land area can be under cultivation at any one time. But if the area of land needed for food production rises and the swidden plots coalesce or succeed one another too swiftly on the same site, unless there is a deliberate replenishment of nutrients through manurial treatment, fertility is likely to be quickly lost (as Fig. 17.2(b) illustrates). Conway (1973) records that in Thailand over-exploitation of this kind has led to the abandonment of three to four million hectares of land. Dimbleby (Chapter 1 above) points out that in Britain, where soils are generally robust, upland areas still display lowered fertility following forest clearance in Bronze and Iron Ages and intensive use with inadequate nutrient replenishment thereafter. The conversion of 'stable' to 'pioneering' modes (as defined by Harris) can therefore bring about degeneration in nutrient levels and productivity. The critical point is whether intrinsic properties of climate, soil and ecosystem and the characteristics of the land management adopted favour a new stable system under continuous agriculture (as in much of western Europe) or a degenerative system (as in many semi-arid tropical lands). One system of continuous usage is illustrated in the third line of Table 17.1, derived from areas of India with Monsoon rainfall, supporting a substantial human population (including some in the cities) without any input of fossil fuel energy.

One of the remarkable features of man's agricultural history is that, as it has proceeded, the number of species forming the staple food resource has actually dwindled. In the hunter-gatherer stage a wide range of plants and animals was certainly taken. But man has taken into cultivation under 100 plant species and under 50 animals and any single culture depends on only a few of these. This narrowing is understandable when it is recalled that it resulted from the superimposition of an added series of constraints; the species not only had to be palatable, but also had to be manageable by a not very sophisticated civilisation. Moreover, once a species had successfully come into domestication, the very success of the process imposed something of a barrier to the addition of further species. Fig. 17.3 illustrates this. It suggests that the possession of a seed crop or manageable mobile meat source conferred such an advantage in terms of food return/unit of effort that agricultural and pastoral groups could move relatively freely wherever their crops would grow or animals graze. Even if a new area chanced to support a wild herbivore

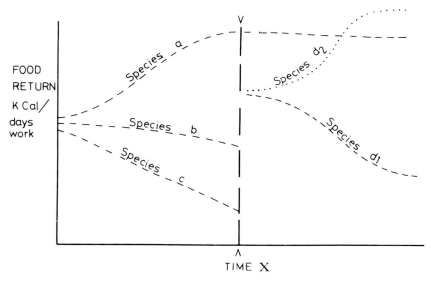

Figure 17.3. Energy and effort values of hunting and domestication. Species a, b, c, in initial centre of population: a domesticated, b and c reduced by hunting. At time X, population migration. Species d, a newly encountered wild herbivore, has considerable potential for domestication: its probable actual reduction by hunting follows curve d_1 but under potential domestication would follow d_2 and ultimately be more productive than species a.

that, within a century or two of domestication might be 10 or 20% more productive than the existing stock, this was still unlikely to have any effect since it was the immediate comparison that mattered and the wild animal was more likely to be hunted as a competitor than evaluated as a new domesticate. Social traditions, originating as practical codes of experience, could well have further discouraged experiment.

Increased agricultural productivity has come from the development of agricultural technology – S_4 in Fig. 17.1, and line 4 in Table 17.1. Intensive cultivation coalesces. Diversity is reduced – in the actual cropped land to perhaps 10% of the original, since the crops are commonly genetically uniform and grown in large blocks – and the main accompanying species are opportunistic 'weeds' and a restricted range of invertebrates. A large energy offtake is possible, supplying cities at a distance. But the flow of nutrients from the soil to crop, city, sewer and sea greatly exceeds natural replenishment (for phosphate at least tenfold) and this intensive agriculture is only possible through the use of fertilisers in whose making fossil fuel or other non-solar energy is used. Such energy supplements are also needed to control competitive plants and plant-feeding insects, and to sustain a mechanised cultivation, processing and distributive system.

The great successes of modern agriculture have come through more
and more productive use of the best lands, on which extensive systems
of this kind are economic. If for any reason the nutrient budgets are not
balanced, degenerative processes can set in even here (represented by
S_5 of Fig. 17.1,) and this happened on some English chalklands when
the corn boom of the late nineteenth century collapsed. The
degenerative system can itself become semi-stable (as in British upland
heather moors with over leached acid podzols, fire-climax grasslands,
or saline or arid desert). Over long periods, however, natural
restorative processes tend to increase its diversity and nutrient level.
Acid podzolic soils under upland heather moor in east Scotland can, for
example, be converted back to acid brown soils after some 40-50 years
under birch woodland, the trees drawing nutrient salts from the deeper
layers of the soil and depositing them in surface leaf litter which
sustains an increased soil fauna, including earthworms that further
distribute nutrients.

Many of the most fertile areas of the world naturally support forest
or, where water tables are high, wetland (swamp, marsh, fen, bog or
fen woodland). Forests are not ideal habitats for hunter-gatherer
hominids. Most of the edible fruits are borne high in the tree canopy
or in occasional openings, especially along streams. The annual
production of green matter on which herbivores depend is
concentrated high in the canopy also. There are relatively few ground-
living herbivores. Most of the plants and animals handy for hunter-
gatherers to use are low-growing shrubs or herbs, and most of our
cultivars are also shrubs, herbs or grasses, but from seasonally arid
grasslands and scrublands or, in a few cases, from salt marshes, rather
than forests. It is not surprising, therefore, that the expansion of
agriculture has involved the progressive replacement of forests by
ground-level vegetation, notably grasslands – vegetation which has
some features akin to those of early stages in seral processes leading to
forests. Such vegetation has a relatively large annual growth
increment in proportion to the standing crop, contains a higher
proportion of annual opportunistic species, is often less diverse
botanically, supports many more medium-sized herbivores like those
man has domesticated, and is readily opened up to provide habitats
for the other species we grow. Wetlands, although less tractable
because they often need substantial drainage to be suitable for
cultivation or grazing, have the attraction of ready water supply and
have also been brought under human management from early times.

The encroachment of man on the forest and wetland systems has
been the main cause of altered ecological structure over much of the
world, and it has brought secondary changes because forests have
properties of water retention, protection of soil against erosion by
water run-off, a capacity to create a humid micro-climate under the
canopy and a longevity that helps to create stability in areas of
fluctuating climate. Wetlands likewise equilibrate water run-off. The

replacement of both systems tends to threaten soil and microclimatic stability.

Food production on land has thus progressively altered the structure and diversity of ecological systems over broad tracts, especially in the lowlands. It has led to the replacement of two dominant systems – forest and wetland – by more open, less multi-layered, herbaceous plant communities. In areas of vulnerable soil and climate, especially in upland zones and areas of unreliable rainfall, it has frequently led to nutrient and soil depletion and to degenerative changes, many of which have either led to the loss of land from agriculture or to cropping at below the level that could have been sustained had management been wiser. In areas of robust soil and reliable climate, intensive cultivation has led to spectacularly enhanced food yields from a narrow range of species, and at a continuing cost in terms of energy injected to balance the system and prevent degeneration.

Fig. 17.4 summarises the process and sets out the data in Fig. 17.1 another way. The core of the diagram is an extremely over-simplified model of almost any ecosystem. Man alters the system in two broad ways. First, he alters the actual composition of the flora (shown by the sequential off-setting of the 'primary producers' box through S_1 to S_4) and likewise changes the fauna, off-setting the secondary producers

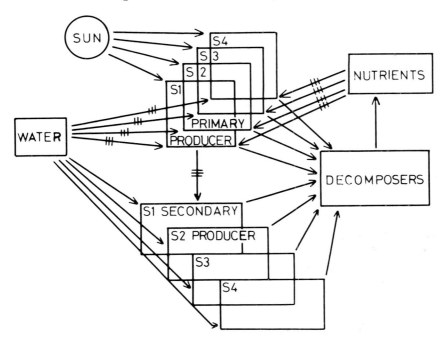

Figure 17.4. Schematic diagram of man's impact on ecosystems. S_1-S_4 represent changing plant and animal components, while processes most commonly altered by man are marked by man are marked by barbs on the arrows.

component to various degrees. Second, he alters the rates of certain processes – chiefly the supply of water and nutrients, but also the supply of material from primary to secondary producers.

Over 70% of the earth's surface the situation is quite different. The oceans·yield about 60-80 million tonnes of food per annum, all of it as animal protein secured by a process which is still one of hunting and gathering. Over-cropping has depleted the stocks of some marine animals – notably the larger whales and the most sought-after fishes – and caused some marginal changes to the structure of ecosystems, albeit with little change in ecological diversity. More managed cropping of the sea, feasible only in inshore basins capable of enclosure, is still in its earliest stages.

Food production: the future

Continuing population growth and the need to raise the standard of living in many parts of the world demand increased food production. This can be done:

(a) by expanding the areas under cultivation
(b) by enhancing the efficiency of production
(c) by using novel food sources or production processes.

Only some 5% of sunlight reaching the earth's surface is absorbed by a green plant. Only 1% of the energy absorbed by plants is converted to useful carbohydrate. Expansion of the area covered by plants is therefore an attractive concept. At present, however, losses from cultivation through degenerative processes (such as salinisation and expanding arid lands) about balance such gains. 'New lands' apparently available for cultivation, moreover, include much marginal land with brittle soils. Unless resources for extensive (and expensive) irrigation and land management are available, too much should not be expected from this method. More may be achieved in the sea. In 1970 it was suggested that conventional fishery might be expected to yield 80-100 million tonnes/year (as against 60 in that year) while extending cropping to the Antarctic krill might raise the total to 150 million tonnes (Gulland, 1970). Intensive 'cultivation' or fish-farming of the inshore seas also offers scope for enhanced production.

On land, increased production efficiency in plants cultivated on stable, robust soils still offers substantial prospects; other chapters (14, 15, 16) in this volume demonstrate what is attainable by genetic selection, irrigation and the development of a sound human 'infrastructure'. Supporting 'ecological' aids through the selective breeding of nitrogen fixing bacteria and mycorrhiza that enhance the efficiency of root systems may become increasingly useful. Recent findings suggest that cultivation systems that do not disturb the soil profile by repeated ploughing for weed control may have advantages over those that do. In addition, selective breeding of more efficient herbivores can improve conversion of plant to animal matter. As a simple (in theory) social economy, if less high-quality plant food were processed through animals to sustain the excessive meat consumption of many developed countries there would be substantial potential gains in world food availability.

Beyond this, we can use our wealth and imagination to toy with the third potential way of enhancing food production, for example through:

(a) new plant producers
(b) new animal producers
(c) new ecological systems of production
(d) new 'infrastructures'.

As to the first, much has been written of the new capacity of the technologist to extract protein from the leaves of plants not now grown commercially. This research is generally associated with Pirie (e.g. 1958). It offers the prospect of cropping whatever plant species could sustain the highest biological productivity on a given soil rather than an ill-adapted cultivar that happens to be digestible. Biochemical processing systems may also have more efficient conversion ratios than cows and are less likely to be poisoned by plant toxins. The system can also crop a diverse natural vegetation which may be more resistant to environmental stress. But the process is self-evidently a technology, needing the input of fossil fuel, and its economic efficiency is still open to question.

Short of this point, few can doubt that we could find new strains of plants we could use if we tried. Certainly with wild animals the pointers are clear. W.H. Pearsall (1962) demonstrated long ago that, in East Africa, wild range supports a comparable biomass of herbivores to improved pasture. Cropping wild herbivores could be cheaper in Rhodesia than improving the pasturage and grazing cattle (see Jewell, 1974 for a summary of recent work). In the past two years Blaxter and others have demonstrated that Scottish red deer can yield as much meat per acre as sheep on impoverished highland *Calluna* moorland. Even more bizarre prospects exist if we consider cropping invertebrates. Earthworms, for example, can contribute 80% of secondary production in some systems. In history, man has used only a small part of the living diversity of the world for food; the cultivars and livestock we use perform well on the best soils but we might well find new species more appropriate to the more marginal areas which have not sustained continuous agriculture in history or may now be opened up for the first time. We might also deliberately construct systems that sustain stability and diversity. For example, a broad-leaved tree layer appears to be biologically desirable on most lands.

Tree roots draw up nutrients from the soil and leaf fall returns them to the surface layers, sustaining the soil fauna that, together with percolating rain waters, moves them back down the profile. Trees can yield nuts, fruit, fibre and timber. The olive grove, coconut plantation, oil or date palm grove or even open birch wood make ecological sense, either standing above a pasture (as highland birchwoods or lowland orchards can be used to harbour sheep and as oakwoods once supported pigs) or above cropped ground. Maybe such trees, planted in broad swathes or strips to allow mechanical cultivation of the intervening land, should be a feature of future farming? In the northern temperate zone we have drained our wetlands – the natural, biologically productive condition of river basins – yet with the high rainfall and low evaporation of such regions, should we rule out the development of a high-yielding wetland crop (a kind of cold-climate rice) which also helped to conserve water run-off? There are few cases of deliberate design of systems that are as efficient as possible in biological and energetic terms to which technology has been adjusted. These speculative examples may not work, but we now know enough to analyse the principles that lie behind them. Should we find that radically new forms of land use are possible, however, the human side of the system must not be neglected; new types of farming and of food demand a new type of farmer and consumer.

The place of conservation

Behind any choices about food production systems lies the fundamental need to balance the equation between energy inputs to and outputs from an ecological system. Should output exceed input, degenerative processes are inevitable. How energy is put into the system is only partly under our control. How it is taken out is wholly within our power. The processes depend on the number of people we have to sustain, the way of life they demand, and our ingenuity.

Conservation is a policy for regulating the rate at which we derive a yield from environmental systems. At its broadest, it ensures that such systems are not over-exploited and pushed into degenerative change. Within this definition, however, there are many subsidiary actions, and in the present book the term has consequently been applied in many different ways, for example covering:

(a) the retention of areas of unaltered natural ecosystems
(b) the protection of soil fertility
(c) the preservation of genetic diversity
(d) the preservation of ecological diversity
(e) the retention of certain visual landscape patterns
(f) the retention of certain land use patterns or management systems
(g) the restoration of degraded environmental systems.

Evidently, this list is neither of like attributes nor comprehensive. But all relate to control over the extent to which the components of the basic ecosystem in Fig. 17.4 is altered. Some (a,c,d,e) constrain the degree to which the initial series of primary or secondary producers is altered. Others (b,f) may affect the extent to which the nutrient and water supply rate is altered, and the extent to which man removes nutrients from the system through cropping the productivity of primary and secondary producers.

Overall, there can be no conflict between agricultural development and the wider concept of conservation in the sense of regulating man's impact upon ecosystems so that degenerative changes, excessive nutrient loss and ultimate impaired productivity are avoided. Development of land for sustained food production depends upon these same controls. As a generalisation, the following forms of conservation do not appear in principle to conflict with development for food production:

1. *Conservation preceding development*

   (a) retention under natural vegetation of land not needed for intensive use
   (b) conservation of ecological diversity, genetic diversity, soil stability, water run-off and landscape quality in such areas.

2. *Conservation parallel to development*

   (a) conservation of soil nutrients and fertility
   (b) conservation of soil water balance and stability
   (c) maintenance of genetic diversity in useful species.

3. *Conservation following development*

   (a) restoration of degraded areas under natural or semi-natural vegetation cover.

Such conflicts as arise are almost entirely due to disputes over the extent to which either:

   (a) land should be excluded from development, or
   (b) food production should be held back to permit other uses to be sustained.

The first of these conflicts is unlikely to be acute where the exclusion is clearly of practical value to food production elsewhere (for example where forest is retained on hills with brittle soils so as to prevent erosion and flash floods). It is more likely to be prominent where land of high potential agricultural productivity is retained under natural vegetation in order to sustain genetic or ecological diversity or aesthetic qualities. Similarly, multiple use of the same area so that a marginal component of agricultural productivity is foregone so as to allow the retention of small parts of the land under wild ecological systems, for game or for visual amenity, will provoke conflict in direct relationship to the demand for the agricultural production and the values set by the community on the alternative uses.

Table 17.2 sets out as a matrix diagram the kind of pattern to be expected. The real situation is, however, more complex and involves a third dimension relating to population density and wealth, the latter evaluated in terms of available food and living standards. As population density and poverty rise, the economic value of food and basic shelter rise also, and the economic value of conserving wild life habitats, landscape amenity and even genetic diversity in the small areas required for potentially useful plants or animals falls, in an extreme case almost to nothing. Conversely, as wealth and standards of living rise, social values set on natural beauty and recreation rise to the point where they become dominant. The resources of

Table 17.2 Matrix of likely levels of conflict between types of conservation and agriculture on various soil types

		SOIL TYPE		
		ROBUST FERTILE SOILS	ROBUST INFERTILE SOILS	BRITTLE SOILS
CONSER-VATION TYPE	SOIL NUTRIENTS AND FERTILITY	NIL	NIL	NIL
	UPLAND FOREST ETC STABILIZING RUN-OFF	LOW	NIL	NIL
	GENETIC DIVERSITY IN GARDENS	LOW	NIL	NIL
	GENETIC AND ECOLOGICAL DIVERSITY IN WILD	HIGH ↓ MEDIUM	MEDIUM ↓ LOW	LOW→NIL
	VISUAL LANDSCAPE	HIGH ↓ MEDIUM	LOW ↓ MEDIUM	LOW ↓ NIL

environment are constantly revalued as social standards alter. Very broadly, the level of protectionist conservation in any country can be expected to be proportional to the production of the area per capita and the wealth per capita. This is one reason why the value judgements of conservationists from affluent countries with no serious population problems and an average expectation of life of over 60 years may strike coolly upon a developing world population with a rapidly escalating population, outstripping growth in its production capacity and facing an expectation of life of around half that of its wealthy neighbour. The general pattern is no more than an application of the relationship well known in economics and summarised for pollution by Beckerman (e.g. 1973), which states that a policy of environmental protection will adjust itself so that the marginal costs and marginal benefits balance.

These differences in value, or social priority, superimposed on natural variations in environment may often dictate radically different actual policies in different places. It is important to recognise that the fundamental systems involved are none the less the same. The components of the environmental system remain those in Fig. 17.4. Human need dictates how far natural systems are replaced by intensively managed substitutes. Economic valuations are one way of expressing those human needs. In this connection, however, much may depend on the descriptive method adopted, just as it does in science. For example, an affluent nation with a low population density may adopt a deliberate policy of retaining 30% of its land under

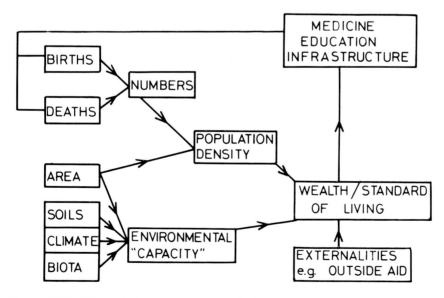

Figure 17.5. The principal components of the social system determining land management choices.

natural forest as a 'bank' against future needs. What is the cost? There is little direct cost: nature manages the land for nothing and all that may be required is a fire watch and a little wild life management, amply repaid by the sporting returns and yields of a carefully controlled harvest of mature trees. But if the forest is on good soil the opportunity cost (that is, the value foregone by not developing the land) could be enormous. Conversely, the opportunity cost of a degraded moorland could be very small, yet rational land use might well demand its restoration at a direct cost out of all proportion to its apparent value. There is also no agreed methodology for setting a value in economic terms on natural beauty, rarity or genetic diversity. Western developed nations expend a more or less comparable share of their Gross National Product (1-2.5%) on environmental protection; in financial terms, wild life and genetic conservation appears to cost a good deal less in terms of recurrent expenditure, but landscape conservation, judged as a component of the overall process of land use planning, is almost impossible to evaluate. Clearly there is room for more research on methods of evaluating environmental resources and options as an aid towards ensuring the right balance of use for the social and environmental circumstances of the place and time. Some balance between alternatives will inevitably be struck but, without a proper analysis of the systems involved and an attempt to quantify their components, it may be a balance that is not obviously logical.

Guidelines and principles

The first general principle that emerges from this analysis is that there is no universal rule that uniquely dictates what a particular piece of land shall be used for. Identical areas, with identical soils, climates, floras, faunas and potential productivities, may be intensively farmed in one country and made a nature reserve in another, and both judgements can be logically right. But it is equally evident that just as a simple model can be constructed of the main components of an environmental system, so too can a basic model be constructed of the social system that determines choice. Fig. 17.5 is a crude model of this kind. It indicates as a logical consequence that any decision on the 'right' use of an area should be reached within the context:

(a) of the intrinsic environmental properties of the land and its ecological and agricultural potential
(b) of the socio-economic conditions in the community.

Before development (or in the context of a review of planning policy) a survey of some kind is needed to describe and measure environmental features such as:

(a) terrain
(b) climate (including growing season)
(c) rocks
(d) soils (including nutrient levels, turnovers and factors leading to vulnerability or misuse)
(e) vegetation (including natural primary productivity and potential sustainable yield under various managements)
(f) fauna (including natural secondary productivity and alternatives under different management systems)
(g) habitats required to sustain various degrees of genetic and ecological diversity.

Such surveys must obviously be objective, based on adequate scales of sampling and must define the range of variation in the areas and not just the average conditions.

Such basic survey data need to be linked to social issues such as:

(a) what population must be supported in the area now and in the future
(b) what food, water, timber and other environmental resources must be supplied
(c) what other needs must be met, for example for shelter or recreation
(d) what wealth or free energy is available to supplement or substitute for agriculture
(e) what technological, scientific and other social resources are available
(f) what built-in social attitudes constrain choice.

From such information, land use strategies can emerge. Obviously in a heterogeneous environment a mosaic pattern of farmland, forest, urban development and conserved 'wilderness' will normally result. Pressures must be very high to push the margins of food production to coincide with the total available acreage. But the relative extent of the components of the mosaic depends critically on the balance of social demand and environmental resources. In this sense, the balance between food production and conservation depends not upon an inherent conflict but upon the outcome of the operation of a common model, whose components vary in their numerical value with changing circumstances.

*REFERENCES**

Beckerman, W. (1973). Pollution control: who should pay, and how much? *In* Clayton, K.M. and Chilver, R.C. (eds.). *Pollution Abatement.* David and Charles.

Conway, G.R. (1973). Aftermath of the green revolution. *In* Calder, N. (ed.). *Nature in the Round.* Weidenfeld and Nicolson.

Gulland, J.A. (1970). The development of the resources of the Antarctic Seas. *In* Holdgate, M.W. (ed.). *Antarctic Ecology.* Academic Press.

Institute of Ecology (1971). *Man and the Living Environment.* Workshop on Global Environmental Problems. The Institute of Ecology.

Jewell, P.A. (1971). Managing animal populations. *In* Warren, A. and Goldsmith, F.B. (eds.). *Conservation in Practice.* John Wiley and Sons.

Likens, G.F., Bormann, F.H., Johnson, N.M., Fisher, D.W. and Pierce, R.S. (1970). Effect of forest cutting and herbicidal treatment on nutrient budgets in the Hubbard Brook Watershed ecosystem. *Ecol. Monogr.*, **40**: 23-47. (see also Institute of Ecology, 1971).

Martin, P.S. (1971). Prehistoric overkill. *In* Detwyler, T.R. (ed.). *Man's Impact on Environment.* McGraw Hill.

Odum, H.T. (1967). Energetics of world food production. *The World Food Problem*, **3**: 55-95. (see also Institute of Ecology, 1971).

Pearsall, W.H. (1962). The conservation of African plains game as a form of land use. *In* LeCren, E.D. and Holdgate, M.W. (eds.). *The Exploitation of Natural Animal Populations.* Oxford, Blackwell.

Pirie, N.W. (1958). Unconventional production of foodstuffs. *In* Yapp, W.B. and Watson, D.J. (eds.). *The Biological Productivity of Britain.* Institute of Biology Symposium no. 7.

* References cited are, so far as possible, reviews in wide-ranging compilations, which in turn lead to a broad span of primary literature.

18. Temperate and tropical: some comparisons and contrasts

R.W.J. Keay

The problem of balance between environmental conservation and agricultural development arises in all the main ecological regions of the World, save those such as the driest deserts, the highest mountains and the coldest polar regions in which agriculture is patently impossible. In the symposium on which this book is based the main emphasis has been on the United Kingdom and on tropical regions ranging from lowland rain forest to semi-arid lands. Comparisons between the conservation/development balance in moist temperate Britain and that in tropical regions can be valuable and stimulating, but the differences – ecological, social and economic – are substantial and must be borne in mind if comparisons are to be valid.

In considering the essential differences between a developed temperate country and a less developed tropical country, it is logical to start with the climate and the natural ecosystems. High temperatures lead to rapid turn-over in tropical ecosystems, so that in a forest as much as 90% of the nutrients in the system are in the standing crop; in the temperate forest a much greater proportion is in the soil. Rainfall in the inter-tropical countries varies from almost nil to the highest in the World (e.g. up to 10 metres a year in Cameroon) and it comes in the growing season when it exceeds evaporation and causes leaching in the soil; furthermore in most of the inter-tropical regions the rainfall is concentrated in one or two rainy seasons (when erosion as well as leaching may be serious), separated by severe dry seasons when evaporation greatly exceeds precipitation. In temperate regions natural and agricultural ecosystems draw on a reserve of water in the soil accumulated during the winter and there is relatively little leaching during the growing season. Furthermore the tropical dry season favours burning of natural as well as man-modified ecosystems on a more extensive scale and more regularly than in temperate regions.

Although most of lowland Britain was, like much of the tropics, originally covered by forest, it was an ecosystem dominated by very few species of trees and was generally much poorer in species of plants and animals than its tropical counterparts. The climax ecosystems of the vast savanna and steppe areas of the drier tropics are very difficult to trace, due to centuries of extensive burning, but may well have been, like those of the moist tropics, species-rich forests of various kinds.

When man was only a hunter and gatherer, his impact on the natural ecosystems was presumably slight, save for his use of fire which in the tropical areas with a marked dry season would have had an influence out of all proportion to his numbers. Later the cultivation of plants and the domestication of animals led to a much more serious impact on natural ecosystems, magnified by the sharp increase in human population which these innovations made possible.

Granted that many primitive agricultural plants and animals had common origins in south-west Asia, how was it that agriculture developed and thrived in Europe, China and other temperate regions but languished in most tropical regions? It is fashionable today to blame poverty and colonialism for the under-development of the tropics, but the truth is more probably ecological. Clearing of forest, at least partially, by primitive axe and fire was a prerequisite of cultivation in both temperate and tropical regions. In the first years after clearing, agricultural crops benefited from the nutrients accumulated in the soil throughout the countless years of forest cover. Thereafter the situation would vary greatly according to the nature of the soil and climate. Robust soils, their nutrient level sustained, albeit at a lower level, from minerals in the underlying sub-soil and/or rock, are found in tropical as well as temperate regions, and so too are soils which quickly and more permanently lose their forest-derived fertility. In both regions man sought to restore fertility by allowing natural recolonisation and replenishment in systems of shifting agriculture, and in limited areas by using animal and human excreta. In both regions too there are examples of field systems carefully and laboriously terraced to reduce erosion and maintain fertility. However, rapid turn-over rates, due to high temperatures, and intensive leaching, due to concentrated rainfall, would naturally make the farmers' task more difficult in the tropical regions. Furthermore, there is a very important difference in the biology of the grass which in both regions sooner or later invades much of the land after forest clearing. In temperate regions the relatively short grass remains green during the moist winter and provides grazing for herbivores which contribute substantially to the protein content of human diet. In tropical regions the tall rank grass dries up and is frequently and widely burnt in the dry season providing scant sustenance for the herbivores. While many of the wild herbivores survive by browsing as well as by moving to moister areas, the herded cattle and sheep are less well adapted to the tropical environment and must be moved to moister areas where grass may still be found.

These are some of the ecological factors which have, over the centuries since man first domesticated plants and animals, made settled mixed agriculture a lot more difficult in both moist and semi-arid tropics than it has been in temperate regions. There are, however, other serious difficulties, especially in water supplies and health. By and large, water for man and his animals is much more easily available throughout the year in temperate regions than in the tropics. Marginal semi-arid tropical regions are especially sensitive to annual or cyclical fluctuations in rainfall.

The species-rich ecosystems of the tropics have, moreover, a long list of pathogens and their vectors which afflict man with many debilitating and deadly diseases – malaria, trypanosomiasis, filariasis, leprosy, yellow fever, dysenteries, to name only a few. Some of these and other diseases certainly occurred also in the temperate regions but the markedly different endemic disease situation must always be taken into account when making environmental comparisons between the two regions.

Reference has been made to the sharp rise in human population brought about by man's success in cultivating plants and domesticating animals some 10,000 years or so ago. Another marked rise in Europe took place in the eighteenth century, largely as a result of improved food supplies; the population of Britain, for instance, trebled between the years 1700 and 1850. Improvements in hygiene led to further rises in Europe in the nineteenth century, with medical care, especially through immunisation and chemical therapy, leading to still further rises in the twentieth century. By contrast the rapid increase in the populations of the less developed tropical world in the 20th century has been initiated more by improved hygiene and medical care than by increased food supplies.

Of course much has been done in the twentieth century to improve food supplies in tropical countries, but difficulties have often arisen because the scientific advice behind these efforts has inevitably relied very much on experience gained in temperate countries. In retrospect it is indeed regrettable that so little effort was made to understand the natural ecosystems and the traditional methods of agriculture which, though far from perfect and supporting only a low standard of living for a disease-burdened population, had achieved a rough balance with the environment, except for certain areas where soils had been degraded too far for man to bother further. But in the late nineteenth and early twentieth centuries when botanists and agriculturalists, trained in temperate countries, were laying the foundations of agricultural departments in tropical countries, ecology as a science had not started. Much of the early effort in tropical agriculture was directed towards plantation crops such as tea, coffee, cocoa, sisal, oil palm and rubber, and later on groundnuts, which yielded produce for export and thereby provided much needed funds for other developments. There was a similar emphasis in tropical forestry: a very few species of fine timber cut for export, and efforts to establish plantations, mostly of exotic species, but far too little effort applied to understanding the natural forest ecosystems and to utilising the trees cut in vast quantity for the development of agriculture, communications, etc.

Well-meaning modern efforts to increase food production in tropical countries, spurred on by the needs of rapidly growing populations or the hope of quick profits in pioneer agriculture, continue to run into serious difficulties because of inadequate understanding of tropical ecosystems and farming methods. For instance, pastoral expansions into semi-arid marginal lands during favourable years in the rainfall cycle have been hit by successions of dry years, new wells have led to soil erosion and degradation of grazing lands, and agricultural development schemes have failed to take social needs adequately into account.

Some efforts are now being made to study traditional farming systems in a holistic manner, and these are greatly to be welcomed. Soils, methods of maintaining fertility, energy inputs, agricultural production, human nutrition and health, economics and especially social patterns and aspirations all require study in an integrated manner. The complex assemblages of food plants, grown under the light shade of palms and other tall trees without the aid of artificial fertilisers and machines driven by fossil fuels, in the swidden plots of tropical forest areas are a striking contrast to the wide open fields of a single grain crop so typical of modern agriculture in temperate lands. In these days when some people in the developed wealthy countries of the temperate regions are growing tired of pollution and the pressures of urban life, the tropical swidden plot understandably has a romantic appeal. An ecological understanding of traditional agricultural systems in the tropics must, however, recognise that their rough balance with the environment has been struck at the expense of low standards of living and of population densities kept low by disease and malnutrition. Any humane approach to the problems of tropical countries must start by alleviating disease, malnutrition and poverty, and by coping with the rise in population which will inevitably follow. This must mean increasing food production preferably by skilful adaptation of traditional farming methods and increased productivity from existing agricultural areas. Scientific studies of traditional methods are therefore of the greatest importance.

In the less developed tropical world the objectives of agricultural development are reasonably clear – more food of various kinds – but the scientific bases for achieving the objectives are seldom adequate. This, in large measure, is due to the complexities of the ecosystem and to the natural reluctance of people to change their ways and to work harder, even though it may be for their own good. Much the same applies in the developed temperate world but here the objectives are less clear and we can, for the time being at least, afford to think about environmental quality, the balance of our diet, the balance between home-grown and imported food, and how and where we want to live and work. The pressures on us are economic, political and psychological rather than hunger and disease. Agricultural methods in Britain have changed in the past because of socio-economic pressures, and it could be that the trauma of the past two years will bring further changes. Greatly increased costs of fertilisers and problems of waste disposal might favour a trend back to less specialised and smaller farms. Greatly increased costs of fuel might lead to greater use of horses, and perhaps, if sufficient people really want to return to the land, more labour-intensive methods. Increased grain prices and efforts to feed the Third World might lead to a change in the balance of our diet, with more cereals grown for human consumption and less for our meat. Such a scenario is perhaps a little nearer to, but still very different from, traditional agriculture in the tropics. It would, by conventional terms, mean a somewhat lower standard of living, but would be beneficial in terms of human health and perhaps of happiness and environmental quality.

In both temperate and tropical regions there are strong scientific, aesthetic, educational, and to some extent economic, reasons for setting aside adequate samples of natural and other uncultivated ecosystems. The case for such conservation must, however, be made in the light of the different ecological, economic and psychological situations.

The recognition that it is right and desirable to conserve examples of wild ecosystems has developed most strongly among the better educated relatively wealthy people of the industrialised parts of the temperate regions. To them the sight of plants and animals in the wild is a precious privilege enjoyed in places very different from the cities and suburbs where they spend most of their lives. Attitudes are usually very different among people who spend their lives in places, both tropical and temperate, where large tracts of wild ecosystems remain. In such situations clearing the forest has been a prerequisite – almost a synonym – of development, and it is not easy for people living in these areas to appreciate the case for nature conservation especially if poverty, hunger and disease are prevalent among them. Indeed it is largely because of the difficulties of agriculture and the prevalence of endemic disease that the tropical regions still have quite large areas of natural or partly natural ecosystems. Virginity in these ecosystems is much less wide-spread than casual observation would suggest. Thus detailed studies in apparently mature tall tropical rainforest may well reveal evidence of past disturbance by shifting cultivation or even habitation, and the vast savanna areas of the drier tropics are as they are because of grass fires lit by man. Nevertheless, the present pace of development and the importance of these species-rich ecosystems in world strategy for nature conservation make it urgent to preserve adequate samples before they disappear or become drastically changed by man. The sites for such reserves can conveniently be chosen in the course of land use surveys which should precede the opening of large new areas to agriculture and sustained yield forestry. In this way nature conservation can take its rightful place in the development of a tropical country. Environmental conservation in the more general sense should be part and parcel of rational agricultural and forestry development.

SUMMARY OF DISCUSSION IN PART VI

The discussion after Holdgate's paper was of considerable interest, although much was held back until the general discussion which came later. The chapter by Keay was not discussed as it did not form part of the original programme although several points in it were touched upon.

The clear message emerging in this section was that, as Thorpe expressed it, if one seeks a balance in man-land relationships one has to prepare balance sheets in terms both of the present and of projections into the future. Inputs and outputs are one kind of balance that must be looked at, whilst another kind is the balance between the various functions of the land, its carrying capacity, and the needs of society. The most important balance for this present volume is that of environmental conservation and agriculture, even though this juxtaposition of two items is probably always an oversimplification. We shall return to this in the final discussion.

Waddington picked up the discussion by making what he called a philosophical remark, namely that inputs into natural systems are always complex and outputs are highly complex also. He felt that agriculture as a way of life had failed to get its message across to the academic, scientific and intellectual world, namely, that the basic character of its thought was always multidimensional. He recalled the conversations on the farm where he was brought up, about the rotation of crops and their production simultaneously in terms of multilayer agriculture – a term used by Holdgate. Under the fruit trees two other crops were often grown, adding up to three levels of crops on one piece of land. The thought was always multidimensional, not only in the space of several years, in a time dimension, but of several crops at once in a space dimension. For this reason Waddington felt that Holdgate was wrong in reducing everything to economics. It may work well in some areas, but where we look at land use and development we have reached the limit of one-dimensional thinking. To take another example, the land of Tuscany has rarely fewer than three crops at any one time, with chestnuts, peach trees, bushes and ground crops each exploiting a different level.

Waddington was convinced that all the long-lasting agricultural developments were very multidimensional, and in many ways showed even greater multiplicity than the natural ecosystems.

This view, in the editor's opinion, would accord very well with David Harris's conclusions on the multiplicity of crop types in tropical swidden agriculture, where, as he expounds it, the farmer is blending introduced and native plants at different canopy levels to create an ecosystem not very different from the naturally occurring ones. It is also worth remembering the classical maize/beans/squash agriculture of the Mexican and Central American *milpas*, where every available ecological niche is efficiently exploited. Surely these points, backed up by the views of an internationally distinguished biologist such as Waddington, should suggest some of the ways in which agriculture in the tropics should be directed in the future.

19. General discussion

J.G. Hawkes

The discussion on which this chapter is based was intended to draw together the thoughts and conclusions stemming from the previous sections of the conference and to provide a brief for Dr. Holdgate who was to report to the plenary session the following day (see Chapter 20). The meeting was chaired by Lord Justice Scarman and was opened by Dr. R.W.J. Keay. In setting out this summary I have attempted to provide a synthesis of the various themes discussed and the conclusions drawn from them by the participants, rather than to present the material in strict chronological sequence.

A large part of the discussion on the natural environment and man's role in modifying it was centred on the soils, their fragility or stability, their degeneration and their recuperation.

Hutchinson began by pointing out the interesting contrast between the stable soils of India and the rather unstable ones of east Africa. In Uganda he had opened a research station in the lush elephant grass vegetation and in ten years the soil became utterly useless. In India, by contrast, a much more intensive and exploitative agricultural system has been practised for 4,000 years without doing the damage that was done in Uganda in ten years. Agricultural systems which are permanent are so because of the robust soils on which they are established. Those of western Europe are similarly robust, as are those of the alluvial areas of N.W. to N.E. India, which never really degenerate however badly they are treated. On the other hand, the rain fed soils of Africa need a shifting swidden cultivation with the abandonment of land after a few years to allow deep rooted trees to re-mobilise whatever little nutrients still exist in them. It therefore follows that we should aim towards an intensification of agriculture on the good lands, those with robust soils, so that we shall not need to use so much of the poor land which can only carry a crop for a short time in between long periods of regeneration.

Kemp took up this point by suggesting that centres of intensive agriculture may have developed in the past only in regions with really robust soils through the trial and error of earlier swidden cultivation. He drew attention to the land use surveys of Brazil where the robust Terra Roxa soils were being sought and agro-villas and agropolises settled on them. By contrast, the majority of the Brazilian soils were fragile and poor, and made up of easily leached sands with the majority of the nutrients in the forest trees themselves. When the forests were removed fertility was lost very rapidly and fertilisers were quickly leached out.

Dimbleby had reservations about Kemp's point that selection for robust soils was made at the swidden stage, since he felt that notwithstanding the fragility of some soils, agriculture had persisted on them and had brought them to virtual dereliction, as on the heathlands in this country. Man often continues to exploit, in Dimbleby's view, and keeps changing his methods to meet the lower nutritive values until in the end the soils are exhausted.

Limbrey considered that there was good evidence to show that early soils were downgraded and podzolised, and were only later upgraded, illustrating her point by reference to work in Orkney. Liming and marling over the past 2-3,000 years in Britain has had a very marked influence in soil improvement. She felt therefore that temperate climate soils should not be considered as inherently stable but only stable in relation to a large labour input. Erosion has had a beneficial effect, paradoxically, in moving soils down into the river valleys, thus forming rich alluvium. This took place because of the ploughing and degradation of the hill slopes, and she thought that the same process might be taking place in tropical soils, though she had no evidence on hand to support this.

Holdgate put the problem of soil degradation into simple economic terms. If the people working such fragile soils had no alternative choice, and had no means to effect soil improvements, what else could they do but finally cause complete soil dereliction? Surely here was an area where socio-economic rather than scientific variables were going to be more important. Dimbleby, however, felt that the lack of options was not so relevant in the earlier periods when populations were small, since the early agriculturalists could move from place to place. Probably much damage was due to inherent dangers such as fire susceptibility. Generalising is dangerous, since today and even in historic times it has been possible to restore soil damage; what could have been almost irreversible in earlier times has today been turned to good use.

Scarman felt that it would be valuable to place industries and cities on the fragile soils and develop the green revolution on the robust ones. Unfortunately, as was pointed out in an earlier chapter, the historical development of land use in most parts of the world has made this virtually impossible, though there could be useful exceptions.

Developing the theme even further, Hutchinson suggested that soils, like plants and animals, needed to be domesticated, and that although we have been successful with plants and animals we have not been very good at domesticating soils. Referring to the comments of Dimbleby and Limbrey, he contended that we had, however, been reasonably successful at domesticating the soils of Britain over the one or two millennia during which they have been cultivated. He described an imaginative research project in Africa in which, by the use of livestock, legumes and some phosphatic fertilisers, it had been possible to raise the poor soils of Uganda to a level where a continuous and improving output of cereals and meat was obtained. So, after this very exciting demonstration, Hutchinson felt that he would not accept any soil, however degraded, as being totally incapable of recovery. Natural regeneration in old industrial areas can be seen in Britain as in the Forest of Dean, Northamptonshire ironstone workings and parts of South America. So the lesson he would draw from this is that we should use some areas well and very intensively, whilst others we should never touch because, with this pressure, we should destroy ourselves as well as the environment in which we live.

Hawkes felt that with very strong mountain slope erosion in parts of South America, which brought about total disappearance of soil and even subsoil, little could be done to restore what had completely disappeared. Limbrey agreed with this, though she believed that soils could be regenerated very fast from subsoils, and this was in fact what had happened after the last ice age in northern Europe.

After this very lengthy discussion on soils, the question of land use surveys was brought up by Thorpe and continued by Harris and Holdgate. Thorpe felt that, though costly, these should be the focus of the new exploration of our globe, to chart and re-chart so as to determine a little more accurately which of the complex of physical, biological, socio-economic and political factors were affecting the situation. But, as Bennett said, will anyone be able to pay for such surveys? Harris also felt pessimistic about them since he had worked with 'western experts' in the tropics engaged on surveys of this type, who paid no attention to the needs and aims of the local populations whose land use development was being discussed. A statement from the meeting should, he felt, strongly qualify our encouragement of such surveys by stressing that they are only really useful if done in terms of the local value systems that operate in the society for which development is being considered. Rather than setting up surveys with western expertise it should be axiomatic that local people participated in them, with social as well as environmental scientists included. Western attitudes to patterns of development are very different and not necessarily relevant to those of the peoples of other parts of the world in this respect, who may be much better adjusted than we realise to their soils and traditional patterns of land use.

Harris returned to the point discussed by him and Hawkes in an earlier session on the valuable lessons to be learned through a study of tropical swidden agriculture. He referred to tropical New Guinea where there had been for many years an intensive root crop plus tree crop cultivation system. The tree cover is *Casuarina*, which helps to restore nitrogen fertility in the soil. A return to mixed cropping with trees (cf. Waddington, p. 251) or an introduction of trees where they do not already exist might be important in helping to promote this sort of restoration of nutrient levels and to provide ecosystems more similar to the natural ones.

Keay referred to the protective element in conservation, and took the thoughts of the meeting to the protection of the sea, a topic that had been omitted from the structured programme through lack of time. Obviously what is taking place on the land has a great effect on the sea, so that, by and large, it seems quite clear that the different parts of our environment, land, sea and air, cannot be discussed separately. So far, we hunt and gather the products of the sea. We have not begun to farm them but by the time we do there is a danger that it may be too late.

Holdgate felt that the sea ought to have received more comment during the meeting and reminded participants that 80 million tons of protein per year were removed from it. Scarman asked whether agricultural techniques could be applied to the sea, to which Holdgate replied that inshore farming could be accomplished but not offshore farming. He felt that it was important at the Conference on the Law of the Sea to consider whether the 200 mile zone should be accepted or not, since countries were more and more concerned with mineral rights and ought also to be concerned with off-shore pollution.

Scarman agreed that nations have got to accept greatly extended sea frontiers in order to begin sea farming. He thought that in the end the 200 mile frontiers would be accepted but not without a struggle. The hunter must give way to the farmer, in the seas as on the land. However, he thought that conservation problems, especially those of the whale and the salmon, were more difficult, since these lay far outside the 200 mile limit. Unfortunately the international will to conserve these organisms was regrettably lacking at present.

Scarman further considered that it was very odd and very self-centred for us to think of the whole world as nothing more than *man's* environment. Should not man take a more modest view, saying 'I am part of the world and I shall fit myself into it so that I do not in the process destroy it.' After all, man still carries with him the hunting and gathering and aggressive instincts that he developed several hundreds of thousands of years ago when he was a much less powerful figure than he is now. The problem is to get him to adjust to his new circumstances. Lester agreed, saying that he and many others feel that we should not only have regard for our fellow human beings but for all our other fellow creatures. We have a common concern, a ·common responsibility to the rest of creation. We should not utilise it totally selfishly for our own anthropocentric purposes.

With this Frankel concurred, though in a later part of the

discussion. A time scale of concern must be formulated in conservation. We must attempt to conserve evolutionary dynamics and evolutionary potential by setting aside relatively large and diverse biosphere or nature reserves. However, this implies an economic input, and the competition between this objective and the agricultural one is a question that must be resolved.

Keay felt that the balance between agricultural production and environmental conservation in Britain was correct, though Gane had earlier expressed doubts on this. The important things to watch in this country are not so much government action, which follows changes in economic factors, but rather the economic implications of changes in world markets and prices which will affect agriculture and hence individual and public thinking about what is important and what is not.

Scarman felt that a tremendous advance in the battle for conservation had been won as far back as 1947 in England and Wales with the passing of the Town and Country Planning Act. There is also something very similar for Scotland. Since 1947 the legislation has compelled land use to be in accordance with permission granted only after consideration of all factors. The Act has deficiencies and there are failures, but he asked delegates not to forget its triumphs. From this Act one lesson stands out very strongly – one must have ongoing machinery for a continual dialogue between scientists and legislators. The Act provides a context for that dialogue and brings compulsion and sanctions for those things which scientists think are important. Scarman felt that such legislation was the luxury of an advanced society and could not so easily be imposed on emerging countries. Nevertheless the lessons could be seen, and international agencies, to whom emerging countries looked with respect, were able to do a great deal. It seemed to him that the law was of great importance in helping scientists to formulate environmental policies, upon which the scientists had first to agree amongst themselves.

Turning now to the subject of genetic diversity, Bennett made the point that we have hardly begun to explore the degree to which genetic diversity can serve man. We have concentrated on perhaps no more than 100 species of plants at a liberal estimate, but there are many others that can serve man, not only for industry but for food. We can regard plant cover as part of man's environment for recreational value and indeed we do. However, in different parts of the world there are different potentials for production and output, and the unevenness in the world distribution of these potentials is largely a social one.

Frankel later referred to organisms of direct use to us as domesticated plant species which can be preserved at relatively small cost, perhaps no more than a few million dollars. With animals it is somewhat more difficult and expensive. All this conservation, so far as plants are concerned, can be carried out in no more than half a generation. The problem of wild species is much greater since here we are involved with setting aside natural reserves, which are expensive and competitive, as was mentioned earlier. In every case there is economic and social competition between reserves and agriculture. The matter is of ultimate advantage to man, since wild areas contain genetic resources which the future may require, and they can easily be surrounded by areas which we need even now for education, recreation and tourism. So even in economic terms the costs of buffer zones around wild-life reserves may be compensated by the money from tourism.

Hutchinson also came back to the problem of genetic resources. In three of our major crops, cotton, wheat and rice, the great recent advances have come from exploitation of diversity within the advanced cultivars, rather than the introduction of genetic material from centres of origin or primitive sources. The bacterial blight resistance in cotton came from West Africa, not from America where the cottons originated. The Norin dwarfs, which were the basis of the dwarf wheats, came from advanced cultivars from China and Japan – similarly with the dwarf rices that form the basis of the IRRI dwarf rice varieties. We need to bear in mind this diversity and do all we can to preserve it, but we have in recent years, particularly in western Europe and in North America, done serious damage to our prospects of maintaining that diversity. In the interests of economic advance we have established varietal right legislation, and in the EEC we are engaged in making sure that none but the most advanced varieties are allowed to be sold in the area, thereby very greatly restricting the diversity that is available to us. We are in fact selling our birthright for a mess of pottage. One can see how this has come about: the variety rights legislation was dominated by two factors, the idea that the man who has bred a variety has a right to profit from it and, complementary to that, the idea that a variety must be pure. We have gone a long way towards getting pure seeds, from the days when it was almost impossible to buy pure seeds of a cereal except from an experimental station in this country, to the present when nothing is impure. However, we have overshot the mark, to the extent that it is now against the law to sell anything that is not absolutely pure, and this is not necessary or even desirable. One can see that in the legal profession a clear brief is required on what kind of legislation should be enacted, and that it should be legislation that can conveniently be carried out. There we have perhaps been at fault, in not making quite clear what are the limits to which we can profitably define a variety in the purity in which we ought to maintain it. We are in very serious danger, in Hutchinson's view, of considerable retrograde steps in eliminating the remaining diversity in our crop plants, particularly by conforming to this legislation.

He therefore hoped very much that we should emphasise the importance of the diversity that exists in our advanced cultivars, as well as the diversity that remains in unexplored or little explored regions.

Hutchinson's point was taken up by Bennett who, remembering that when Gane spoke earlier of resources, plant, land, animal and energy alike, we had to speak to governments, argued that scientists did not know too well how to communicate with legislators, since each spoke a rather different kind of language. She felt that perhaps one of the things that should engage the attention of scientists, if good resolutions were to be carried forward into legislative action, was that they should learn to speak clearly to legislators. This problem is continually arising in FAO.

Scarman was able to pursue this point further, and his legal background and experience were again most useful to the conference. He stated that he had lived the whole of his life with the Sale of Goods Act, 1893, and with the legislation dealing with the guaranteed purity of the packet of seeds one buys in the shop. There was of course a great emphasis, economic, social and legal, on purity of the product – giving the customer what it is he thinks he is ordering. What Hutchinson called diversity in describing the necessity of preserving advanced varieties as well as natural species, in legal terms appeared to be getting something that the customer did not order. It was clear to Scarman, as a layman and as a lawyer, that there was great importance, scientifically and perhaps – in the long term of evolution – economically, of retaining diversity in the advanced varieties that the farmers and others used in this country. The problem was somehow or other to get across this idea to civil servants, administrators, lawyers and, ultimately, politicians. There is a message for conservation, even though it is a little subtle. The general public is beginning to see that conservation of, for instance, building and architecture can only be achieved by sacrificing the more immediately beneficial use of the site or its redevelopment – because there is a benefit in retaining that piece of architecture that does not necessarily have to be measured in terms of cost-benefits. So also there is the same message in regard to conserving the environment. He was not by any means pessimistic that the legislators on the other side of the fence would not get the message, but he stressed that it was the scientist's duty to pass the message on. If a scientist asks for a declaration of policy he would say: 'Yes, provided you make clear to the legislators and others not skilled in your discipline what it is you want, bearing in mind the great danger that was shared by the laws of the Medes and the Persians: – once something is declared it is apt to become doctrine and once it becomes doctrine it is heresy to depart from it.' This must not be allowed to happen, since one has to retain flexibility in what is being said. One proceeds, of course, from hypothesis to hypothesis; one is acting, and asking the legislator to act, upon assumptions that are only partly verified or may ultimately be falsified. This is the central problem. If the scientist speaks in the language of policy rather

K

than in the language of hypothesis he may mislead, and the law may turn out to be something other than what he envisaged.

Holdgate, as a civil servant, agreed with this wholeheartedly, since he was not long ago responsible for advising the government on the protection of the environment from pollution, acting as a link-man between scientist and civil servant. The problem was not simple, since the way the scientist communicates by means of a scientific paper is totally inadequate for putting on the desk of a Secretary of State. The scientific world knows that science is a matter of balancing probabilities and this is a message that must somehow be conveyed to the legislator.

We now come to the last part of the discussion, in which an attempt was made to strike a balance between the various needs and pressures of environmental policies. As was stated earlier by Holdgate, a decision on the right use of an area of land should be reached within the context of its properties, its ecological, agricultural or other potential, and the socio-economic conditions of the community living in it.

Many of the points touched on by previous speakers were referred to by Owen when he said that industrial wealth was essential in order to achieve the surveys and development needed for this country and the Third World also. Obviously the matter of energy was vital to all the deliberations of the present session, since without financial, mineral and energy sources, conservation or development in a planned and meaningful way were both out of the question.

Keay spoke about the dissatisfaction with the balance that exists between conservation and development, but the problems are how to suggest modifications and how to determine the desirable features in an improved balance. In his view we should press for policy declaration by governments in relation to land use, since if a government formulates such a policy the way is then clear for implementation. This focuses the mind of the scientific community and draws public attention to the importance of land use issues. A number of speakers also agreed with an earlier point that a very intensive use of land may very often be necessary in order to conserve other areas for recreation and for nature or other kinds of reserves. Owen felt that land should have a dual or even a multiple use where possible. He cited areas such as derelict mining sites, the Norfolk Broads, etc., and Bennett later mentioned Colebrookdale, where the vegetation had come back into a formerly very heavily industrialised landscape. Bennett went on to point out that industrial activity was like agricultural activity – it could destroy, but in some places regenerative forces were at work.

Thorpe went on from this to stress the need for the reclamation and rehabilitation of derelict land. It could then be used for housing and leisure purposes, thus easing pressure on good agricultural land.

Hutchinson believed that the balance of land use has changed in our own life-time and will surely continue to do so in the future. We need then to be flexible in our farming strategies. For instance, the specialisation of our agriculture in eastern England by putting the land almost entirely under cereals means that it will be very expensive to get back to a position where, if we have energy problems, we could economise on nitrogen fertilisers through the use of clover lays and livestock farming. The fences and hedges have all disappeared and it will probably be too expensive to reinstate them. Nor have we the buildings in which to keep the cattle during the winter. It would seem that a very positive decision for this conference would be to pay a great deal of attention to the maintenance of all those factors that contribute to flexibility in land use within the farming system. This is one of the important features of balancing our options, by providing more general, flexible systems instead of specialist ones.

Some of the final decisions coming from this conference were:-

(i) that careful planning of land use was essential but with as flexible an approach as possible

(ii) that genetic resources of crop plants, domestic animals and forest trees, as well as their wild relatives and other material of potential interest, should be conserved both in banks and in wild-life reserves

(iii) that decisions and techniques based on experience in temperate countries should not be applied to the tropics without proper care

(iv) that soils and vegetation had, in many instances, powers of recuperation when properly treated or even when left completely alone

(v) that soils, like domesticated animals and plants, could also be 'domesticated'

(vi) that all decisions for future land use and development policies should be based not on scientific policies alone but also on socio-economic ones

(vii) that proper dialogues should be developed between scientists and legislators, it being the scientist's responsibility to formulate his ideas clearly so that legislators are able to express them with equal clarity.

The conference ended on a note of cautious optimism, as expounded more fully by Holdgate in the next chapter. It was concluded that flexible land use policies were necessary for both developed and developing countries, reflecting scientific, political and socio-economic views, and capable of change under altered circumstances where necessary.

The conference finally stressed that, in its view, development and conservation were not to be regarded as two irreconcilable opposites. On the contrary, they should be thought of as two aspects of a single environmental strategy. Such a viewpoint could lead nations to keep ecological considerations in mind when planning the uses of their land and natural resources for a future in which conservation was regarded as an integral part of the process of development.

PART VII
CONCLUSIONS

20. Final summing up

M.W. Holdgate

The theme of this book is the conservation and development of the natural environment. It is thus about the management of the natural resources of the land and especially the use of that land to produce food. At the outset, it is worth re-emphasising how fundamental man's dependence on natural environmental systems is and will be for as long as we can foresee. The energy that drives the world's living systems, ourselves included, comes from the sun and is trapped by green plants. Innumerable tiny and inconspicuous micro-organisms we commonly forget cycle the oxygen, nitrogen, carbon and other nutrients upon which we depend.

Implicit in our title is a question: 'Is the conservation of these vital functions of the biosphere at hazard from agricultural development and other processes?' More widely, are developmental and conservationist pressures capable of reconciliation? There is something of a novelty in posing this question at all. Over much of history, and still over much of the world, mankind has been impelled by nature and its vagaries. Now we have a consciousness of choice about our future environment. This choice has been granted by development. It was the assurance of food supply that early agriculture gave which allowed urban development, leading to technology and what we now call civilisation. Now we have, in the developed world, the wealth, scientific skills, industrial and technological capacity and social organisation to plan ahead. We should not assume that we have these freedoms for ever. We may have no more than a breathing space. Energy demands and demands for natural resources certainly cannot continue their present exponential rate of growth for ever: sooner or later the curve must reach an asymptote. We need to plan now how to guide the process towards stability.

This book opens with a record of the history of the agricultural development which has generated our civilisation. The chapters by Dimbleby, Harris, Thorpe and Brothwell trace man from the rare hunter/gatherer, altering little, through the axe-wielding fire-raiser capable (and guilty) of over-killing his hunting grounds to his own detriment, to the cultivator and the domesticator of stock. Several authors point out how fragile soil fertility can be. In a natural forest, the nutrients washed out in the rivers are balanced by those brought in by rainfall and the weathering of rock, but after clearance, losses may exceed natural replenishment ten-fold. In some tropical forests at any one time 90% of all the nutrients in the system may be locked up in the standing crop of trees and if that is burned not much is left. In east Africa, grassland soils with good rainfall can be 'brought to their knees' after only ten years of use. Fortunately, not all areas are like this. In India and in the temperate regions such as extend over much of Europe, there is land that still yields good crops after several millennia of continuing cultivation. But in the tropics there is much land whose soil is brittle and the luxuriance of tropical forest often masks an infertile and intractable soil. The wealth of the superficial vegetation is here a delusion.

Traditionally, such land has been cropped by shifting or 'swidden' cultivation. In many presentations this sytem is castigated as a villain upon the world's stage. However, Harris's paper demonstrates that it can be stable if, after a plot is exhausted, it is given long enough under natural forest for the restorative powers of nature to rebuild fertility. Some so-called primitive people crop their plots with a careful mixture of species, maintaining diversity and at the end speeding the restorative process by deliberately planting appropriate wild trees on plots before they abandon them. But where these areas of tillage coalesce or where there is not time for replenishment, problems arise. In Britain, as Dimbleby's chapter demonstrates, we still have uplands and sandy heaths whose fertility is impoverished because of exhaustion through unwise forest clearance several thousand years ago followed by cropping without adequate manurial or fertiliser treatment.

Modern intensive agriculture substitutes large areas of virtual monocultures of single crops for the smaller scale and more diverse systems of primitive man. It balances the energy and nutrient budget of the land, but demands fossil fuel energy to support mechanised cultivation, to provide fertilisers replacing the nutrients we channel from soil to crop to city to sewer to sea, and to control natural competitors and pests. Modern intensive livestock farming is likewise energy-demanding as a process.

Modern monocultural agriculture has greatly reduced the numbers of species of plants and animals in the areas where it prevails. Many people have deplored this loss on aesthetic grounds (as Davidson does in his chapter), although Hooper's contribution suggests that there is less evidence that it matters scientifically. The removal of hedgerows from eastern England, for example, seems unlikely to have led to the loss of any species of the regional fauna and flora, and hedgerows are not so important as reservoirs of wild-life as has sometimes been thought.

Looking to the future, it is clear that we need to expand agricultural production in order to feed the present world population better and in order to feed the increase in population we know we are going to have. This book does not discuss human population increase or the means for its regulation, although Bennett does express the view that population growth tends to slow as the wealth created by development rises, perhaps because people no longer lose half their children in infancy and because social services mean that they do not need to have six offspring in order that one or two survive to support them in age. In Bennett's language, 'the train of population growth has brakes that it will apply before it hits the buffers'. This only follows, of course, if development can raise living standards by generating wealth faster than it is consumed by mounting numbers. Whatever view is taken of that optimistic projection, however, there will be a need for more food in the foreseeable future. The chapters by Hutchinson and others indicate that this food could be produced in several ways.

Cultivation might be extended over a larger area and better crops might be developed. The chapters in this book indicate some doubts about the first of these. The new lands available to us may not be those with robust soils. More confidence can be put in the second. The present skills of the farmer and the crop breeder can continue to enhance yields especially on the best soils, and maybe we can widen the range of species we grow. Several chapters (especially by Bennett, Burley and Kemp, and Frankel) stress what a tiny part of the diversity of nature man has so far domesticated. We use, intensively, under a hundred plants and under fifty animals.

Originally, our ancestors no doubt chose their crops because they grew well under simple conditions and yielded plenty of fleshy, nutritious matter which our systems could digest raw or with simple cooking. Today, we recognise, theoretically at least, that our crop plants and stock may not be the best species we could derive if we look systematically at the world's living systems. Pioneering, of course, has its hazards; Thorpe, in his paper, proposes the thanks of humanity to that unknown forebear who demonstrated the unwisdom of eating deadly nightshade. But new and even bizarre food species might give better yields for the intractable and marginal lands that we may have to use. Earthworms account for 80% of the meat production in some systems. There is a possibility of bypassing the herbivore altogether and directly processing protein out of leaf material. Although this is a well-known technique, it does, however, have an energy cost and its technology does not seem to have reached take-off point.

In ecological terms, a multispecies and multilayered system, that is, one with trees and ground level components, might be more stable and more desirable than a simpler one-layered monoculture, although the economics may not necessarily point towards it without social and

K*

technological changes. We should also note that while such developments, and the continued application of the knowledge we already have, could enhance the world's food supply, there are elements of waste which as scientists we cannot approve in what we do today — like feeding good fish protein to cattle or pigs. This process sacrifices 75% of the food energy and is an expensive way of changing a food flavour.

We can learn a good deal from the recent experiences of the developing world. In many countries of the Third World there is neither the wealth nor the time for thorough scientific analysis before development. People have an expectation of life of 35 years or so; one cannot tell such people that new farm lands must not be cleared from forest because scientists have not yet named the trees. But there are areas where forest conservation to bind the soil, to slow down water run off and to provide timber is none the less vital. King's paper points out that the areas of harsh famine in recent years in the Sahelian region, Ethiopia, Pakistan and Bangladesh are all areas with brittle soils on which deforestation has been overdone.

The situation in India, described by Hutchinson, Harriss and Singh Gill, permits optimism. Since 1950, agricultural production has doubled. This has been a steady upward progression, concentrated on good land, irrigated on an increasing scale. It has not been spread diffusely over the whole sub-continent. It has been a process of evolution. The 'R' on the second word of the 'Green Revolution' is, as Hutchinson points out, a misnomer. The Green Revolution has not just been a simple process of sowing a miracle seed and having the grain harvest double over night. The soils have been improved steadily since the late 1940s by better management. This has provided the opportunity for the new, high-yielding wheats and rice which came in when the soils had reached a point where they could be sustained. And the key to this success, which is paralleled elsewhere, in the Philippines for example, is the infrastructure of sound social organisation, education, and the right kind of innovative cultivator. Without these things science can do little. That is why, perhaps, the Green Revolution is patchy in its greenness, when considered geographically.

It is logical to turn from these types of optimism about development to conservation. In this book, the term is defined broadly as the avoidance of unnecessary dissipation of the wealth of the environment; avoidance of the overuse or misuse of natural resources to our detriment. 'Conservation' is an overworked word and it is none the less used in these pages in many senses as Gane's and Holdgate's papers demonstrate. For example, there can be conservation before development in order to set aside areas we do not immediately need, to conserve their fertility under the natural balancing processes of nature until we need to tap it. Conservation also encompasses setting land aside so as to preserve a diversity of genetic and ecological resources (as Frankel describes in the chapter on the MAB programme) and to sustain forest cover on soils and catchments which are unsuited to intensive development and yet valuable in balancing the run off of water and hence playing a part in sustaining fertility on lower ground.

Often such reserves are needed in parallel with development, providing hydrological control, timber, genetic and ecological diversity, and aesthetic quality. Conservation is also an element in active agriculture, since this demands the protection of the soil and its nutrient resources. There is another kind of useful conservation in the deliberate retention of samples of earlier land use systems from which we may still have something to learn. After development there is yet another kind of conservation in the restoration of derelict land. Not all these make the same kinds of demand on us in terms of land or in terms of cost, but all have their place in the system.

To produce more food we may need new kinds of crop and livestock, and this, too, demands a type of conservation – that of genetic resources. We continually go back to the wild relatives of our modern cultivars or to primitive varieties of our present crops and livestock for genetic traits that help adaptation to new areas and needs. This is likewise important for forest crops – and we should recall that wood not only builds the dwellings of much of the world but fuels half the world's cooking. We just cannot say on what varieties and species we may depend later. Apparently outmoded strains of sheep and cattle are coming back into use (as Henson's chapter explains). Sometimes we may feel that we really will not want certain species – many people would say this about blow-flies or mosquitos and certainly we cannot conserve stocks of everything. But it is an evident folly to allow the extinction of potentially valuable trees, herbs and animals before we have even described, still less evaluated, what we are losing. There are tropical forests today where unknown species that may have pharmaceutical value are probably being eliminated before their existence has been recognised.

There are, of course, many methods for the conservation of the world's genetic resources. Some conservation must be done *in situ*; this is true for trees, forests and wild species, and the demand for land can conflict with development for agricultural and other purposes. On the other hand, some conservation can be carried out away from the original habitats, in botanic gardens, seed banks and zoos and here the conflict is less and the process cheaper. Frankel's paper points out that it would not be difficult to conserve the range of genetic diversity of our present crop plants in a few decades of effort at no vast cost, given the social and political will.

This raises another general point. Development and conservation are, in many of their aspects, part of the same process. This is obviously true for the conservation of forests on brittle soils, regulating run off and preventing erosion. It also applies when the fertility of lands not yet needed for agriculture is sustained under natural cover, when genetic diversity is conserved, soil fertility maintained or the restorative capacity of nature sustained. All these elements should be built in to development plans. But conflict can arise over alternative uses of fertile land suited for development, especially where the population density is high and its wealth low, and the optimism in this book must be admitted to be a generalisation. There are areas of the world with high population densities and low wealth, and in these areas genetic and ecological diversity will be hard to conserve, even though the clearance of every scrap of land that can yield a few blades of something edible may be regarded as unwise by scientists in more favoured nations.

Ideally, a mosaic of land uses would be the rational outcome of this kind of philosophy, in which each part of an area was used as near to its optimum as possible and sometimes for several purposes. An agricultural region can retain small areas, maybe only a few per cent of the total, of wild life habitat and of areas of natural beauty, recreational in its deepest sense, and it can be right, assuming that the country's wealth can allow it, to drop the productivity of the primary, agricultural land use marginally in order to sustain these other valued forms of land use as well. Just how you balance the equation, however, depends on the individual case. Gane's and Davidson's papers show how this approach may be fitted to the British situation, while Holdgate attempts a wider generalisation.

There is no doubt about the overall need to retain the richness and restorative power of nature while achieving the development that will raise the quality of life of the world's population. How does one strike this balance? One evidently necessary practical step is to carry out land potential and land use surveys and evaluations: first, before development, to evaluate the intrinsic feature of the environment and define the options for its use and, second, in areas already developed or even degraded, to document the trends they are displaying, their potentials if managed differently and the needs for remedial action. In this kind of survey we would also need to encompass the constraints that might be required on other social activities, including industrialisation, since this, if uplanned or inadequately controlled can generate pollution that might reduce the growth of forests or the productivity of crops. Often it *is* wise to use intensively the best land whose soils are robust and climate predictable and to avoid extensive and maybe over-demanding use of poor land with brittle soils. This latter kind of situation is where, in logic, we should put the cities. In Britain, the sandy Surrey heaths or the Breckland rather than the good farmland would clearly have been the area for the new towns: the modern industrial state is very often superimposed without very much rationality upon the market town network of the earlier agricultural community. The early towns are where the good land was, but the industrial towns could rationally have been put on the bad land. But although it might be attractive to re-cycle some of our less desirable cities under forest for a couple of centuries, there are obvious practical constraints!

Such surveys must, in any case, be quantitative and not anecdotal. They must use rigorous statistical techniques. They must be formalised and well enough documented to be repeated a century hence, obviously by somebody else. One must not have controversy over whether the apparent difference arises because a surveyor fifty years ago used a silly method and generalised too much or because the change is a real one. Such surveys will provide a scientific base for the 'balancing act' of judgement. But we are concerned with *man* and environment. We need also to appraise human needs and for this the surveys need to involve the people of the region under survey. The detached western expert, seeking to sell or impose his own values on a different culture in a different environment in a different continent, has been demonstrated to be a menace in many parts of the world. Sir Joseph Hutchinson provided, in discussion at the conference from which this book comes, one horror story of an order from India for a mass of heavy machinery that could only have been of museum value in the area for which it was sought, 'because it was the modern way of doing things.'

In this survey of human needs and attitudes, many human parameters need appraisal. They include the size of the population the area is going to have to support, what those people's needs are for health, food, shelter and other basic essentials and what social, aesthetic, cultural or spiritual values must be sustained in that community. People are driven by beliefs, among them some which we may castigate as food fads, but which none the less may prohibit the development of new agricultural resources, even if our medical wisdom suggests that they would be good for people. We need to know how much wealth is likely to be available for the development and support of agriculture and where the industry that will create this wealth is located. Here we should recall that it is industry that has, through technology, created the wealth that has given us the breathing space and opportunity for planning we now have: we must plan industrial development but cannot afford to abolish it. We need to know what energy supplement for agriculture is available. Finally we need to know what communication system, management and other social infrastructure is required, what educational needs there are and, last, what economic costs are going to be. Too often scientific discussions like those recorded in this book take place in isolation: economic contributions are needed because when these things are said and done, the economic evaluation is the 'balancing act' that is most easily related to administrative machineries.

Together, the environmental and the human surveys constitute a plan. Producing plans on paper is easy. They are not so easy to implement. For this reason, while the value of such exercises is evident from this book, they should *not* become a block to development while they are being drawn up and approved. It is a matter of social and political will to apportion the due share of national wealth and administration to implement a plan. Sometimes a short term gain may need to be foregone for a long term advantage and for this reason plans need to be endorsed by Governments, to whom the scientists must sell their judgements rather more efficiently than they do at present. We shall not get to heaven in one jump: and even the heaven on earth of which we are speaking will doubtless be attained only in part, and slowly. In evaluating the environment, however, we can at least draw attention to some things that must *not* be done. These are things where there is a very high probability, if not certainty, of actions bringing disaster – such as deforesting mountains with brittle soils, strongly seasonal rains and a great proclivity to erosion, or allowing urban developments on the best lands. Conversely, we can stress some things that *must* be done such as the maintenance of certain irrigation levels, the consequent avoidance of excessive salinity in the soil, and the maintenance of nutrient inputs. Within the framework of a plan some flexibility is essential; there must be options in time and in space. There will be uncertainties, and room for continuing adjustment based on value judgement. A plan should not fossilise or constrain choice or become doctrine like the law of the Medes and Persians spoken of by Lord Justice Scarman, who chaired the final session of the conference from which this book stems: something that cannot be altered, even when it is clearly wrong. Our policies need redirecting as experience unfolds and, for this reason, monitoring and feed-back are essential.

Finally, we must recognise that even environmental scientists are constrained by history. The world's frontiers may make very little environmental sense and yet we cannot sweep them away. This book does not discuss the sea, except briefly to note that it too has a potential for increasing the food supply of the world, but the protein yield of the ocean could probably be doubled without overtaxing its resources, and in the future the intensive management of the shallow seas might well bring great benefits. At sea, man is still a free-ranging hunter/gatherer and at times a piratical one, yet we still seem unable to agree on a framework of international law that will allow strict management of valuable oceanic resources.

Plans based on a single area or single nation will not solve the problems of world poverty or hunger. We know areas where conservation is not practicable today because of poverty. National resource plans need to be linked to wider plans, and here the international agencies have their role. In Europe the Environment and Agriculture Programmes of the European Economic Community are seeking to do just this. In the world as a whole the Food and Agriculture Organisation of the United Nations has an evident key role. Obviously the work of these agencies will not prevent some famine and some waste of environmental resources but it should reduce it, and confine it.

It is right to look forward in a mood of cautious optimism. Ecological and genetic wisdom could sustain more people than the world at present holds and at a decent standard. But for this we need development, guided by the principles of constructive conservation, to generate wealth and raise living standards, a process which is the most proven way of stabilising population. It is not a new finding that agriculture and conservation policies can *only* be designed and can *only* be evaluated in a wider socio-economic and socio-political context. Often this is where the determinant factors in this whole situation clearly lie, and for this reason this book covers only part of its field. But even if it does not reveal the whole truth, it does at least bring to light some determinant constraints.

INDEX

Index

SOCIAL SCIENCE LIBRARY

Oxford University Library Services
—Manor Road
Oxford OX1 3UQ

WITHDRAWN

Tel: (2)71093 (enquiries and renewals)
http://www.ssl.ox.ac.uk

This is a NORMAL LOAN item.

We will email you a reminder before this item is due.

Please see http://www.ssl.ox.ac.uk/lending.html
for details on:

- loan policies; these are also displayed on the
  notice boards and in our library guide.

- how to check when your books are due back.

- how to renew your books, including information
  on the maximum number of renewals.
  Items may be renewed if not reserved by
  another reader. Items must be renewed before
  the library closes on the due date.

- level of fines; fines are charged on overdue books.

Please note that this item may be recalled during Term.